Pale Horse at Plum Run

"And I looked, and behold a pale horse,
And its rider's name was Death,
And Hell followed with Him"

REVELATION 6:8

Pale Horse at Plum Run

THE FIRST MINNESOTA AT GETTYSBURG

———

BRIAN LEEHAN

MINNESOTA HISTORICAL SOCIETY PRESS

www.mnhs.org/mhspress

Manufactured in the United States of America

10 9 8 7 6 5 4 3 2 1

∞ The paper used in this publication meets the minimum requirements of the American National Standard for Information Sciences—Permanence for Printed Materials, ANSI Z39.48-1984.

International Standard Book Number
0-87351-429-7

Library of Congress Cataloging-in-Publication Data

Leehan, Brian, 1959–
    Pale horse at Plum Run : the First Minnesota at Gettysburg / Brian Leehan.
        p. cm.
Includes bibliographical references and index.
    ISBN 0-87351-429-7 (alk. paper)
    1. Gettysburg (Pa.), Battle of, 1863.
    2. United States. Army. Minnesota Infantry Regiment, 1st (1861–1864).
    3. United States—History—Civil War, 1861–1865—Regimental histories.
    4. Pennsylvania—History—Civil War, 1861–1865—Regimental histories.
    5. Minnesota—History—Civil War, 1861–1865—Regimental histories.
    I. Title.
E475.53 .L48 2002
973.7'349—dc21
                                                                          2002003555

To Alexander—
the next generation to carry the story

Pale Horse at Plum Run

PREFACE

"That these dead shall not have died in vain"

A CHILLY RAIN FELL. Rain always seems to follow me onto Civil War battlefields. I have visited many in the past quarter century, and most of my
visits have been under steel-gray skies in intermittent monsoons. It has
always reminded me of the stories from soldiers of the period of how the
skies seemed to open up the night after a great battle. Some thought the
enormous clouds of battle smoke rising into the sky had something to
do with it. The even more scientifically challenged thought it might be
connected to all the roaring and thundering of the weapons shaking the
rain loose from the sky. I think it just as likely that God was weeping over
the whole sorry mess.

My previous visit to Gettysburg had been more than a decade before,
long enough that I couldn't conjure up a mental image of the field over
which my state's premier regiment, the First Minnesota, had charged on
July 2, 1863. I recalled many other sites on the battlefield, but this stretch
of Pennsylvania turf remained elusive to my mind's eye. I drove into the
small parking lot behind the enormous Pennsylvania monument, and
my eyes fixed on the Minnesota monument about one hundred feet
away: a stair-step granite base leading to a rectangular column and the
word "Minnesota" in prominent, raised letters at the base.

At the top of the column is a silent metaphor for the First Minnesota
and especially its performance at Gettysburg: a bronze soldier in charge
bayonet position. It stands solid, determined, immovable, and frozen in

Looking west down the slope of Cemetery Ridge. The tree line was not there during the battle. Plum Run snakes through the bottom of the swale, about thirty to forty yards into the trees.

Looking northwest from the First Minnesota's position in the Plum Run ravine. Plum Run cuts across, left to right, in the left background where the low bushes are growing.

the perpetual forward motion of running into the oncoming rebel horde to the west with bayonet pointed at their hearts. Rain streaked the monument and dripped from the soldier's forage cap and face, like tears for his fallen comrades. A short walk in the steady rain and I was there—alone on that hallowed ground.

I was grateful to find that the site was still an open field, unlike many other parts of the battlefield. The field slopes down three hundred yards to the shallow ditch of Plum Run, a small stream that meanders through much of the southern part of the battlefield. What was scrubby brush and small saplings along its banks at the time of the battle is now a dense forest of mature timber. Fortunately, by the time of this publication, some of these woods will have already been removed. The Gettysburg Military Park management plans call for the rest to be taken out in the next few years, returning the site to its July 1863 appearance.

The dense green canopy extended fifty yards on either side of the stream at the time of my visit. It was midafternoon, but the overcast day made it dark as twilight among the trees. The soil was sodden and spongy in places. Here was the real killing ground, among the flat boulders and along the banks of Plum Run.

The American Civil War took hold of me when I was about eight or nine years old. My childhood fascination with uniforms, flags, and battles has given way to the more subtle study of the politics, strategy, motivations, and culture of the period. But, as with all military history, the blood and the battle smoke are never far away. Ultimately a war is decided on the battlefield, and a country's civil war is certainly the most personal to its people.

The personal connection drew me to these places and the history of the war fought here—a sad and tragic period of fratricidal insanity, where we chose sides and killed and died on our own fields, hills, valleys, and mountains for two very different ideas of what the United States was and should be. Historian James McPherson makes the observation, "Five generations have passed, and that war is still with us." It will probably still be true in another five generations—or ten—or twenty. The war was a fundamental and defining event of our country, even more so perhaps than the American Revolution. The Revolution brought us together, the Civil War tore us apart, and the "peace" and the reuniting that ensued were cobbled together by force.

The issues of the war are as fresh as the current news cycle: state's rights versus all-encompassing federal power, race relations, majority versus minority rights, Democrat versus Republican (although the philosophies of the two parties seem to have switched 180 degrees in the intervening 140 years).

The young state of Minnesota sent eleven infantry regiments into the federal armies. Only the First Minnesota served in the main eastern army, the Army of the Potomac, and fought at Gettysburg. The regiment was considered one of the best-drilled and best-disciplined combat units in the Army of the Potomac. Having been a member of the Old First was a point of justifiable pride to the survivors throughout their lives.

Minnesota was in its third year of statehood when Fort Sumter fell. The fort surrendered at 7:00 P.M. the evening of Saturday, April 13, 1861, after a thirty-four-hour bombardment from the Confederate batteries ringing the harbor of Charleston, South Carolina. The governor of Minnesota, Alexander Ramsey, was in Washington, D.C., at the time. By 9:00 A.M. on Sunday, April 14, word had spread that the war had begun, and Ramsey was already at the office door of Secretary of War Simon Cameron. He offered one thousand men from the state of Minnesota to suppress the rebellion. Cameron was gathering documents in his rush to get to the White House. He told Ramsey to sit down and write out and sign his official offer, which Ramsey did.

In Minnesota, as elsewhere in the country, there was confusion and concern but also an overarching feeling of patriotism and a desire to fight to hold the Union together. The state militia at the time was for the most part organized more along the lines of a social club than a military body. Some units were armed, uniformed, and drilled with regularity, but some existed more-or-less only on paper. The law indicated that the federal government could call state militias into federal service for ninety days in an emergency. Still there was perplexity and reticence from many who did not want to leave families and businesses behind for an uncertain future.

One of the better organized militia units, the Pioneer Guard of St. Paul, met in the local armory on the evening of Monday, April 15, 1861.

The guard's armory occupied the third floor of a stone building on east Third Street, between Cedar and Minnesota Streets. A lively discussion ensued as to the fate of the unit. Many were ready to sign up immediately, and many were adamant that the government could not force them to go to war. Some suggested the unit must enlist as a whole, while others suggested that men could choose individually whether or not to join. Finally the commander of the Pioneer Guard, Captain A. T. Chamblin, told them, "It's up to the company to say what you are all going to do."

A blank notebook was passed to the front of the room and set on a table. The first man to step forward and sign was Josias Redgate King, a twenty-nine-year-old surveyor who had come to Minnesota the year before statehood. King said, "Here's one for the war," and signed the book. Thereafter King always claimed to be the first man to volunteer to put down the rebellion of the southern states, since Governor Ramsey was the first to offer troops to the government. King signed up for what would become Company A of the First Minnesota Volunteer Infantry, and his service to save the Union was all the more poignant because he was a native Virginian, home of the Confederate capital and the native state of Confederate General Robert E. Lee.[1]

The regiment truly was an American body of men: immigrants as well as first- and second-generation Americans from eastern states—hearty pioneer stock who had moved to the territory, or new state, for adventure and a new start in a new land. They were loggers, printers, rivermen, carpenters, house painters, and cobblers—tradesmen of every kind. They were farmers, newspapermen, lawyers, and legislators. Their first colonel, Willis Gorman, had been the second territorial governor of Minnesota (Alexander Ramsey had been the first).

They enlisted for the original call: three-month's duty. Almost immediately upon being mustered into federal service, they were mustered out of service and asked to reenlist for three years or the duration of the war. Some did not reenlist, but most did. The regiment was filled out with new recruits, who were coming in a constant stream to Fort Snelling at the convergence of the Mississippi and Minnesota Rivers. The men fought and served with distinction until mustered out in early May 1864.

The record of the First Minnesota is impressive enough without Gettysburg. But this largest land battle in the history of the Americas, fought in and around a tiny Pennsylvania crossroads hamlet, was truly the making of the history and the mythology of the regiment. There were countless acts of heroism, by individuals and units, in these three days of intense bloodletting, but the First Minnesota ranks at or near the top of the list in courage and in sacrifice.

It is the quintessential story of heroism: a handful of fighting men engaging a much larger body of the enemy and holding them at bay, with the requisite devastation or annihilation. It is small wonder that the regiment, in speeches, newspaper stories, and articles throughout the remainder of the nineteenth century, was constantly compared to the three hundred Spartans at Thermopylae Pass or the celebrated Light Brigade of the Crimean War. One assumes that a comparison to the defenders at the Alamo was deemed distasteful, since Texas had been a Confederate state.

This is the story of the First Minnesota at Gettysburg—a regiment of volunteer citizen soldiers who truly gave what President Abraham Lincoln called "the last full measure of devotion." They were common men in a most uncommon time: individuals, sometimes cantankerous and with plenty of attitude about circumstances but also with a keen sense of duty to their comrades, to their regiment, and to their place in helping to maintain the Union.

Not surprisingly, much mythology about the regiment has sprung up over time. At a certain point in history, facts and figures became set in stone. Even those who knew better began accepting and repeating casualty rates that were too high and numbers engaged that were too low. Some published accounts from the period had the regiment charging into two full brigades—more than one said the regiment charged an entire Confederate division! To their credit, veterans of the regiment rarely made such claims.[2]

It is certainly not my intention to lessen what these men did at Gettysburg but merely to give as accurate a telling as possible with extant records. What they did was enough, without embellishment. As one survivor wrote many years later, "There was glory enough for all."

For the most part the mythology is what survives, despite a very few articles in arcane specialty magazines giving a thumbnail analysis of numbers engaged and casualties incurred. Most written accounts of the regiment at Gettysburg either quote the mythology and leave it at that or go on to make a brief passing comment that the "numbers are in dispute." There is no book-length treatment of these two terrible, seminal days in the First Minnesota's history. I felt strongly that the material was there, waiting to be researched and analyzed, that would yield a more definitive and accurate telling of the complete story. My goal has been to fill a void in the published materials and to do my part to fulfill Lincoln's 1863 admonishment to "we, the living"—"That we, here, highly resolve that these dead shall not have died in vain." They certainly did not, with or without this book, but this is my small contribution to the history and to the remembrance of these brave and devoted patriots who sacrificed so much to save the Union.

I have begun with a general overview of the situation at the end of the Army of Northern Virginia's first invasion of the North, which culminated in the Battle of Antietam in September 1862. The work becomes more specific and detailed as it advances into the Gettysburg Campaign. My intention has been to focus on the First Minnesota, but since any army functions as a team, it is necessary to deal—sometimes in detail—with units engaged around the Minnesotans, since what these units did affected what befell the First Minnesota.

I have, as much as possible, allowed the scene to be set and the story to be told by the men in the First as well as other military units. In maintaining the tone and personalities of these men, I have made as few modifications as possible of spelling, syntax, and punctuation. I personally find the ubiquitous "[*sic*]" distracting when reading quotes. The reader must trust that I, and the copyeditors, know poor syntax or misspellings when we see them—there are sometimes multiple examples of both in the quotes. We have chosen to let them stand unadorned.

The only changes that have been made are for clarity's sake. Reading any stranger's handwriting can often be little different from reading an unfamiliar foreign language. Add to this the peculiarities of nineteenth-century cursive letters and the penchant for some to spell phonetically, and it becomes an exercise in frustration. There is tremendous satisfaction in finally cracking the code, when all of a sudden a particular soldier's letter or journal seems to snap into focus and all—or most—of the words become clearly legible.

This was particularly satisfying with the reminiscences of octogenarian Charles Muller, formerly of Company A. Muller had immigrated from Alsace-Lorraine when in his early twenties, several years before the war. A stone mason by trade, in his eighties he was still writing phonetically in what surely must have been the same dialect that he spoke. Consequently, I have left his reference to running in a zigzag manner the way he wrote it, "zik-zak," and his did's as "dit."

I have made an attempt to keep the narrative flowing and therefore have put a good deal of the analysis and minutiae about the battle, the tactics, and the individuals in the endnotes. There is an appendix covering, in great detail, the issue of numbers engaged and casualties incurred. This has been part of the greatest misinformation and mythology regarding the First Minnesota at Gettysburg. I hope that this appendix can, in some way, lay to rest much of the confusion on the issue. Additionally, there is an appendix on weapons and tactics of the period, which anyone not having a background in the subject might find interesting and informative.

I have also included an appendix covering a general discussion of time keeping and how very different it was at the time of the battle from today. It is general but fundamental information that bears directly on the chronology of events in the battle and helps explain the often widely disparate reports of when certain events occurred. Finally, there is an appendix on the "mythology" that surrounds the regiment—how it developed and how and why it was sustained in the days and years following Gettysburg.

ACKNOWLEDGMENTS

THE BOOK IS THE RESULT of a long and winding journey, beginning in 1991 with preliminary research for my master's thesis in journalism. From that came a forty-five-minute video documentary on the First Minnesota Volunteer Infantry Regiment; a one hundred-fifty-page book that represented a general regimental history, focusing on the regiment's participation at the first Bull Run, Antietam, and Gettysburg; and an intention to expand the whole thing into a full-blown and detailed regimental history. That plan was laid aside in 1993, when I was still editing the documentary. Richard Moe's fine book *The Last Full Measure* was published, and there seemed little reason to expand my general history into a fifth regimental history of the First Minnesota.

But still I dabbled; this remarkable group of men had caught hold of me, and I continued to scan material and make notes off and on. By late 1995 I had resolved to focus the book on the battle that truly brought the regiment glory and martyrdom—Gettysburg. During the following summer, with a toddler underfoot, a full-time job in the research library of a major regional newspaper, and a wife working full time, I began the daunting task of focused and relentless research and writing.

My son is now beginning second grade and is finally convinced that I did not actually fight in the Civil War, despite the fact that I talk about it so much. To Alexander I lovingly dedicate this book, which has been such a ubiquitous part of his earliest years on this earth.

I am grateful to my wife, Angela, for her patience, support, and encouragement. She shouldered extra parenting duties and accommodated much schedule juggling to allow for my seemingly endless research and writing. The book would not exist without her.

The list of thank-yous is necessarily long.

First and foremost, my family, friends, and coworkers at the *Star Tribune*. My manager, head librarian Robert Jansen at the *Star Tribune* News Research Library, was encouraging and patient with my sometimes somnambulant behavior after a long night at the home computer. As a Civil War buff himself, Bob read the finished manuscript and offered helpful criticism and praise.

Other readers at the *Star Tribune* to be thanked are Tom Jones, copy and layout editor; Norman Draper, reporter; Dan Fenner, former manager of the newspaper's Digital Imaging Center; Bonnie Clark, former member of the Imaging Center's gray-room staff; and Brian Peterson, photojournalist. All were generous with their time and helpful with technical advice regarding photography and digital photo reproduction.

Many thanks to the following people for supplying information, photos, and/or copies of letters and journals, many of whom are direct descendants of men in the regiment: Thomas R. Aldritt, Minneapolis, Minnesota; Brigham Bechtel, Leesburg, Virginia; Arlem Bryngelson, Bemidji, Minnesota; John W. Busey, author and historian, Centreville, Virginia; Edgar A. Cadwallader, Kissimmee, Florida; Tom Chirhart, Stafford, Virginia; William Frassanito, author and historian, Gettysburg, Pennsylvania; John F. Gross, Medford, Minnesota; Wayne Motts, licensed battlefield guide and historian for historical artist Dale Gallon, Gettysburg, Pennsylvania; Timothy Smith, licensed battlefield guide and historian, Gettysburg, Pennsylvania; Ivan Stull, Harrisonville, Missouri; Don Troiani, historical artist; Linda Underwood, Adrian, Missouri.

Many institutions and archives and their talented and helpful staff members contributed to this project: Vickie Wendel, Anoka County Historical Society; Stephen P. Hall, archivist, Beverly Historical Society and Museum, Beverly, Massachusetts; James J. Hill Group, St. Paul, Minnesota, and Tom White, curator of manuscripts; Jim Magnuson, Minneapolis Public Library—Interlibrary Loan Department; Jan Warner, director, Morrison County Historical Society; Cynthia Fox and Deanne Blanton, National Archives and Records Administration, Old Military and Civil Records Division; Alice Gingold, reference librarian, New York Historical Society, New York, N.Y.; William A. Evans, archivist III, New York State Archives and Records Administration; Dr. Richard J. Sommers, chief archivist/historian, and Louise Arnold-Friend, reference historian, U.S. Army Military History Institute, Carlisle Barracks, Carlisle, Pennsylvania; William Crozier, director, Winona County Historical Society.

The excellent staff at the Gettysburg National Military Park was tremendously prompt and thorough in their analysis of my questions and forwarding of information. I cannot help but feel, after a while, that someone would call out, "another letter from Leehan—who wants it," as everyone scurried out for coffee or ducked under desks. That certainly never showed in the information I received. My thanks especially to Dr. John Latschar, superintendent of the Gettysburg National Military Park and park ranger/historians Bertram H. Barnett, John Heiser, Thomas Holbrook, and Karlton D. Smith.

Minnesota Historical Society, like the GNP, has an excellent and helpful staff and a superb and inviting facility. I am proud that my state has invested in such a beautiful and functional building as the Minnesota History Center in St. Paul to preserve the treasures of our past. Many on the staff have been helpful, but I would especially like to thank Bonnie Wilson, chief archivist of the Photographic and Audio/Visual Collection; Ruth Bauer Anderson, reference associate; and Hamp Smith, reference associate.

I extend great thanks to two men who have done so much to preserve the history and memory of this great regiment: Steve Osman and Chuck Barden. Both men are longtime members of the First Minnesota reenactment regiment; Steve, in fact, was a founding member. Steve is the site manager of the Minnesota Historical Society's Historic Fort Snelling. This part-original, part-reconstructed stone fort dates to the 1820s and was the rendezvous and training center for the First Minnesota and all Minnesota regiments raised during the Civil War.

Steve offered analysis, information, and advice in the creation of this book. He also supplied me with a copy of the photo of Colonel William Colvill. Steve gave the final manuscript a thorough reading and provided detailed notes about inaccuracies where warranted. He then gave the appendix on weapons and tactics a second reading, after rewrites, to ensure accuracy. However, I still claim all responsibility for any factual errors.

Chuck Barden has researched and collected information on the regiment for many years. He has a wonderful collection of original material and has constructed a detailed database. I thank him for making much material available to me, some as confirmation of my own research and analysis and some information that was new to me.

Also I extend thanks to my new friends at the Minnesota Historical Society Press, especially editor Sally Rubinstein and Press director Gregory Britton. Greg has brought a passion for Civil War titles to the MHS Press, an inexplicably neglected subject until the beginning of his tenure three years ago. Sally contacted me in March 2000 when she discovered I had a nearly finished manuscript. The Minnesota Historical Society Press was always my first choice to bring this book to readers, and Sally has been instrumental in piloting it through the turbulent waters of committees and editing. Sally had great faith in this work, and I am very grateful for her commitment and editing skills. No author could ask for a better experience, and this is a far better book for her involvement.

Finally, many thanks and warmest regards for my friend and copyeditor Dr. Edward V. "Mike" Foreman, D.M.A. "Mr. Mike" has been a mentor, teacher, and general ray of sunshine in my life for many years and through many endeavors. I thank him for his wisdom, his humor, his skillful red pencil, and his friendship.

Pale Horse at Plum Run

— I —

I had been sleeping with a dead man

SEPTEMBER 20, 1862: "This day will long be remembered by me, for about 8 o'clock A.M. the doctors put me on a table and amputated my right leg above my knee, and from then the suffering commenced in earnest."[1]

So ended twenty-five-year-old Color Sergeant Samuel Bloomer's tour of combat duty with Company B of the First Minnesota Volunteer Infantry. This young carpenter's stump would be a lifelong reminder of the agony of Antietam and his personal sacrifice to turn back Confederate General Robert E. Lee's first invasion of the North.

The fall of 1862 found the United States well into the second year of civil war. After a disastrous eighteen months, the federal army finally won a victory along the banks of Antietam Creek in southern Maryland. Lee had tried another of the gambles for which he was becoming famous. He split his army into parts and sent them into Maryland to try and get that border state to rise up and secede from the Union. It would be a significant coup for the Confederate war effort to have the capital of the United States of America—Washington, D.C.—within a Confederate state.

Lee depended on his knowledge of human nature and the temperament of his opponent. His counterpart in the federal Army of the Potomac was Major General George Brinton McClellan, a diminutive West Pointer known affectionately by his troops as "Little Mac."

McClellan was a supreme organizer and a true inspiration and bonding force of the army he created, but he was a hesitant and even timid battle commander.

Fate handed him a once-in-a-lifetime opportunity prior to Antietam. Two of his soldiers found a copy of Lee's battle orders, dropped in a farm field where rebel troops had previously camped. McClellan now had Lee's entire campaign plan before him and knew that Lee's troops were scattered all over southern Maryland and northern Virginia. Still, he cautiously polished his own battle plans, letting a precious eighteen hours slip by with no movement by his army.[2]

Lee, not the kind of audacious opponent who waited on the enemy, quickly drew his army together on the high ground above Antietam Creek and turned to fight. The tactical draw that ensued left the armies facing each other, the rebels too battered to attack and McClellan with two full army corps still in reserve, refusing to continue the battle. The nearly twenty-three thousand casualties at Antietam make it still the bloodiest single day of combat in U.S. history.

Lee withdrew into Virginia, and President Abraham Lincoln realized he had the closest thing he would get to a victory for a while. He used the opportunity to release his Emancipation Proclamation, freeing all slaves in states that were then in rebellion against the federal government. He pressured McClellan to take an aggressive posture toward Lee, to pursue him into Virginia, and to attack again before the rebel army could regain its strength.

But McClellan stayed in his encampment around the Antietam battlefield to rest and reequip his army—and to plan. Even a battlefield visit from President Lincoln could not budge McClellan. Looking at the Army of the Potomac spread over the plain below, a frustrated Lincoln commented to an officer that it was not an army but rather "McClellan's bodyguard."[3] For more than a month the Army of the Potomac remained encamped while McClellan readied himself.

McClellan finally started a sluggish movement into Virginia at the beginning of November, but Lincoln had tired of "Little Mac" and relieved him of command on November 7, 1862.[4] Major General Ambrose E. Burnside, commander of the army's Ninth Corps, was placed in command of the Army of the Potomac. Burnside was affable and liked by the soldiers, but he proved to be a poor choice as a general in command of an entire army.

Lincoln had, in fact, approached Burnside about taking command the previous spring during the army's stay at Harrison's Landing at the end of the Peninsula Campaign in Virginia. At that time, Burnside made it clear that he knew himself well and insisted that he was not competent to lead an entire army.[5] After the command was forced on him in November 1862, he promptly proved it.

Burnside moved the army to Falmouth, Virginia, directly across the Rappahannock River from Fredericksburg. It was his intention to cross the river on pontoon bridges and assault the heights behind the city, which Lee's army had fortified. Fredericksburg was a main terminus for roads and rail lines in northern Virginia, directly on the path to Richmond.

Burnside waited for his pontoons to arrive—and waited and waited. The pontoons finally arrived a week later, while Lee had continued to pull his entire army together and strongly entrench and fortify his Fredericksburg position.[6] Burnside sat in Falmouth two more weeks, brooding over his spoiled plan and calculating alternative strategies. In the end, he reasoned that his original plan would be so obvious that the Confederates would never suspect that he would do it.[7]

Burnside counted on his crossing being masked by the city itself, and he reasoned that with rapid construction of the pontoon bridges and quick deployment and assault by his troops, the rebels would be overwhelmed. The attack was to be a massive frontal assault on the Confederate fortifications. It had to be made over six hundred yards of open ground, cut across the middle by a deep canal. The Confederate battle line was behind a stone wall at the base of Marye's Heights, the high ground, with several lines of infantry and artillery entrenched on the Heights.

On December 13, 1862, wave after wave of Union troops charged the Confederate position, and by nightfall more than 12,500 federal soldiers were dead, wounded, or missing in action. The First Minnesota and the other three regiments of its brigade were spared the slaughter. The rest of the Second Corps of the Army of the Potomac was not.

The Minnesotans, and the rest of their brigade, were saved by their benevolent and beloved commander. Brigadier General Alfred Sully, a former colonel of the First Minnesota, apparently was ordered in at some point late in the day. Having watched the useless butchery for hours, he simply refused to order his men forward. Sully later claimed that the order to advance had been countermanded. However, a man in Company B wrote a letter to the *Stillwater Messenger* newspaper that quoted Sully as saying, "They might court martial me and be damned, I was not going to murder my men, and it would be nothing less than murder to have sent them there."[8]

The regiment was in a forward position on the federal right during the battle, supporting an artillery battery and under continual rebel artillery fire. It was relieved after dark, and the men spent the night sleeping on the sidewalks of Fredericksburg. The next night they were sent out on picket duty in an advanced position in the center of the federal line. They spent the night digging rifle pits on the frozen, open plain. Thomas Pressnell, a nineteen-year-old printer from St. Paul and member of Company C, recalled: "After 3 hours of steady hard work on the trenches I was relieved about 2 o'clock for 2 hours rest. In groping around for a place to lie down I came upon a man covered by a large double blanket. Considering that this blanket was large enough to cover two comfortably, I crept in beside him and in 2 minutes was sound asleep. About 4 o'clock I was awakened by a subdued voice and ordered to 'fall-in.' Observing that my sleeping companion did not move I endeavored to awaken him also, but there being no response to my kicks. I passed my hand over his face and thus discovered that I had been sleeping with a dead man."[9]

Twenty-one-year-old Private Daniel Bond of Company F remembered the ordeal of holding a position on a battlefield at night. On this night, some of the wounded had been lying between the lines for more than twenty-four hours: "I was again obliged, in the stillness of the night, to listen to the heart rending cries of poor wounded men. . . . The weather was very cold, and there were men lying with limbs torn from their bodies, on the cold, damp lap of earth. And the icy grasp of winter was freezing their blood as it flowed from the shattered fragments of their mutilated members."[10]

Burnside pulled his army back across the Rappahannock River and went into winter camp. The beginning of 1863 found the First Minnesota and the rest of the Army of the Potomac living in a grim, frozen tent-and-log city surrounding Falmouth. It was one of the worst periods for this battered, abused, and poorly commanded army and has been referred to as the Army of the Potomac's "Valley Forge."[11]

Sixteen-year-old Charley Goddard, a Winona, Minnesota, boy in Company K, wrote to his mother on New Year's:

Daniel Bond of Company F. Late in life he wrote a vivid, fascinating, if somewhat cantankerous, reminiscence of his company's part in the war.

Camp near Falmouth, Jan. 1st, 1863. Dear mother—I received your kind letter this morning. If you remember we were last year at Camp Stone Md., and I think I enjoyed myself much better than I have here. But I did not come in the Army for enjoyment and I cannot expect it. One year ago last night I was on guard, and on post from 11 o'clock to 1. Had the pleasure of seeing the old year out and new year in and I strained my eyes to see if there was any difference. But the new year looked about the same as the old. That night I let one of my comrades in camp with a bucket of apples and a jug of cidar, but that poor fellow has gone to his last resting place. He was shot at the battle of Antietam in the right breast and died. I would gladly wish him a happy new year, but I cannot....

I take Burnside at his word—he says he cannot command such an army as this, and I think he cannot.[12]

Daniel Bond recalled: "We had but miserable poor quarters this winter owing to the scarcity of timber. Our quarters consisted of a hole dug in the ground, a shelter tent pitched over it. A fireplace dug-out in one side with a little, low chimney over it."[13] Bond's mood in the winter of 1862–63 probably mirrored every man's in the Army of the Potomac. They all had earned the right to be cantankerous. "I have not spoken of a certain peculiarity in my mind at or about this time. That was I was subject to fits of most violent anger, so that at times I came very near striking my officers over the head with my gun. I could not control myself at all. On one occasion when [Artemus] Decker and I were playing at chess, one of these fits seized me and I knocked the board and men all over the tent. This lasted me until the spring."[14]

Determined to do something—anything—to inflict some kind of damage on Lee, Burnside mounted a rare midwinter campaign. He decided to move the army upriver, cross, and try to outflank Lee and drive him out of Fredericksburg. On January 21, 1863, Burnside put most of the army in motion. Almost immediately a cold winter rain started falling and continued to fall steadily for days.

The red, sandy, clay soil quickly turned into bottomless mire. Artillery pieces, caissons, and wagons sank up to the wheel hubs and finally up to the muzzles of the guns. Twelve-horse teams tried to move a single cannon; hundreds of men gathered to try and pull a cannon or wagon along with ropes.[15] The Confederates watched the show from the other side of the Rappahannock, laughing and shouting suggestions. After forty-eight hours the campaign was abandoned, and the infamous "Mud March" ended with the miserable, wet, cold, and filthy Army of the Potomac slogging back to their old camps at Falmouth.

The First Minnesota and its brigade had the good fortune to be camped in view of the rebels across the river. As a result, they were not called on to participate in what was intended to be a clandestine flank maneuver, now turned disaster. Private Isaac L. Taylor of Company E

Patrick Henry Taylor (left) and his brother Isaac Lyman Taylor,
both of Company E

had no particular sympathy for Burnside, but his pragmatic outlook on life and the war left him with little tolerance for the common soldier's tendency to blame everything on the generals. The teacher from Belle Prairie, Minnesota, watched a portion of the exhausted, mud-spattered army march back into camp. With his characteristic droll sarcasm, he noted in his twenty-sixth birthday diary entry—Friday, January 23, 1863: "They have been out during the past three days and look rather the 'worse for wear.' Some of them threaten to 'sit up nights to curse Burnside' for taking them out in the mud and storm. I think, myself, that

This 1861 photograph of officers from the First Minnesota tells the story of the regiment: (left to right) Captain Wilson B. Farrell, killed at Gettysburg; First Lieutenant Samuel T. Raguet, wounded at First Bull Run; Captain Louis Muller, killed at Gettysburg; (seated) Major Mark Downie, wounded at Gettysburg; First Lieutenant Charles Zierenberg, died in September 1862 from wounds received at Vienna, Virginia; Captain Henry Coates, survived the war unscathed.

Burnside ought to be removed for allowing it to rain. If Burnside is not smart enough to out-wit the Lord in these matters, it is clear that he is not the man to handle the Army of the Potomac."[16]

Whether or not it was for "allowing it to rain," Burnside surely set some kind of record for the brevity of his in-and-out performance with the Army of the Potomac; he lasted less than three months. President Lincoln next named Major General Joseph Hooker of the First Corps as commander. Hooker had a reputation for being a courageous and competent officer and had won the confidence and respect of the common soldier. He also had a reputation for denigrating fellow officers and superiors, drinking to excess, and frequenting brothels.[17]

Like many colorful figures, Hooker had a way of generating myths during his own time and after. He was known during the war as "Fighting Joe" Hooker, which was not completely undeserved but still makes him sound more sanguine than he really was. The sobriquet stuck after a newspaper headline during the 1862 Peninsula Campaign was incorrectly typeset. It was supposed to read "Fighting—Joe Hooker," but the dash was left out.[18]

The story circulated long afterward that his penchant for prostitutes resulted in one of their more common slang names. The term "hooker" for a prostitute actually predated the Civil War by nearly two decades. The term came from an area of New York City called "The Hook" that was known for its many brothels.[19]

Despite a promising start and an excellent battle plan to outflank Robert E. Lee's army, Hooker as commander of the Army of the Potomac had a short tenure, ending in military disaster. He left part of his army, including the First Minnesota, in front of Fredericksburg and made a rapid march upriver with the rest. Crossing the Rappahannock about twenty-seven miles above Fredericksburg, he quickly began sweeping down on Lee's left flank. The remainder of the federal army crossed the river and once more assaulted the city to keep Lee's attention divided.

Lee saw through the ruse and again, contrary to conventional military tactics, split his force in the face of a superior enemy. He left a token force to hold the high ground above Fredericksburg and rapidly marched the rest to meet Hooker at a small crossroads hamlet called Chancellorsville.

The Confederates attacked the federal army aggressively, bringing it to a screeching halt. Hooker actually stopped the advance, to everyone's astonishment, and ordered his lines to fall back. The full weight of Lee's reputation and previous victories finally seemed to have gotten to Hooker. Later, speaking of the battle, he said, "Well, to tell the truth, I just lost confidence in Joe Hooker."[20]

Sensing Hooker's fear, Lee again split his force. He sent Lieutenant General Thomas J. (Stonewall) Jackson and his corps on a wide, arcing march to get on the right flank of the federal army. The march took most of the day. Federal pickets, seeing the movement, frantically reported back to headquarters that an enormous column of rebels was approaching the right flank. The reports were ignored or dismissed as really meaning the rebels were in retreat.[21]

In the early evening Jackson's men came roaring out of the woods and smashed the Union right flank, held by the Eleventh Corps, sending a large portion of the Army of the Potomac into panic and retreat. Darkness was the only thing that stopped Hooker's army from being completely routed. The next day Hooker continued to draw in his lines, and the federals finally retreated across the Rappahannock River and started back to Falmouth.

While Lee left part of his force to keep pressure on Hooker, he rushed the rest back toward Fredericksburg to attack the federal troops there. The Union army had taken Fredericksburg and Marye's Heights and was conducting an advance westward to connect with Hooker. Through aggressive fighting and maneuvering, the rebels pushed the Federals back and retook Fredericksburg. Hooker eventually ordered his troops to withdraw.

The Battle of Chancellorsville and the second Battle of Fredericksburg cost Lee dearly in casualties. This was especially true in the loss of Stonewall Jackson, mistakenly shot in the dark by his own troops. Chancellorsville is considered one of Lee's masterpieces of strategy, tactics, and crisis control. He displayed his uncanny ability to read and recognize his opponent's weaknesses and mistakes and to capitalize on them aggressively.[22] Stunned and dazed, Joseph Hooker and the Army of the Potomac stumbled back to their camp around Falmouth.

After inflicting these humiliating defeats, Lee decided once more to invade the North. He knew Union morale was low—the advance of Confederate troops into the heartland would send it even lower and might bolster the growing sentiment in the North for a negotiated peace to end the war.[23] An invasion would also shift the battleground from northern Virginia and allow the farmers to plant and harvest a desperately needed crop. The more immediate benefit to Lee's ragged army would be an area rich in food, clothing, shoes, and other supplies available in an area untouched by the ravages of war. In political terms, military success on northern soil finally might induce Great Britain and the other European powers officially to recognize the Confederate States of America as a legitimate government and separate nation from the United States.

There were still dissenting voices to the plan in both the Confederate government and the army itself. One of the central moral pillars of the war, in the minds of many southerners, was that the Confederacy was fighting against "the Yankee invaders." They were fighting on their own soil against a foreign, invading army. Like the invasion of the previous year that ended with the Battle of Antietam, this excursion was going to take the war aggressively into the country to the north—the United States of America.[24]

— 2 —

The morning of a better hope

IN HIS MEMOIRS, former Orderly Sergeant James Wright of the First Minnesota's Company F wrote: "Someone has asserted that every one must 'eat a peck of dirt during his lifetime.' I have heard some old soldiers say that they had eaten that much in a day."[1] By the beginning of June 1863, more than 160,000 men on both banks of the Rappahannock River were about to add significantly to their peck.

On June 3, Lee began moving his army of roughly 75,000 men north. The scouts and pickets of the Army of the Potomac immediately noted the movement. After it was confirmed that it was a general advance by the entire rebel army, not just a concentration of the forces, Hooker put his own army into motion. On June 10, the federals began following a parallel course with Lee, staying between the rebels and Washington, D.C.

By the spring of 1863, the Army of the Potomac was organized into seven corps. The First Minnesota belonged to the Second Corps under Major General Winfield Scott Hancock. Of the three divisions within the Second Corps, the Minnesotans were in the Second Division, commanded by Brigadier General John Gibbon. The division was made up of three brigades, composed of four or five individual regiments. The First Minnesota belonged to the First Brigade, commanded by Brigadier General William Harrow, of Gibbon's Second Division.

The regiment's commander was Colonel William Colvill, Jr., who had mustered into the regiment at the beginning of the war as captain of

Company F. The thirty-three-year-old Colvill had been a lawyer and a newspaper editor in Red Wing, Minnesota. He had been promoted to colonel of the regiment on May 6, 1863. One of his early orders dealt with the mundane matters of command, typical of the day-to-day tedium of army life in the grim winter camp at Falmouth. The issue was obviously no small matter to the lieutenant concerned, since marching orders were expected at any time.

> "Headquarters, 1st Minn. Volunteers. Camp near Falmouth, Va., June 13th, 1863. Special Order No. 53. A board of survey to consist of Capt. Perium, 1st Lieut. Demarest and 2nd Lieut. DeGray will convene at this camp without delay for the purpose of examining a blanket issued to 1st Lieut. Heffelfinger, Commanding Co. D, by the Regimental Quarter Master as a 'Rubber Blanket' and which the former refuses to accept as such. They will report as to whether said blanket is 'Rubber' or 'Painted'—By order of Col. Colvill, Commanding, John Pellar, Adjutant"

Lieutenant Christopher Heffelfinger was a twenty-nine-year-old house painter from Minneapolis. Whether his "gum blanket" dilemma was resolved is not known, but on the evening of the next day, June 14,

the First Minnesota and the rest of Harrow's brigade departed their winter camp. The brigade was marched about five miles, halted, and waited in formation about an hour, then was about-faced and marched back to the Rappahannock where it arrived around midnight. The men promptly were posted for picket duty. They started again the next morning and experienced what was remembered as probably the hottest day of marching the Minnesotans ever endured.

This photograph of Colonel William Colvill, Jr., was probably taken during his recovery from the Gettysburg wounds. In marked contrast to earlier photos, the face is leaner, the eyes show a strain and haggard weariness that come from chronic and severe pain.

The men already were exhausted from the ten-mile march, counter-march, and a night of lost sleep from picket duty. They managed to catch a few hours' sleep in the middle of the sweltering day after their brigade caught up with the rest of their division. By 2:00 P.M. they were back on the march, down a road that was bordered by dense trees and foliage. It was like a hot, humid, dusty tunnel with no air circulating. Orderly Sergeant James Wright, who was a twenty-three-year-old student at Hamline College in Red Wing, Minnesota, when the war began, wrote: "It was one of the heart-breaking marches of our experiences and many men wilted in the scorching heat and dust like mown grass. There were many prostrations; men staggering from the ranks and falling as if shot. There were a number of cases of fatal sun-stroke, and some dying almost as quickly as if struck by a bullet in a vital part. All of the ambulances were filled with helpless men and those left behind were coming in all of the first part of the night."[2]

The entire march from the Rappahannock to Gettysburg and on through the battle was noted by many as having some particularly warm and humid days. There was no light-weight, summer-issue uniform, and everyone was clad in wool, with wool or heavy cotton underwear (if it was worn), and leather accoutrements, and they were

Orderly Sergeant James Wright reenlisted and served to the end of the war, obtaining the rank of captain.

First Lieutenant Christopher Heffelfinger commanded Company D at Gettysburg.

lugging thirty-five to forty pounds of arms and equipment.[3] On the train trip to Gettysburg for the fiftieth anniversary in 1913, Chester Durfee, formerly of Company K, recalled, "June 30, 1913, Arriving at Hagerstown, Maryland—4:15 P.M. Here is the old stomping ground where we experienced some hardships on our terrible, long, hot, dusty march to the battlefield of Gettysburg, Pennsylvania in 1863—just 50 years ago today. I, for one, do well remember while marching along here with the blood trickling down my poor chaffed limbs to my shoes."[4]

The First Minnesota and the rest of its division made about eighteen miles on the first day's march. Their brigade decided to make an early start on June 16 to avoid the heat, and they set off at 3:00 A.M. We can wonder what they thought they were saving themselves, because they were made to march until 6:00 that evening.[5] At 10:00 A.M. on Sunday, June 21, they reached Thoroughfare Gap in the Blue Ridge Mountains, where the regiment got a four-day rest. They were assigned to guard the pass and provide information to the wagon trains that passed through.

During this lull for guard duty, Sergeant Philip Hamlin of Company F, a twenty-four-year-old farmer from Pine Island, Minnesota, penned a contemplative letter home to his parents. Musing on the cause for which he was fighting and what the future might hold, Hamlin wrote:

> Thoroughfare Gap, Virginia, June 23rd, 1863. Dear Friends: We are halted at the base of the Bull Run Mountains about 10 miles from Manassas. This is beautiful country. It is sad to think that a picture so lovely is marred by the hand of war. Here each road and stream and mountain gap have been the witnesses of scenes of violence and blood, and still the work is not stayed.
>
> But in spite of the desolation caused, a great work is being wrought in the midst of this by the blasts of war. And when peace comes, if it should be decided in our favor, these lands will be held cheaply and we shall see organized free labor colonies coming in purchasing the soil and establishing here their institutions and civilization. It would be a glorious sight to see a young and free civilization springing-up here where slavery has wrought ruin.
>
> The morning of a better hope than has ever lighted the hearts of the people of this land.[6]

Guarding the gap provided free time for men not on picket duty. On the third day of their stop, Colonel Colvill sent for Orderly Sergeant

James Wright and invited him on a trip to the Bull Run battlefield, about ten miles to the east. Wright was pleased to be asked, as the regiment had marched through the battlefield during the dark night of Saturday, June 20. The men strained in the blackness to make out what they could of the place where they had their "baptism of fire" nearly two years earlier, but as Wright said, it had been so dark that, "one could scarcely distinguish a man from a mule six feet away."[7]

Others had planned to go as well, but only two other horses could be obtained, so Wright and Colvill's orderly, twenty-four-year-old Private Milton L. Bevans of Company F, accompanied the colonel. They were cautioned to "keep an eye out for bushwhackers" and started on their journey. The men obtained lunch—hot biscuits and fried ham and eggs—at either the Robinson or Van Pelt farmhouse on the battlefield. They were asked to pay for the meal but were offered all they wanted to eat. Wright noted that it was a nice change from army field rations.

The men surveyed the battlefield more closely after their meal, taking in the debris of both battles that had occurred there—the one they participated in back in 1861 and the second Battle of Bull Run under Major General John Pope in 1862. The area was still littered with rotting and rusting portions of clothing, damaged weapons, and equipment, as well as the contents of shallow graves that had been washed open by the rain or rooted-up by hogs. James Wright noted, "On a recently cut stump some grim jester has set a skull, as if in mockery of a real sentry. Much of the skin was still on it—dried and shrunken—and a bullet had passed through it from the right temple to a point above the left ear. There was nothing to indicate the color of the uniform he had worn—or the flag he had followed. I rode away from this grinning, ghastly exhibit of a mutilated, dissevered head, with the unpleasant reflection that my own might be transferred to a stump before the war ended."[8]

The men started back to Thoroughfare Gap, keeping a cautious eye open for rebels. They heard a smattering of musketry in the distance, too far away to be able to discern the direction. Becoming uneasy, they planned for what to do if attacked. Embracing the adage that "discretion is the better part of valor," they decided to run if they could and fight with the revolvers they carried if they could not. To their relief they finally rode through the federal picket line, and Wright remembered:

"The day had been pleasant, without dust or oppressive heat, and no 'Johnny Reb' had fired buck-shot at us or tried in any way to molest us; just the same, the day had not gone without some anxiety and we were glad to get inside the circle of protecting rifles."[9]

By mid-June advanced portions of Lee's army already were plundering southwestern Pennsylvania with little opposition. During the night of June 24 the sky clouded over and a light rain began to fall. The First Minnesota and the rest of the Second Division of the Second Corps were to be the rear guard in the movement out of Thoroughfare Gap. The rain continued intermittently throughout the day of June 25, and when it was not raining the air was still thick and misty.

The march went peacefully for a while, and then a series of minor attacks started on the rear and flanks of the column. These harassing attacks, by Confederate Major General J. E. B. Stuart's cavalry, tried to capture supply wagons and federal soldiers as opportunity presented. The horsemen would swoop in out of the mist and fire a few rounds and then retreat when they met resistance. The First Minnesota had to deploy into a battle line several times when the attacks became sharp enough to press the skirmish lines on the flanks and rear.

By noon the column had reached the small hamlet of Haymarket, Virginia, and Stuart's men became a little bolder and more aggressive. "At 12 m. ["meridian" or noon] as we approach Haymarket some cavalry appear on a bluff south of us, and while the boys are earnestly arguing the question 'are they our men?,' a white puff of smoke and the unearthly screech of a shell closes the debate and a unanimous decision is rendered in the negative. Shells fly about our ears pretty lively for a short time, but our batterys soon get into position and succeed in quelling the disturbance," Private Isaac Taylor of Company E wrote in his diary.[10]

Colonel William Colvill's horse was blown out from under him by a bursting Confederate shell. Colvill managed to kick his feet free of the stirrups and roll away from the frantic, thrashing animal. He got up covered in thick, red Virginia mud but unhurt. The horse did not fare as well—its back legs were gone. Colvill directed his orderly to shoot the animal and to recover his bridle and saddle. Orderly Bevans then went off to find his colonel another mount. Several men in the Second Division of the Second Corps were killed during the shelling, and two men of the First Minnesota—Joseph Walsh of Company B and George A. Kinney of Company G—were wounded.

The most important outcome of the Battle of Haymarket was that J. E. B. Stuart was delayed, and as a result he made a fateful decision. Stuart was a victim of—and a participant in—a series of misunderstood orders, directives, reports, mixed messages, and missing couriers to and from General Lee and from Lieutenant General James Longstreet, commander of the rebel army's First Corps. There is also the distinct possibility that Stuart simply chose to interpret broadly—or purposely misinterpret—his orders so he could cut loose on another of his famous independent raids.[11] He had ridden completely around the Army of the Potomac during the Peninsula Campaign in 1862, a raiding sortie that solidified his reputation as a bold, intrepid, and brilliant cavalry commander.

Stuart was still trying to rescue his reputation from the pummeling it had taken on June 9, 1863, at Brandy Station, Virginia. On that morning federal cavalry, always considered the inferior of the knightly Confederate horsemen, surprised Stuart and his forces and nearly defeated them. It was an enormous blow to rebel egos and an equally enormous lift for the Union cavalry.

After engaging the Union Second Corps at Haymarket, Stuart decided rather than rejoining Lee's army, as his orders seemed to indicate under the circumstances, that he would ride around the federal army once again. He chose to ride east, between Washington, D.C., and the Army of the Potomac, raiding and capturing supplies and prisoners. He left two of his least-liked, and least-competent, subordinates and their cavalry brigades to guard the mountain passes for Lee's army.[12] Stuart set off, and Lee would not see or hear from him again until late in the afternoon of the second day of battle at Gettysburg.

Misunderstandings, lost time, and lost opportunity plagued Lee's entire campaign in Pennsylvania and stemmed largely from his desire for secrecy; he was determined that his plans would not be leaked or divulged. This compulsion was driven, at least in part, by the fiasco of the lost set of written orders just prior to Antietam.[13] Lee was, apparently, even circumspect in discussing his plans with Confederate President

Jefferson Davis and his cabinet.[14] No specific written orders for the overall plan were ever made—officers were informed on a "need to know" basis, nor was there any indication that Lee ever intended to decide on a specific battle plan. Evidently circumstances would dictate the specifics of his campaign into Pennsylvania.[15]

After a twenty-mile march, the First Minnesota bivouacked at Gum Springs, Virginia, on the night of June 25 in a driving rain. The men were ordered to sleep close together and to sleep with their rifles. On the morning of June 26 the First Minnesota and its division were assigned to lead the Second Corps in the day's march. James Wright recalled that the pace and the weather were having the expected effect on the men.

> Our general appearance that morning, as we left the bivouac, was about as animated and cheerful as a lot of rained-on fowls leaving their roost on a back fence to hunt for their morning meal in the wet grass. It was still raining a little; our clothing was wet and spattered and smeared with mahogany colored mud. The moisture, the sand, and the sharp stones of the road, which the wheels of the artillery and the [supply wagon] trains had broken up badly, had been very destructive to shoe leather. Men who had left the Rappahannock 12 days before, with new shoes on their feet, were now practically bare-footed; and there were quite a number with feet so badly bruised or blistered that they walked like foundered horses.[16]

As the day progressed, the clouds cleared and the oppressive heat returned. The men kept marching, "some of the boys were telling stories, others were laughing and others were hanging down thare heads as if in deep meditation—and all at once our 'official' company singer, J. G. Sonderman, begin to sing and the whole company dit wake up as if they had been dreaming in a sound sleep. Almost every one that had a singing voice dit fall in with Sonderman so that almost the whole company was singing," recalled Private Charles Muller of Company A.[17]

By June 28 the Army of the Potomac was concentrating at Frederick, Maryland, about twenty-six miles south of Gettysburg, Pennsylvania. General Hooker was frustrated in not being allowed to abandon Harpers Ferry, Virginia, and use its garrison to attack the rear of Lee's army and his supply wagons.[18] He was also required to stay between the Confederates and Washington, D.C. He felt that all his best military options and strategies were being thwarted by the civilian government. In frustration, he submitted his resignation, which Lincoln quickly accepted.[19] "On this day it was noised through the army that General Meade had superceded Hooker. But we had become so accustomed to change, and even defeat, that nothing could distort our equanimity. We could neither be depressed by disaster nor elated by success," wrote Private Daniel Bond of Company F.[20]

A change in commanding generals on the eve of an expected major battle was enough to make anyone uneasy—especially the new commanding general. Forty-seven-year-old George Gordon Meade was a West Point graduate from a prominent Philadelphia family. He had been a reliable and successful division and corps commander, commanding the army's Fifth Corps. In light of the current crisis, Lincoln liked the fact the Meade was a Pennsylvanian—saying a man was "likely to fight harder on his own dung heap."

Meade quickly developed a plan using the tactics that Lee himself employed to such devastating effect, particularly in the last year of the war—fortify and entrench a position and make the enemy attack you. Meade selected as his position a line running parallel to Big Pipe Creek in northern Maryland, about five or six miles from Pennsylvania. In fulfilling its part in this plan, the First Minnesota marched on the morning of June 29 and crossed the Monacacy River, this time with their division leading the corps.

A misdelivered set of marching orders caused the Second Corps to be four hours late starting, and the men were driven relentlessly on the warm day to make up the time.[21] After about three hours of hard marching, the regiment came to small, knee-deep Linganore Creek, a tributary to the Monacacy River.[22] A couple of logs were in place across it, hewn flat on top for local pedestrian traffic.

In an attempt to prevent a bottleneck at this crossing, the inspector general for the Second Corps—Lieutenant Colonel Charles H. Morgan—posted himself there. He directed all regimental commanders to march their men rapidly straight through the creek without using either of the logs to cross. All of the veterans of the First Minnesota knew the misery of having to march on a hot day in soaked shoes and socks, and they were not looking forward to raw and blistered feet.

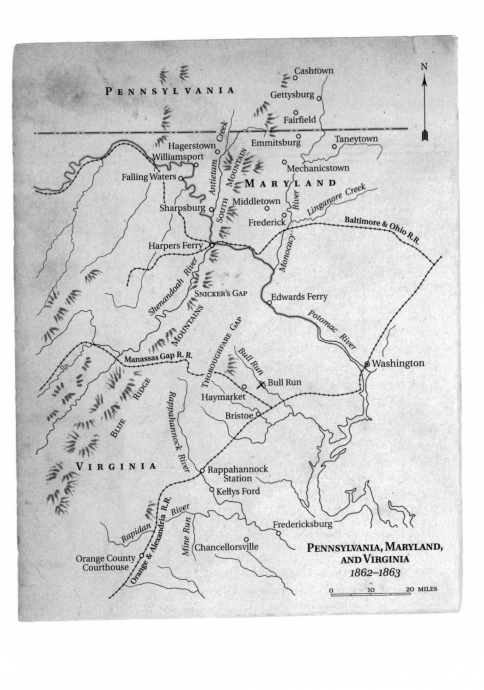

N

PENNSYLVANIA

Cashtown

Gettysburg

Fairfield

Emmitsburg

Taneytown

Hagerstown

Williamsport

Mechanicstown

Falling Waters

MARYLAND

Sharpsburg

Middletown

Frederick

Baltimore & Ohio R.R.

Linganore Creek

Antietam Creek

SOUTH MOUNTAIN

Monocacy River

Harpers Ferry

SNICKER'S GAP

Edwards Ferry

Shenandoah River

Potomac River

BLUE RIDGE MOUNTAINS

THOROUGHFARE GAP

Manassas Gap R.R.

Bull Run

Washington

Bull Run

Haymarket

Bristoe

Rappahannock River

VIRGINIA

Rappahannock Station

Kellys Ford

Rapidan River

Orange & Alexandria R.R.

Mine Run

Fredericksburg

Orange County Courthouse

Chancellorsville

PENNSYLVANIA, MARYLAND, AND VIRGINIA
1862–1863

0   10   20 MILES

Colonel Colvill received the order from Morgan and gave the command for close-order march. A few of the line officers, and some of the men, saw an opportunity to scamper across one of the logs. Regimental historian William Lochren, a thirty-one-year-old Irish immigrant and Minneapolis attorney, admitted to doing this himself.[23] Morgan saw them crossing on the log and was angry that his order had been ignored. There were similar log-crossers in the Fifteenth Massachusetts, which followed the Minnesotans.

James Wright stated that some of the Minnesota boys delivered a few catcalls toward Morgan as they were passing through the water, which could not have helped Morgan's demeanor. However, when the Fifteenth Massachusetts was given the order to march through the stream, Wright recalled that, "Before the regiment was half across there was a pretty strong 'barnyard chorus' behind us and we all knew that it was a 'benefit' for the inspector general—and he knew it, too!"[24]

A halt was ordered three miles down the road. The men of the brigade were in column of battalions, with about twenty feet between the lines. As Morgan rode past toward the front of the column, he was given a collective "groan," according to Lochren, by some of the men of the Fifteenth Massachusetts. However, James Wright wrote that a few of the First Minnesota boys had a part in it as well.

Morgan immediately vented his outrage on Colonel Colvill and Colonel George H. Ward of the Fifteenth Massachusetts and had them both placed under arrest. Colvill spent the rest of the journey to Gettysburg riding behind his regiment instead of at his place in the front. Lieutenant Colonel Charles Powell Adams, a thirty-two-year-old newspaper editor from Hastings, Minnesota, took command of the First Minnesota.[25]

For the men in wet footgear, it was as bad a day as any could have expected—another sweltering day of heat and humidity and a numbing thirty-three-mile march. While passing through Uniontown, Maryland, the regiment was pleased to find that this particular Maryland town—unlike Baltimore—was indeed a "Union" town. Twenty-one-year-old Private Edward H. Bassett of Company G wrote in his diary, "When we came through Union Town last night, the women brought out bread, milk, cakes and pies and gave to us, and very few would take any pay.

They all gave freely. They had no warning of our approach, and were happy to see us as they had expected the Rebs."[26]

Orderly Sergeant James Wright noted that the farther they marched north from the Potomac River, the more accommodating the citizenry was:

> Instead of it being exceptional to get a friendly greeting it became quite general. Flags, handerkerchiefs, aprons and sun-bonnets were waved from windows, door-steps and front-yard fences as we tramped hurriedly on. These things had a soothing effect on our disturbed feelings, and a little later, when we made a short halt, women and children came with baskets of buttered bread and *real* doughnuts, pails of water and jugs of buttermilk, the boys cheered them with hearty goodwill. This was not long after noon and the halt was but brief. Then we trudged on again through the long, hot afternoon. The weight on our weary shoulders felt as if it was increasing with each rod we traveled, and it was in vain that we "hunched up" the right shoulder or the left, or shifted the rifle more frequently from one to the other; it was there just the same and bore down incessantly.[27]

The regiment halted at 9:00 P.M., just past Uniontown, seven or eight miles from the Pennsylvania border. Many of the men were so tired that they dropped down on their blankets after falling out of ranks on the roadside. They did not even bother to carry out the ritual of every federal soldier—boiling a cup of coffee at every stop on a march.

Fate was to have a subtle revenge on Lochren for his log crossing. Having just dropped to the ground, sound asleep, he was almost immediately awakened by the regimental adjutant, Lieutenant John Pellar, with orders to go out with a picket detail for the night. Lochren wrote that he felt exhaustion had just about reached its limit, but there was nothing he could do to avoid it.[28] First Lieutenant Thomas Sinclair, commanding Company B, took charge of the picket detail. The thirty-one-year-old Irish stonemason from Stillwater, Minnesota, formed his worn-out men, and they all stumbled three miles farther in the dark to find their posts for the night.[29]

Fate also granted the men of the First Minnesota one last day's rest before the beginning of their real ordeal. On June 30 they remained in place near Big Pipe Creek north of Uniontown. The companies made out their bimonthly muster payrolls on which, William Lochren pointed out, so many would never draw pay. Private Isaac L. Taylor of Company E noted in his diary, "Tuesday, June 30th, 1863; Light showers and sunshine alternate. Mustered for pay in the A.M. In the P.M. I go 'out around' to farm houses and get bread, butter, milk, eggs. etc.; A good Union lady gives me a quart of apple butter. We live on the 'top shelf' today. The boys are enthusiastic in their admiration of Maryland generally and the nice bread and nice girls in particular."[30]

Things were developing rapidly north of the state line. The rebel army had been ravaging southwestern Pennsylvania since June 23, meeting scant opposition from local militias. General J. E. B. Stuart's cavalry was still looking for a way to get back to the rebel army. Without his most trusted cavalry commander to bring information, Lee felt blind to the movements of the federals.

Lee had split his force and sent them about their plundering and gathering with the intention of finally taking the state capital, Harrisburg. He immediately ordered his scattered army to rendezvous at Gettysburg, six miles north of the Maryland border. Gettysburg was a junction for ten major roads, and Lee did not necessarily intend to fight there but rather to concentrate his forces and move on to do battle with the Army of the Potomac elsewhere.

At the same time, Meade sent Major General John Reynolds and his First Corps, along with the Third and Eleventh Corps, toward Gettysburg. They were to make contact and mask the Union army's concentration on Big Pipe Creek. The advance portion of Reynolds's force—cavalry under Brigadier General John Buford—moved into Gettysburg from the south on the afternoon of June 30 just as Confederate patrols moved out of town going west.

Buford posted heavy picket lines covering the north and northwest roads and waited for the expected attack the next morning. In the evening, he could see the campfires of a Confederate division in the distance, northwest of the town. He instructed his officers to have the men fight dismounted, as infantry, saying, "They will attack you in the morning and they will come booming—skirmishers three deep. You will have to fight like the devil until supports arrive."[31]

Early on July 1, bad luck again befell the marching orders for the Second Corps. This time Lieutenant Colonel Morgan's bodyservant unknowingly had knocked the tissue paper set of orders into the wet grass while packing Morgan's things. Morgan frantically searched his tent until he noticed a yellow lump on the bottom of his servant's boot. Examining the yellow paste, Morgan knew it was the remains of the orders.[32] The corps had been roused at about 3:00 A.M. but waited around until a new set of orders could make it back from headquarters.

At either 6:30 or 7:30 A.M.—there are conflicting diary accounts— the First Minnesota finally left their bivouac north of Uniontown and marched back through the town. There they took a road to their right, marching northwest toward Taneytown, Maryland. They arrived in Taneytown shortly after noon. James Wright recalled that he thought he heard firing before reaching the town, about thirteen miles from Gettysburg, but they did not hear anything during their one-hour stop.

At this time General Winfield Scott Hancock was ordered by General Meade to ride to the field at Gettysburg as fast as he could. Hancock was to be Meade's personal representative in the field until the commanding general arrived. General John Reynolds, first commander on the field, had been killed by a Confederate sniper early in the fighting, which prompted Meade to send Hancock.

The men of the First Minnesota were on the move again shortly after 1:00 P.M., and this time they were ordered to march at quick time and to keep the ranks well closed-up. Almost immediately after the march resumed, everyone heard the distinct rumble and roar of distant artillery. It became louder the farther north they traveled.

James Wright remembered, about halfway between Taneytown and Gettysburg, "We crossed a higher ridge which gave a more extended view than we had had for some time, and we could see and hear enough to satisfy us that there was real fighting going on. A heavy and well-sustained artillery fire was generating great masses of smoke which was rising and expanding into white clouds as the wind carried it away. On this the late afternoon sun was shining, making the hills appear as if covered with snow—but none of us imagined there was a snowstorm there."[33]

— 3 —

The best we had in the shop

THE FIRST RIFLE SHOT CRACKED in the still morning air at dawn on July 1, 1863. As the battle opened, the dismounted Union cavalry troopers using their breech-loading carbines held back the rebels. The battle escalated as the race continued for more Confederate and Union troops to arrive on the scene. The rebels won the race, overwhelming the federal troops, and pouring into town from the north and northwest.

By nightfall of July 1, the Union army had drawn up into a fishhook-shaped battle line on the high ground southeast of the town. The right flank was anchored on Culp's Hill, across Cemetery Hill, and southward down Cemetery Ridge. The Confederate army faced them in a wide arc through the town of Gettysburg and south along Seminary Ridge to the west of the federal position.

Around 4:00 P.M, the rapidly marching Second Corps began to run into the refugees from the battle. Accounts mention that these men were the "camp followers"—cooks and noncombatants of various kinds, civilian refugees, as well as "skeedadlers," men who simply looked for any opportunity to leave the fight and keep going toward the rear. All had tales of utter defeat and rout of the Army of the Potomac. William Lochren mentioned with some contempt that most were wearing the crescent-moon insignia of the Eleventh Corps. This ill-fated corps did not have much reputation left after they were routed by Stonewall Jackson's flank attack at Chancellorsville.

The Eleventh Corps had been commanded earlier in the war by the German immigrant Major General Franz Sigel. These men, many of them also German immigrants, were known for proudly declaring, "I fights mit Sigel!" The corps had been commanded since March 31, 1863, by Major General Oliver O. Howard. After Chancellorsville and Gettysburg, the corps became the butt of a classic bit of scathing soldier humor as the proud statement was reworked and repeated mockingly by others as, "I fights mit Sigel, but I runs mit Howard!"[1]

The First Minnesota continued its rapid march north. Somewhere between nine and ten o'clock on July 1, the Minnesotans formed in line of battle, stacked arms, and bivouacked for the night. Given their proximity to the battlefield and the results of the day's fighting, there appears to have been some initial indecision as to whether the men should stay or move onto the battlefield proper. Relating a scene that must have been maddeningly frustrating for the exhausted, hungry soldiers, Company K's Sergeant Mat Marvin, a twenty-four-year-old farmer from Winona, Minnesota, wrote in his diary of this night, "Three times we got permission to have fires & twice they were put out; four times we made coffee & three times we threw it away and packed up & fell in. At last the order came to build brest works, that we should stay all night."[2]

Twenty men were sent out on picket detail and, as Mat Marvin indicated, the rest of the regiment was ordered to build barricades, or breastworks—an order that was obeyed selectively. John W. Plummer of Company D, a twenty-three-year-old plasterer from Minneapolis, wrote, "as we were pretty tired and couldn't really see the necessity of work that far from the field, we boys did not build any, but laid down to sleep."[3] The bivouac was east of the Taneytown Road, roughly three miles south of the town of Gettysburg and

John W. Plummer, shown later in the war as captain of Company F, Eleventh Minnesota

about one-half mile southeast of Big Round Top in the southern portion of the battlefield. Today the area encompasses the field southeast of the intersection where Wright Avenue crosses the Taneytown Road and becomes Howe Avenue.[4]

James Wright remembered the moment:

> Those not required to watch [not assigned as pickets] hastened to make coffee and, this done, to bestow themselves for the night as best they could, near the stacked guns. This was a brief matter as they simply looked for a smooth spot, as any animal might, spread their blankets and laid down with their heads on their knapsacks; then covering their bodies with the unoccupied portions of the blanket and their faces with their old slouch hats, they slept. Pregnant as the situation was with possibilities for the morrow, and they were not forgotten or ignored, I do not think much time was spent in their consideration, by those not obligated to keep awake. We had been on our feet since soon after three o'clock that morning and had marched 20 or 22 miles and it felt good to stretch ourselves on the ground and be at rest.[5]

While Wright, and others, might not have anything but sleep on their minds, having a brother as a bunkmate was naturally conducive to hushed conversation in the dark, especially with a battle imminent. Reliving a scene he and Isaac obviously had experienced since childhood, twenty-four-year-old Sergeant Henry Taylor of Company E would write in his diary, "Wednesday, July 1st, 1863; Bivouacked at 9:00 P.M. Made coffee; built barricade of fence rails and lay down to sleep. The full moon frequently showed itself through the clouds. My brother and I talk of the expected battle tomorrow and mutually agree that should we survive this battle we may hope to see friends and home again."[6]

Orderly Sergeant Wright was roused by his captain, twenty-seven-year-old John Ball of Winona, at 1:00 A.M. on the morning of July 2. Sergeant Wright was told to wake the men and form the company. Colvill remembered the time as 2:00 A.M., and Sergeant Henry Taylor's diary mentioned the time as 3:00 A.M. The exhausted soldiers of the First Minnesota formed in column and marched north on the Taneytown Road.

The regiment moved out so early, and so quickly, on the morning of July 2 that the picket detail did not make it back to join the march. First Lieutenant Jasper N. Searles of Company K was on detached duty, commanding the Second Corps Second Division ambulance corps. The

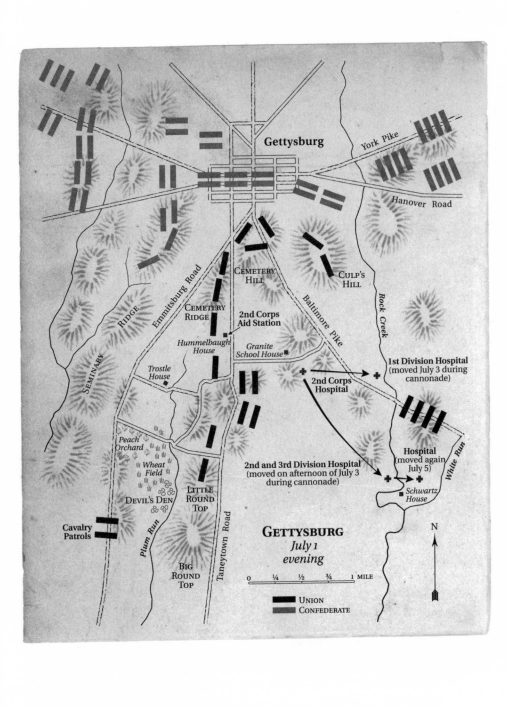

Gettysburg

York Pike

Hanover Road

CEMETERY
HILL

CULP'S
HILL

Rock Creek

EMMITSBURG ROAD

CEMETERY
RIDGE

2nd Corps
Aid Station

Baltimore Pike

RIDGE

Hummelbaugh
House

Granite
School House

1st Division Hospital
(moved July 3 during
cannonade)

SEMINARY

Trostle
House

2nd Corps
Hospital

Hospital
(moved again
July 5)

White Run

Peach
Orchard

Wheat
Field

2nd and 3rd Division Hospital
(moved on afternoon of July 3
during cannonade)

Schwartz
House

DEVIL'S DEN

LITTLE
ROUND
TOP

Cavalry
Patrols

Plum Run

Taneytown Road

BIG
ROUND
TOP

GETTYSBURG
July 1
evening

0   ¼   ½   ¾   1 MILE

N

UNION
CONFEDERATE

twenty-three-year-old druggist from St. Anthony, Minnesota, came up later in the morning with his train of ambulances and found the twenty men from the picket detail. Searles took charge of them, and these men did not reconnect with the regiment until that night when they helped Searles's ambulance crews in the removal of wounded from the battlefield.[7]

Everyone suspected they were in for a considerable fight that day, but as Wright noted, "If any one had a premonition that we had reached the culminating battlefield of the war, and that that day was to be the saddest, bloodiest, grandest and most glorious day in the history of the regiment, I do not recall that I heard it suggested. I do remember that some of us thought we ought to have been allowed to make coffee before marching, and 'growled' about it."[8]

At about 5:45 A.M. the regiment reached a point on the road about one hundred yards south of Mrs. Lydie Leister's farmhouse. The small, whitewashed, two-room house along the road was being used as General Meade's headquarters. The entire Second Corps deployed here on the federal left center. The men left-faced and marched up the eastern slope of Cemetery Ridge.

Captain Jasper N. Searles,
first lieutenant of Company K
at Gettysburg

Alonzo Pickle,
who turned twenty the day of the
regiment's charge at Gettysburg

General Alexander Hay's Third Division was deployed north to Ziegler's Grove on the northern tip of Cemetery Ridge, then stretching south was General John Gibbon's Second Division and the First Division of General John Caldwell. The First Brigade of the Second Division, of which the First Minnesota was part, was held in reserve to the rear of the left of the Second Division, just behind the crest of the ridge. The brigade was formed in a close column of regiments: each of the four regiments was in one long double-rank line, creating a column with about twenty to thirty feet between each regiment.[9]

Private Daniel Bond of Company F wrote of this moment, "We were quickly posted, extra ammunition was distributed and the order of the day was read. There was not much talk, but the countenances both of men and officers seemed expressive of a determination to give them 'the best we had in the shop.'"[10] Private Alonzo H. Pickle of Company K must have mused on the perverse joke fate was having at his expense. The Quebec native and farmboy from near Rochester, Minnesota, was leaving behind his teens on this day. It was his twentieth birthday, and he undoubtedly was wondering if he would see another.[11]

Colonel William Colvill was well aware what the day would bring, and he was not about to sit in the rear under arrest. He rode to where his brigade commander, Brigadier General William Harrow, was standing. As he remembered the event, forty-one years later, he saluted and said, "General Harrow the prospect is that we are to have a battle today. I should like to have command of my regiment, I would be greatly obliged to you if you would relieve me from arrest."[12] Harrow told Colvill that he was right about doing battle that day and that he was released from arrest. Colvill rode back to the regiment and informed Lieutenant Colonel Charles Powell Adams that he was no longer under arrest and could now take back command. Whether Adams was being a stickler for army regulations, or there was something else going on, is anyone's guess, but he told Colvill that he was unwilling to relinquish his command without orders from above. Colvill rode back to Harrow to discuss the problem. Harrow sent a member of his staff back to relieve Adams and reinstate Colvill.[13]

For the most part, Colvill was well liked and respected by the men who served under him, but there was apparently some tension among the field officers. Private Charles Muller of Company A was an admirer of Colvill. The thirty-one-year-old immigrant stonemason from Alsace-Lorraine wrote, "Some of our officers dit not like him, but the men dit like him just the better because we know that he is not a coward."[14] Orderly Sergeant Wright wrote, "He was a man of iron nerve and will; but he was not a man without feelings and sensibilities . . . he certainly could face danger with the greatest show of indifference of any man I ever knew; and he was there in an emergency and ready to meet it without fuss or flourish."[15]

Wright also mentioned that as the regiment finally was getting a chance to boil coffee and eat breakfast, a newly freed Colvill showed up; "He was received with a spontaneous outburst of cheering and clapping of hands. The welcome he received ought to have pleased any man and no doubt did please him, immensely, but he only said: 'Keep still, boys. Damn-it, can't you keep quiet?' All the same, we all knew very well that he appreciated the reception we had given him and was much gratified with it."[16]

About this time Company L, the Second Company of Minnesota Sharpshooters, was detached from the regiment and sent north to the Ziegler's Grove area, near Lieutenant George A. Woodruff's Battery I, First U.S. Artillery. Using their breech-loading Sharps rifles, they sniped at and harassed the Confederates across the farm fields on Seminary Ridge.[17] Now that the regiment was posted, Company C also left to go to division headquarters to serve as provost guard.[18]

Since arriving on Cemetery Ridge in the early morning, the First Minnesota and the rest of the Second Corps were subjected to intermittent artillery fire. The gunners of Confederate Lieutenant Generals James Longstreet and A. P. Hill were firing from Seminary Ridge to the west and southwest of the Union line while Lieutenant General Richard Ewell's gunners were likewise employed firing at federal troops on Cemetery Hill and Culp's Hill from the north and northeast. The central position of the Second Corps made it the unhappy recipient of the rebels' tendency to overshoot when aiming their artillery. Many of the projectiles crossed in midair over the area occupied by the First Minnesota. When they came close, there was little the regiment could do but hug the ground and endure.

Private Muller remembered the episode, "Early that morning we could hear some firing on our right, and soon afterwards we could hear some cannon firing in our front, and some shells went over our heads. But very soon some of them busted in our front and some of our men were badly wounded. It is quite a peculiar feeling for a man to stand there on level ground for 3 or 4 hours and be shot at all the time and not being able to defend yourself."[19]

In a letter written shortly after the battle, John Plummer of Company D wrote that the artillery firing did not really start in any significant way until about two o'clock in the afternoon. He stated that there was "sharp skirmishing" on the Union line to the front and an occasional discharge from a federal artillery piece, but that the brigade spent the morning and early afternoon, "making coffee and cooking, and filling up the inner man, preparatory to the coming struggle."[20] Miraculously, only one man of the First Minnesota—Sergeant Oscar Woodward—was killed, and Sergeant Oliver Knight (and possibly several others) was wounded when a stray shell exploded in the ranks of Company I.[21]

The Second Corps held the center of the Union line, but trouble had been brewing on the left flank since early morning. It would become one of the longest debated and most controversial actions of the war. The issue centered on the placement of Major General Daniel Sickles's Third Corps. General Meade thought he had made his orders clear— General Sickles always contended that the orders designating his position were not and that they left him broad personal discretion on how and where to place his corps. The colorful Daniel Edgar Sickles, a former congressman, was a tough Tammany Hall politician from New York City. His military experience and training were limited to a brief period as a major in a New York militia unit before the war.[22] He had proven to be a courageous and aggressive commander in combat, but a "politically appointed" general nonetheless. His courage could not compensate for his lack of military experience, and that was nowhere more apparent than in his performance at Gettysburg.

Sickles's corps was supposed to be the left flank of the army, posted to the left of the Second Corps.[23] Whether or not Sickles ever had troops on the high ground of Little Round Top, to the south, is disputed. Undoubtedly, in the morning he had troops massed near the base of Little Round Top and along the properly designated battle line on Cemetery Ridge.[24]

The ground south of Gettysburg is uneven, and it is hard to say which is the best high ground on this particular part of the battlefield. Ultimately it comes down to what can be defended, and Little Round Top is certainly the highest relatively clear ground in this area. The land drops off from Little Round Top into a broad swale where Plum Run flows, and immediately starts to rise again toward the Emmitsburg Road, where Sherfy's peach orchard is located, soon to be known in history as simply "the Peach Orchard."

There is also a timbered ridge, Houck Ridge, that runs west and north from Devil's Den, a huge jumble of massive bungalow-size granite boulders about eight hundred feet southwest of Little Round Top. Farmer John Rose's twenty-acre wheat field butts up against Houck Ridge. Like the Peach Orchard, Rose's field would become known down through time as simply "the Wheat Field." Both, like "the Corn Field" of Antietam, became synonyms for human butchery of phenomenal proportions. Several woodlots in the area, and a rough and scrubby area along Plum Run, kept Sickles's artillery from having clear fields of fire if posted on the Cemetery Ridge battle line.

Around noon General Sickles authorized one hundred sharpshooters under the command of Colonel Hiram Berdan, with the Third Maine regiment as support, to cross the Emmitsburg Road and reconnoiter the Confederate position. About six hundred yards west of the road, while moving into farmer Emanuel Pitzer's woodlot, they encountered the Tenth and Eleventh Alabama Regiments of Confederate Brigadier General Cadmus Wilcox's brigade. A sharp firefight ensued, and after sustaining sixty-seven casualties among the sharpshooters and the Third Maine—and realizing he had taken on an entire brigade—Berdan withdrew back across the Emmitsburg Road.[25] Sickles now had the information he was looking for: the rebels were not just skirmishing on his front, they were massing for an attack.

To add to his worries, the battered troopers of John Buford's cavalry division, which had been patrolling Sickles's left flank and the Emmitsburg Road south of his position, were withdrawn. They were sent to the rear to rest, refit, and guard the supply trains. Sickles sent word to

Meade that he now had no protection or advance warning of any kind on his left flank. Meade assured him the cavalry would be replaced and ordered more cavalry to the area. The replacement cavalry never arrived, a serious oversight on someone's part.

Shortly after 2:00 P.M. Sickles took it upon himself to ignore, or at least broadly interpret, Meade's orders and deployed his men as he saw fit.[26] He had begun posting artillery farther out from the Cemetery Ridge battle line and continued strengthening his skirmish line on the Emmitsburg Road throughout the morning. Now he left the high ground of Little Round Top vacant and pushed his First Division under Major General David Birney forward to cover Houck Ridge, the Wheat Field, and the Peach Orchard.

Later, between 3:00 and 4:00 P.M., Sickles moved his Second Division, commanded by Brigadier General Andrew Humphreys, to the right of Birney and extended his line north along the Emmitsburg Road. This configuration created a right angle in his battle line at the Peach Orchard, and his right flank was unattached to the left flank of the Second Corps, with a five-hundred-yard, east-west gap between them. Sickles's advance produced a dangerous situation that flew in the face of military tactical training and tradition, as well as common sense: each corps now had an unprotected flank "in the air."[27]

— 4 —

What meaner place could man be put in?

ROBERT E. LEE had not been idle; he was forming his battle plan on the spot as the situation developed. Not having intended to fight on this ground and not really knowing the lay of the land well, he was searching for vulnerability in the Union line. J. E. B. Stuart's cavalry was sorely missed. Two separate early morning reconnaissance parties brought back information that the Union left flank did not extend to the Peach Orchard or Little Round Top areas. These reports would strongly influence Lee's battle plan for the day, but it is inexplicable how the parties—especially the second one, returning at about 7:00 A.M.—could have missed the federal activity and the skirmishing fire.[1]

Between 11:00 A.M. and noon Lee formed and set his plan— a massive assault on the Union left flank by General James Longstreet's First Corps. After the attack had developed, a division of General A. P. Hill's Third Corps was to attack the Union center on Cemetery Ridge.[2] While Lee was slow in formulating his plan, he was also poorly served by many of his subordinates.

Longstreet was reluctant to attack until he had his full corps in position. He was allowed to wait for one more brigade but finally had to attack without one entire division. The poor reconnaissance also required a slow and stealthy march to avoid detection once it was realized the federals were all the way out to the Emmitsburg Road. Foot-dragging, miscommunication, and poor information resulted in an attack being ordered around noon, to be launched as soon as possible, finally commencing at 4:00 P.M.

Longstreet's and Hill's assaults were structured to progress in a trip hammer movement from the right, or southern, portion of their line through to the left. Each brigade was to move out after the brigade to its right had advanced and become engaged. This attack en echelon was eventually to involve the entire Confederate line up to its left-center, attacking the federal line until someone was able to punch through.[3] General Richard Ewell's Second Corps would attack Cemetery Hill and Culp's Hill, the "bend" and the "barb" of the fishhook-shaped Union line, as soon as Ewell heard Longstreet open the attack on the right. Keeping the entire federal line engaged would prevent Meade from moving troops to aid a weakened or collapsing portion of his line.

While the Confederates planned and deployed, sharp skirmishing continued along the front out on the Emmitsburg Road. Artillery rounds kept passing over and occasionally exploding near the First Minnesota. General Meade finally received word of Sickles's forward movement to the Emmitsburg Road, and he galloped to the advanced position as fast as he could. He found Sickles and began to question him hotly about the unauthorized advance. Sickles insisted that his orders had left him the latitude to use his judgment on the field and to move forward as he did. Meade made it clear that the advance was certainly not within his orders.

Sickles was just offering to pull his men back to their original position when Confederate artillery opened fire on his corps. General Meade told him that it was too late to withdraw and that the Confederates massing to his front would definitely not let him withdraw in an orderly fashion without attacking. Sickles was to hold on, and Meade would send reinforcements as he was able.[4]

It was now about four o'clock in the afternoon, and the Confederates of Longstreet's First Corps and elements of Hill's Third Corps had begun their massive infantry assault on both faces of Sickles's line with a twenty- to thirty-minute artillery barrage on the federal position. General Andrew Humphreys mentioned that the artillery started as his division was moving forward toward the Emmitsburg Road line.[5]

At about 4:30 P.M. Brigadier General John C. Caldwell, commanding the First Division of the Second Corps, was ordered to move his troops

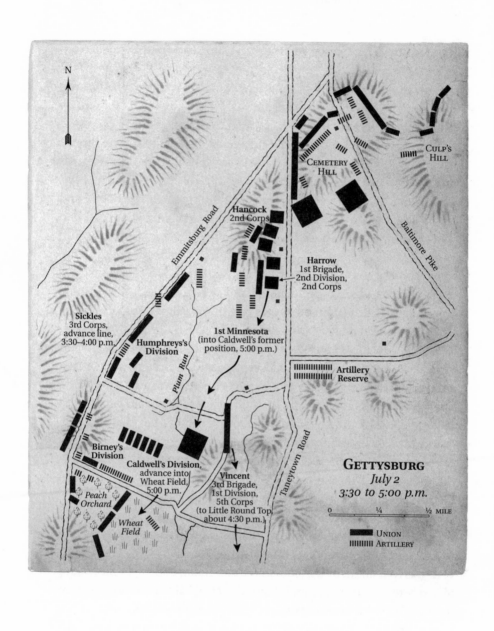

N

Cemetery
Hill

Culp's
Hill

Baltimore Pike

Emmitsburg Road

Hancock
2nd Corps

Harrow
1st Brigade,
2nd Division,
2nd Corps

Sickles
3rd Corps,
advance line,
3:30–4:00 p.m.

Humphreys's
Division

1st Minnesota
(into Caldwell's former
position, 5:00 p.m.)

Plum Run

Artillery
Reserve

Taneytown Road

Birney's
Division

Caldwell's Division,
advance into
Wheat Field,
5:00 p.m.

Vincent
3rd Brigade,
1st Division,
5th Corps
(to Little Round Top,
about 4:30 p.m.)

Peach
Orchard

Wheat
Field

Gettysburg
July 2
3:30 to 5:00 p.m.

0   ¼   ½ MILE

██ Union
||||||||| Artillery

forward in support of Sickles's Third Corps. Caldwell's troops were barely under way when they received orders to return to their former position. The entire Fifth Corps had come in on its left to support the Third Corps. By 5:00 P.M., severe fighting from Little Round Top to the Peach Orchard was causing the thin federal line to buckle.

Once again, Caldwell was ordered to move, this time to the aid of the Fifth Corps. His troops trotted south at the double-quick and were promptly fed into the meat grinder of the Wheat Field.[6] By the end of the day, repeated charges, repulses, and countercharges would yield a grisly harvest in this twenty-acre tract. More than four thousand dead and wounded men were sprawled on a carpet of ripe, flattened, bloody wheat.

Meanwhile tension increased on the Second Corps line. With Caldwell's division gone, General John Gibbon pulled apart his reserve brigade to try to close the enormous gaps in the line created by Sickles's move forward. The First Minnesota was taken out of reserve to patch the hole in the line created by Caldwell's movement, one undersized regiment filling the gap left by a division. The Eighty-second New York and the Fifteenth Massachusetts were sent forward to the Emmitsburg Road and posted to the right, or north, of the Codori farmhouse. The regiments pulled down fences and erected a makeshift breastwork in an attempt to make the flat, exposed position a little safer.

Gibbon also posted Battery B of the First Rhode Island Light Artillery on a small rise about five hundred feet behind the two regiments. The battery faced northwest, which covered the two regiments' right flank but did nothing to protect itself from attack from the south, or left.[7] At this time the two regiments and the artillery battery were the only protection for the five-hundred-yard, east-west gap in the line between Sickles's Third Corps and Hancock's Second Corps. Gibbon ordered up the last regiment in his reserve, the Nineteenth Maine, to take a position on the battle line directly in front of their reserve position.

When the Minnesotans were called up, they were marched forward and to the left to support Captain Evan Thomas's Battery C of the Fourth U.S. Artillery on the crest of Cemetery Ridge. The regiment was about 350 yards south of the Nineteenth Maine. Thomas's battery consisted of six bronze Napoleon twelve-pounders, which were not yet in action.

The battery was posted on a slight swell of high ground that faced roughly due west, part of a slope that extended for about three hundred yards across two irregularly shaped farm fields and ended at Plum Run. The dry stream bed contained a scattering of rocks, boulders, scrub brush, and small trees. From Plum Run the land rose for about six hundred yards until it reached high ground at the Emmitsburg Road.

The First Minnesota passed to the rear of Battery C, and the men lay down to the left of it. It soon became evident that the battery was a prime target for the Confederate artillery or at least the rounds that overshot their targets out on the Emmitsburg Road. Colonel Colvill moved the regiment forward so that it was partway down the west slope of Cemetery Ridge. He was depending on the rebel artillery's habit of overshooting a target to provide protection for his men. The regiment was now to the left and slightly in front of Battery C.

The First Minnesota had a front row seat for the drama unfolding on the Third Corps line. Except for the smoke, they had a relatively unobstructed view all the way to the Emmitsburg Road and the Peach Orchard. A number of men in the regiment, including Colonel Colvill, mentioned an eerie optical illusion caused by the smoke of thousands of muskets and dozens of cannon discharging. The day was fairly humid and the air was relatively calm, elements that combined to create curtain walls of thick battle smoke that quickly extended upward into the partly cloudy sky. The smoke, coupled with the light and shadow on that part of the battlefield, made all of the combatants in the distance seem extremely tall. It was as if the men on the battle line along Cemetery Ridge were watching a struggle between giants on the distant forward line.[8]

James Wright left one of the best descriptions of the view and the experience:

> Crashing, crushing, stunning discharges of artillery made the earth vibrate beneath us. Rolling, tearing, crackling volleys of musketry; Union cheers and Confederate yells, mingling with other noises of the strife, burst out from the concealing clouds of smoke in that indescribable mixture of sounds commonly called the "roar of battle." Along the lines of the contending forces there was a whirling tempest of fire and smoke, and about them gathered clouds of sulphurous vapor—into

which the reinforcements plunged and were lost sight of, and out of which came streams of wounded and the fragments of broken regiments. It was with feelings of anxiety, beyond words to express, that we watched the awful scene before us, listened to the tumultuous sounds, and wondered how it would end.[9]

Observing the severe beating that Humphreys's division of the Third Corps was taking on the Emmitsburg Road, General Hancock of the Second Corps attempted to reinforce the east-west gap in the line. He rode to the left flank of the Nineteenth Maine, dismounted, and grabbed the soldier on the far left in the front rank. It was a private named George T. Durgin of Company F, and Hancock trotted the man eighteen or twenty yards forward of the line and a little to the left. He placed the Mainer on top of a small spur of high ground that had an excellent panoramic view of the center and federal left of the battlefield.

The spur, a continuation of the summit of Cemetery Ridge, gently sloped to the northwest, but dropped more sharply to the west and southwest. It was lightly wooded on its southwest end and on the slope that ended in a drainage rivulet that ran across the fields southwest into Plum Run. Above the din of battle, Hancock shouted in Durgin's face, "Will you stay here?" to which the short, stocky private looked up into the imposing general's face and shouted back, "I'll stay here, General, until hell freezes over!" It was the kind of answer and attitude that pleased Hancock. Smiling, he ordered the Nineteenth's colonel, Francis E. Heath, to dress his regimental line on Durgin.[10]

Hancock remounted and rode off to order up another artillery battery. He sent Lieutenant Gulian V. Weir's Battery C, Fifth U.S. Artillery, to a small rise of ground south of the Codori barn, in front of the Nineteenth Maine's position. It is not entirely clear whether Weir's battery was sent before or after the posting of the Nineteenth Maine. About the same time another artillery battery, commanded by Lieutenant John J. Turnbull, was being rushed to aid General Andrew Humphreys's line on the Emmitsburg Road.

Whether Weir's, Turnbull's, or another's, some artillery battery went scrambling to the front at a gallop, leaving Colonel Heath of the Nineteenth Maine to deal with the fact that it was going to pass directly through his regiment.[11] Heath had the regiment split toward the rear, allowing the battery to go through. Hancock was enraged enough at this to gallop out and dress down the battery's commander, roaring that "if I commanded this regiment I'd be God Damned if I would not charge bayonets on you!"[12]

Three hundred and fifty yards to the south the First Minnesota hugged the ground on the west face of Cemetery Ridge. The battle raged back and forth from Little Round Top on the far left to and along the Emmitsburg Road directly in front of the Minnesotans. It was nearly a two-mile-long line of thundering hell-on-earth.

Shortly before 6:00 P.M. the battle truly began directly to involve the Minnesotans. James Wright noted that they began to receive small-arms fire that was not necessarily stray shots, "Occasionally a bullet knocked up the dirt in front of us, and it was soon observed that they were coming from some point on our left front, and that they were increasing in frequency. It was believed that a line of skirmishers, or a body of sharpshooters, had reached the cover of bushes and fences across the hollow and should be looked after."[13] Colonel Colvill detached Company F, commanded by Captain John Ball, and sent it forward and to the left as skirmishers to try and stop the rifles firing on the regiment.[14]

The First Minnesota now had eight of its regular ten companies in line on Cemetery Ridge. Company F was out skirmishing, and Company C was at division headquarters, having been assigned as part of the division's provost guard the previous January. The actual number of men present for duty in those eight companies has been disputed to this day. The low figure of 262 has been cited for years because it is the number given in the earliest regimental history, written by former Second Lieutenant William Lochren of Company K. If that was accurate, there were a lot of men who cannot be accounted for because that figure does not fit the rest of the extant records. In fact, there could have been as many as 324 men in the eight companies. The actual figure was probably around 289.[15]

The rebel yell sounded over the battlefield as the Confederates continued to batter the overextended Union line. For all of the pro-and-con postwar analysis of Sickles's movement forward, it obviously had the effect of a giant breakwater for the gray tide washing over it. The Confederate assault was being bled—drained of energy and men—but at the cost of the entire Third Corps of the Army of the Potomac and large portions of other corps.

The federals stood to the grim work. When the Peach Orchard salient finally caved, the federal withdrawal was conducted, for the most part, as a fighting retreat. Artillery crews actually used the force of the recoil of their guns to help back them across the field, pulling them away by hand because so many draft horses had been killed.[16] What remained of the infantry lines would reform, deliver a volley, and continue back toward Cemetery Ridge for a few yards while reloading. The rebels were paying dearly for every foot of ground they gained.

Upon receiving Colonel Colvill's orders, Company F of the First Minnesota stood and stepped out from the regimental line, and the line closed up behind it. The men took a few paces forward and then did a left face, marching by the left flank until they cleared the left of the regiment. Company F then deployed to its right front, heading southwest in the direction of the Abraham Trostle farm. They were subjected to continually heavier incoming fire, and it was probably during this advance that Private James Bachelor was hit in the foot.[17]

The company advanced partly down into the swale of Plum Run, moving about 250 yards to the southwest of the regiment's position. The right of the line was on the edge of marshy ground that extended down to the run, and the left rested on a snake-rail fence that enclosed one of Trostle's fields. The right of the line had the advantage of stones and boulders, both those deposited by nature and those piled up from past clearing of farm fields. The men welcomed the cover, and those who had none lay down nearby on the ground.[18] The rebel minié balls came "hissing over us, cutting the weeds and bushes, plumping into the ground and spatting against the stones," recalled Wright.[19]

Three hundred and fifty yards to the southwest of Company F, General Sickles sat on his horse in the barnyard of the Trostle farm. Whatever his good intentions may have been in moving his corps to the forward position, he could only watch the shattered, bloody results stream past him. One colonel, whose horse had been killed in the Peach Orchard, came trudging past Sickles, carrying his regimental colors and leading the twenty men from his command he was able to gather in the smoky confusion. Sickles wailed, "Colonel, for God's sake can't you hold on?" to which the teary-eyed colonel choked out the simple, tragic reply, "Where are my men?"[20]

Shortly after 6:00 P.M., Sickles received firsthand experience of what had happened to most of the colonel's men.[21] Still mounted, and on the same high ground by the Trostle barn, he was struck by a solid-shot cannon ball that smashed into his right knee and glanced away, not even disturbing his horse.[22] Sickles calmly puffed on a cigar as he was taken from the field on a stretcher, his shattered lower leg still attached to his body by a few shreds of flesh. In an odd but typical gesture, Sickles donated his amputated limb to the Army Medical Museum in Washington, D.C., and visited it periodically until his death in 1914. The bones are still there on display.[23]

While the Confederates were in high spirits from their success, their lines were becoming progressively more ragged and intermixed. Brigadier General William Barksdale, a portly firebrand politician from Mississippi, commanded the brigade of more than sixteen hundred Mississippi troops that had smashed the Peach Orchard salient.[24] Barksdale pivoted his three left regiments, the Eighteenth, the Thirteenth, and the Seventeenth Mississippi, and trekked north up the Emmitsburg Road to attack Union General Andrew Humphreys's division on the left flank. His right regiment, the Twenty-first Mississippi, continued east to

Brigadier General Cadmus Marcellus Wilcox, C.S.A.

engage Union troops and an artillery battery that had fallen back from the Peach Orchard and that were trying to reform.[25]

Barksdale's advance was the signal for Brigadier General Cadmus Marcellus Wilcox's brigade of Alabama troops, posted to the left of Barksdale, to move. Wilcox's command, numbering more than seventeen hundred men, was deployed in an odd configuration due to its earlier encounter with Hiram Berdan's sharpshooters and the Third Maine.[26] It had also been the right flank of the Confederate army at its initial deployment earlier in the day. The right regiment, the Eighth Alabama, nearly was perpendicular to the rest of the brigade, facing almost due south.

Because of the placement of Wilcox's brigade when he began his advance and because of Barksdale's sweep northward into Humphreys's left flank, Wilcox was forced to shift his troops to the left, or north, to avoid running into Barksdale's men. His three left regiments, the Ninth, the Fourteenth, and the Eleventh Alabama, marched at the double-quick by the left flank. Wilcox said, "Having gained four-hundred or five-hundred yards to the left by this flank movement, my command faced by the right flank, and advanced," quite a run for men moving into combat on a summer day.[27] The next regiment to the right, the Tenth Alabama, was able to advance straight forward and connect with the right of the Eleventh Alabama.

The far right regiment presented a special problem. The left flank of the Eighth Alabama was pointing in the direction they needed to attack, east toward the Emmitsburg Road. The regiment's commander, Lieutenant Colonel Hilary A. Herbert, said that the order to advance came quickly, and it specified that he was not to take time to change front but rather to execute that maneuver on the move. Herbert said: "It [the regiment] went forward by the left flank. As we rose a hill [the high ground rising to the Emmitsburg Road] we received a severe fire and I ordered the regiment to 'change front, forward, on the tenth company,' which was executed at a double quick, the men firing as they came in to line."[28]

This maneuver required the men to make a running forward sweep to the right, pivoting on the front company like a giant door closing. The result of this complicated maneuver, executed under fire and in the smoke and chaos of battle, was to separate the Eighth Alabama from the rest of Wilcox's brigade by about two hundred yards.

While Wilcox's other regiments slammed into the Union battle line on Emmitsburg Road between the farmhouse of Peter Rogers and a spot about thirty or forty yards south of Daniel Klingle's farmhouse, the Eighth Alabama crossed the road south of Trostle's farm lane.[29] This put the Eighth behind the swath cut by Barksdale's brigade, causing them to maneuver to avoid colliding with Barksdale's separated Twenty-first Mississippi and still try and reconnect with their own brigade. After crossing the Trostle farm lane, collapsing Humphreys's left flank, and observing Cadmus Wilcox's advance, Barksdale's brigade pivoted again to continue east toward Cemetery Ridge.

The necessity of avoiding a collision of the two brigades caused Wilcox's brigade to continue a slight shift to the northeast, while Barksdale's brigade moved east but also slightly to the south. This created an increasing divergence of the two brigades the farther they advanced.[30] The grinding combat, rocks and boulders, fences and trees, and pivoting movements of Barksdale's brigade were all taking a toll on the coherence and alignment of his battle formation. The Confederates were winning, but it was beginning to look as if their troops were in as much disorder as the Union lines they were pursuing.

Barksdale was in his element and aggressively pressed his attack. Earlier in the day he had begged both his division commander, Major General Lafayette McLaws, and corps commander, General James Longstreet, to let him cut loose and start his attack. Both told him to be patient until all was ready.[31]

Now that the assault was under way and successfully pushing the Yankees back, Barksdale allowed no stopping for any reason. Two of his brigade's colonels asked permission to stop and reform, and Barksdale bellowed, "No! Crowd them—we have them on the run. Move your regiments." At one point he held his sword high, pointing forward, and roared, "Brave Mississippians, one more charge and the day is ours."[32]

Back on the east side of Plum Run, Company F of the First Minnesota peered through the smoke and continued to see federal troops falling back. This handful of Minnesotans would be one of the small, solid pockets of resistance to the rebel juggernaut. They held their ground, and their fire, as minié balls hummed past their heads and smacked into the rocks and dirt around them. A number of men from the retreating Third Corps, who obviously still had fight left in them, joined the Company F battle line.[33] Finally it seemed the bulk of the retreating federals had passed and, as James Wright recalled, "As soon as we were thus satisfied that the fellows we could now see coming down the opposite slope were enemies we proceeded to treat them as such, and 'got busy' at once."[34]

Company F poured lead into the oncoming rebels. The men noticed that the enemy line was shifting to their right. This was obviously the right of Wilcox's line, minus the Eighth Alabama, making the diverging northeast movement away from Barksdale's brigade. These rebels seemed to be on the edge of rifle range, and Wright mentioned that the range was too great to be effective.[35] It did not make much difference because doing anything was preferable to doing nothing. Wright wrote, "It was *more* satisfactory to be trying to do something than it was to lie on the ground under the howling shrieking shells, or wait inactive, but we do not wish to be understood that there was anything *very satisfactory in being shot at.*"[36]

Captain Ball dispatched Private Jonas P. Davis back to the regiment to report the company's situation to Colonel Colvill and ask for further orders. The men then saw another rebel line moving almost directly toward them, but the track of their march would take them to the left of Company F. This was surely Barksdale's brigade, and its line of march would take it very close to the left of the company of Minnesotans, well within rifle range. The men began to pour a concentrated and effective fire into the left flank of the passing line, causing even more disorder among the rebels. Ball shifted the company farther left, up to the higher ground. The left of Company F's line was strung out along a portion of the snake-rail fence bordering Trostle's field, and the entire company continued to rake the rebel line with rifle fire.

Back on Cemetery Ridge the First Minnesota continued to hug the ground. Their comrades from Company F had been out only a short time, but the rifle fire on the regiment was not slackening significantly. There was far too much lead in the air for some of it not to find its way to the crest of Cemetery Ridge. The regiment was not having the satisfaction of at least shooting at something—anything—as the men of Company F were. We can only speculate about the level of anxiety, tension, and frustration that must have been building as the men lay on the field, passive targets for stray artillery rounds and minié balls.

The First Minnesota's fellow-brigade regiment, the Nineteenth Maine, was facing the same situation just a few hundred yards north. Private Silas Adams of the Nineteenth's Company F wrote after the war, "Now and then [the Confederates] would pitch a shell over among us, striking in our midst, killing a few and wounding many more. All we had to do was to lay there and anticipate the next one and guess where it would strike and who the next victim would be. The thoughts that passed through our minds during the hours we lay there were not pleasant in their contemplations, for there is relief when one can 'up and at 'em,' but here it was anticipating the next one, and not being able to strike back. What meaner place could man be put in?"[37]

Second Lieutenant William Lochren of Company K, First Minnesota, recalled the moment, "We stood in full view of Sickles' battle in the peach orchard half a mile to the front, and witnessed with eager anxiety the varying fortunes of that sanguinary conflict, until at length, with gravest apprehension, we saw Sickles' men give way before the heavier forces of Longstreet and Hill, and come back, slowly, at first, and rallying at short intervals, but at length broken and in utter disorder, rushing down the slope by the Trostle house, across the low ground, up the slope on our side, and past our position to the rear."[38]

Lochren probably was standing, as he indicated. It was not unusual for officers in the Civil War to continue standing even when their men lay down for protection. Like it or not, the officers were expected to be an inspiration to the men, and displays of courage—sometimes insanely foolish ones—were not uncommon. Field officers routinely led charges on horseback, making them tempting and easy targets. The corps of officers in both armies was severely depleted at Gettysburg.

In all likelihood by this time, the order had come down to "fix bayonets."[39] It was becoming apparent that they would be needed.

The world was coming apart along the Emmitsburg Road.

— 5 —

My God, are these all the men we have here?

WINFIELD SCOTT HANCOCK had earned the sobriquet "Hancock the Superb" for his performance during the Peninsula Campaign in 1862. His feat at Gettysburg matched or surpassed it. Superb is the word—the man seemed to be everywhere on the battlefield, making decisive, in-the-nick-of-time decisions while being a solid inspiration for the troops. Given the placement of the Third Corps and the subsequent Confederate attack, it was truly fortuitous for the Army of the Potomac to have Hancock's corps beside it.

After placing the Nineteenth Maine forward and Weir's battery southeast of the Codori farm, Hancock dealt with multiple requests for support for the Third Corps. General Humphreys, still fighting for his command's life on the Emmitsburg Road, sent to Hancock for two regiments. Hancock passed the request to Gibbon, who sliced his line still finer and dispatched the Nineteenth Massachusetts and the Forty-second New York into the curtain of fire and smoke along the Emmitsburg Road.[1] General Meade then asked Hancock to send an entire brigade to help General Birney, throwing more of his men into the morass in which Caldwell's division already was falling.

Hancock sent word to his Third Division's commander, General Alexander Hays, to prepare to move a brigade rapidly to the left. Hays ordered Colonel George Willard, commanding his Third Brigade, to report to General Birney, saying, "Take your brigade over there and knock the hell out of the rebs."[2] Willard's command, consisting of the 39th, 111th, 125th, and 126th New York Regiments, was a good choice. All of the regiments' ranks were fairly full, compared to other Union regiments at this point in the war, and, more importantly, they had something to prove.

Shortly after being organized the previous year, the brigade was posted as part of the garrison for the nearly indefensible Harpers Ferry, Virginia. The town, located at the confluence of the Potomac and Shenandoah Rivers in northwestern Virginia, was boxed in and dominated by towering areas of high ground and changed hands eight times during the war. Willard's brigade had the dubious distinction of being there to help surrender the town to the Confederate troops of General Stonewall Jackson on September 15, 1862, two days before the Battle of Antietam.

Despite a gallant fight, Willard's men and the rest of the garrison were surrounded and outgunned. Between 11,000 and 11,500 federal troops had to surrender.[3] Now, nearly a year later, they had finished their terms of parole and had been officially exchanged. On this July afternoon they were so recently assigned to the Third Division of the Second Corps that they still had enviably new uniforms and no blue trefoil corps badges on their forage caps. They were relishing the opportunity to disprove the moniker the 126th New York had unjustly worn, and the entire brigade had felt since the surrender, "The Harper's Ferry Cowards." Willard ordered his regiments to fix bayonets and then begin a running advance nearly a mile south to the crumbling Third Corps line.[4]

Major General Winfield Scott Hancock, "Hancock the Superb," commander of the Army of the Potomac's Second Corps, about the time of Gettysburg

General Meade informed Hancock of Sickles's wound and, in a display of the confidence he had in the man, ordered Hancock to take command of the Third Corps as well as his own Second Corps.[5] General Hancock now had the responsibility for the entire center and left wing of the Union army, quite a burden under the current circumstances, even for Hancock. He turned the immediate, on-the-ground command of the Second Corps over to General Gibbon and then galloped south to catch up with Willard's brigade, which already had passed by in their rush to help the Third Corps.

Hancock and the sweaty, determined men of Willard's brigade crossed behind the First Minnesota and continued south.[6] Rebel artillery rounds, minié balls, and federal soldiers were zipping past them toward the rear. In the area where the left of Caldwell's division had previously been posted, Hancock halted the brigade as he saw General Birney of the Third Corps approaching. Hancock told Birney of Meade's order, and Birney informed Hancock that his new command had disintegrated. Birney was on his way back to do what he could to round them up, but there was no line for Willard's men to support.

Directly in front of Willard's brigade, down the slope and close to Plum Run, Company F of the First Minnesota was still pouring fire into the left flank of Barksdale's Confederates. Soon another portion of Barksdale's ragged line began to approach directly in front of them, causing a hot, head-on fire fight.[7] With the battle raging on both sides, and now in front of them, Captain Ball felt there was little more his small company could accomplish and ordered it back a short distance. The men halted, faced about, and began firing again; then Ball ordered them all the way back to the top of the ridge.

Company F continued back to Cemetery Ridge, still deployed as skirmishers. Private Daniel Bond recalled that they had to watch their backs and fronts, as they were compelled to fall back through a federal battery that was firing. If this was the case, it must have been a portion of Lieutenant Colonel Freeman McGilvery's cobbled-together Plum Run Line of guns.[8] Reserve Artillery officer McGilvery had collared fragments of withdrawing batteries, and he added a fresh battery from the reserve as an anchor.[9] McGilvery's guns did excellent and heroic service in stemming the Confederate assault at this point in the federal battle line.

As the men of Company F crested the ridge, they closed up to the right to avoid a charging infantry line moving down the slope on their left, just north of them. James Wright recalled that one officer of this charging line, "was short, and fat and 'game as a rooster' but very much excited. He was swinging his hat in one hand and his sword in the other, shouting in a hoarse voice: 'Forward, boys, forward!' "[10] Wright recognized the regiment passing them as the 111th New York of Willard's brigade.

While the men of Company F were still fighting down toward the base of the slope, General Hancock quickly took in the situation before him. The Third Corps had come apart and was withdrawing. All Hancock could see to the left and right of Willard's brigade was smoke and retreating federal soldiers, although the solid First Minnesota was less than one hundred yards north, shrouded by the pall of smoke. He could also begin to see the ragged line of Confederates pursuing the retreating men of the Third Corps. Hancock ordered Willard to deploy his brigade facing west and attack down into the swale.

Willard had marched his brigade down from Hay's line in close column by division, maintaining the same formation they had while in reserve for Hay's division.[11] This meant that the brigade was in two columns of two regiments each. After deploying to face the Confederates, the two front regiments were the 125th New York on the left and the 126th New York on the right. Willard kept the two rear regiments in reserve, the 39th New York on the left and the 111th New York on the right. He posted them farther out to cover the brigade's left and right flanks.

Willard began his charge down the slope toward Plum Run and the advancing rebels of Barksdale's brigade. Watching the New Yorkers from Cemetery Ridge, Hancock noticed another rebel line through the smoke. It was advancing to the right of Willard's two regiments. Once down the slope this new enemy line could be a real threat to Willard's right flank, so Hancock rode to the 111th New York. He ordered Colonel Clinton MacDougall to charge the advancing rebel line and hold them off the right flank of the 126th New York. MacDougall moved his regiment farther right, or north, to make sure it would not collide with the 126th New York, then advanced down the smoky, shell-torn slope.[12] He struck what was either the right of Cadmus Wilcox's brigade, a portion of the left of Barksdale's brigade, or perhaps a part of each.

Hancock sent an aide to Meade and requested more reinforcements for this part of the line. He continued a short distance to the right until he came upon General Humphreys. He informed Humphreys that he, Hancock, was now commanding the Third Corps and ordered Humphreys to try and gather as many of his retreating men as he could and establish a line in the area formerly held by Caldwell's division.[13] Hancock could not have had a lot of confidence in the prospect of Humphreys's men helping much, later writing, "The number of his troops collected . . . was very small, scarcely equal to an ordinary battalion, but with many colors, this small command being composed of the fragments of many shattered regiments."[14] This meant that scarcely two hundred men had rallied, and these were probably not very steady under the circumstances.

In the roaring, smoky chaos, Hancock saw a slightly more organized column of men moving toward Cemetery Ridge. The shadowy, dark, crouching forms were inching forward within the curtain of battle smoke amid the scrubby brush and trees on the west side of Plum Run. He galloped down toward the run's swale to meet and to attempt to rally them, thinking they were a portion of Humphreys's men still making it back to the ridge.[15]

He was met with a ragged peppering of musketry. Miraculously the rebel rifle fire missed Hancock, but hit his only remaining aide, Captain William D. W. Miller, twice. Hancock shouted to Miller to ride out of it, and Miller got away. Hancock was able to gallop back east, up over a lip of ground that dropped down into Plum Run's swale. He gained the protection of a couple of hundred feet of low ground as he rushed the 330 yards straight up to the crest of Cemetery Ridge.[16]

With the wounded Miller in tow, Hancock reined in when he came upon a small body of dusty blue-clad soldiers lying in orderly ranks on the ground. He dismounted and ordered the regiment's colonel to help stop and rally the still retreating federal troops. While the regiment's officers tried to help, it became obvious that few of these refugees from Humphreys's Emmitsburg Road battle line were going to halt and form.[17] Finally Hancock stopped and looked around in disbelief. "My God, are these all the men we have here?" bellowed the general as he looked at the solitary eight-company formation of the First Minnesota.

— 6 —

Behold! A Pale Horse

THE OFFICERS OF THE FIRST MINNESOTA were all dismounted, their horses held by orderlies to the right and rear of the regiment.[1] According to the standard placement of companies—an established order based on the seniority (commission date) of the various captains—the eight companies of the First Minnesota were formed in double ranks by company in the following order, left to right: D, I, E, A, B, K, H, G.[2] Working with a figure of 289 men in the eight companies at that time, the regimental facing would have been about ninety-six yards wide. They were facing a wall of gray three to four times as wide.

There are several extant versions of what was said and done next. Hancock possibly asked Colonel Colvill, "What regiment is this?" although other evidence suggests not. It was clear that most of the retreating Third Corps troops could not be rallied, so Hancock remounted and surveyed the Confederate advance from Lieutenant Evan Thomas's artillery battery to the right and slightly behind the First Minnesota. Waiting in forlorn hope of reinforcements appearing out of the smoke from the right rear, the general clearly was loath to do what he knew he must. Hancock then gave an order for the Minnesotans to charge, possibly shouting it directly to the regiment, possibly giving the order to Colvill: advance and take the rebel battle flags from the approaching enemy.[3]

As William Lochren wrote, "Every man realized in an instant what that order meant—death or wounds to us all; the sacrifice of the regiment to gain a few minutes' time and save the position, and probably the battlefield."[4] General Hancock wrote later of his order for the charge, "Reinforcements were coming on the run, but I knew that before they could reach the threatened point the Confederates, unless checked, would seize the position. I would have ordered that regiment in if I had known that every man would be killed. It had to be done."[5]

Cadmus Wilcox's brigade of rebels nearly had reached the bottom of the slope from the Emmitsburg Road, which ended in the dry stream

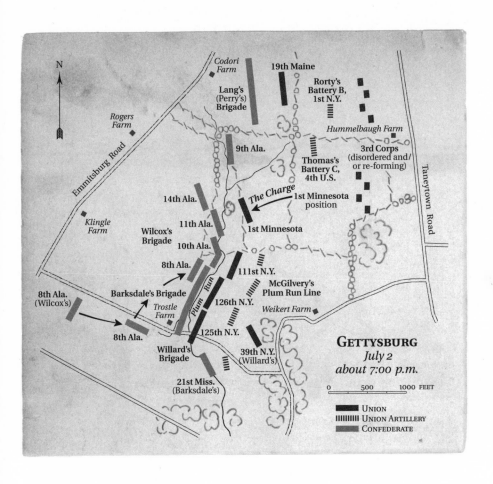

GETTYSBURG
July 2
about 7:00 p.m.

0   500   1000 FEET

■ UNION
||||||||| UNION ARTILLERY
■ CONFEDERATE

bed of Plum Run. The rebels were about 350 yards from the First Minnesota. Wilcox started the battle that day with nearly eighteen hundred men. The Eighth Alabama's separation from the rest of the brigade would have reduced the number by about 477 men. Casualties and straggling to that point would have subtracted another few hundred. In Wilcox's battle report he says that he sent the Ninth Alabama, on his brigade's left flank, to attack and silence a federal artillery battery on Cemetery Ridge. This was probably the four ten-pounder Parrotts of Captain James McKay Rorty's Battery B, First New York Light Artillery, posted fifty or sixty yards northeast of the First Minnesota.[6]

Wilcox sent his remaining three regiments to hit Captain Evan Thomas's Battery C, Fourth U.S. Artillery, posted directly to the right and rear of the First Minnesota. These three regiments were attacking en echelon, with the Eleventh Alabama in the lead and the Fourteenth Alabama behind and to the left, the Tenth Alabama behind and to the right.[7] The Minnesotans were positioned to hit, more or less, the center of the Eleventh Alabama. These three regiments were the part of Wilcox's brigade that the First Minnesota would primarily engage. They could have contended with at least part of the Ninth Alabama as well. The roughly 289 Minnesotans would charge 1,000 to 1,100 Confederates.

To begin the charge, Colvill ordered the First to attention. The men stood and shouldered arms and then center dressed, dressing ranks on the colors.[8] The time was between 6:30 and 7:00 P.M., perhaps as late as 7:15 P.M. Colvill's order was "Forward, double-quick!—March!" The regiment moved out at a slow trot on the command "March," stepping-off on the left foot while moving their rifle-muskets to the right shoulder shift position.[9] Recalling the moment years later, Colvill wrote, "I noticed, as the regiment started, the swinging of the gleaming muskets as the right-shoulder-shift was made to one time and two motions corresponding to the steps of the advance and seemed to emphasize the unity of the start; It was grand. The regiment moved as one man, taking up its swinging gait down the slope."[10]

Outnumbered four or five to one, the First Minnesota silently charged down Cemetery Ridge.

The regiment was close to the western edge of a pasture.[11] Their charge took them out of this field, through a wheat field, and then into the rocky, scrubby area bordering Plum Run. According to maps of the battlefield, there were two fence lines to be traversed—one combination split-rail and post-and-rail separating the pasture from the wheat field and another split-rail fence separating the wheat field from the marshy area. However, no mention was made of having to contend with fences, and there was a reference to tearing down fences to facilitate troop movements in the official reports of Generals Humphreys and Caldwell, both of whom had occupied this part of the battlefield at different times earlier in the day.[12]

The entire distance to the Confederates was now something over three hundred yards. It should have taken the regiment less than a minute and a half to make it to the Confederate line.[13] It is hard to say what kind of obstacle the wheat presented. Probably not much, since no one mentioned getting his feet caught in the wheat or having to struggle through standing wheat during the charge. Private Edward H. Bassett of Company G, a farmer from Rice County, Minnesota, noted that the regiment charged over a "stubble field." He would have been referring to the wheat field, and his diary entry seems to indicate that the field already had been harvested.[14]

Colvill wrote that the rebels of Wilcox's command began to fire on them immediately, but that they tended to overshoot. He maintained in his 1904 story that only twelve or fifteen men were lost on the actual charge down the slope to the stream bed of Plum Run. However, William Lochren contended that many men were hit on the charge and that the slope "was covered with dead and wounded."[15]

In a 1915 recollection Lieutenant Christopher Heffelfinger wrote, "The lay of the ground protected us considerably from the enemy's fire. The regiment charged down the incline; the enemy, be it understood, was on an elevation. Now we came to close action in what is known as a ravine; but the enemy's position being high, the shots went mostly over our heads, and it is a matter of record that most of the killed and wounded were hit in the upper part of the body."[16] Heffelfinger remembered the charge starting before the Confederates had reached the area of Plum Run and its ravine. He said that the rebels were higher on their side of the incline—coming from the Emmitsburg Road—and the First Minnesota was moving fast coming down their side from Cemetery Ridge.

Other men of the First had recollections as well, some written as soon as a few days or weeks after the battle. An "unknown sergeant" of the First Minnesota wrote a letter at the end of July that was published in the *Saint Paul Pioneer* on August 9, 1863. In it he wrote, "Now their cannon were pointed to us, and round shot, grape and shrapnel tore fearfully through our ranks, and the more deadly Enfield rifles were directed to us alone. Great heavens how fast our men fell. Marching as file-closer, it seemed as if every step was over some fallen comrade. Yet no man wavers: every gap is closed-up."[17]

Sergeant Mat Marvin of Company K was one of those who went down during the charge. In his journal he wrote, "We had not fired a musket and the Rebs were firing rapidly. I dropped to the ground with a

Mat Marvin, probably taken shortly after the war.
Marvin poured water from this canteen, which he carried
throughout the war, over his head and wrists after he was shot.

wound somewhat. I picked myself up as quick as possible, where I saw blood on my shoe, the heel of which was tore out. I thought it a slight one, and run to ketch up, thinking no Rebel line could stand a charge of my Regiment, and if the bayonet must be used I wanted a chance in, as it was free to all. I had just ketched-up again when I fell a 2nd time, to faint to get up."[18] Marvin was unable to stand and walk after this second fall. After drinking from his canteen and pouring water over his head and wrists, he crawled back to the Union lines on his hands and knees.[19]

William Lochren recalled, "Silently, without orders, and almost from the start, double-quick had changed to utmost speed—for in utmost speed lay the only hope that any of us would pass through that storm of lead and strike the enemy."[20] Captain Louis Muller of Company E was shot through the head and dropped dead on the field. First Lieutenant James DeGray of Company G fell with a four-inch rip in his skull from a minié ball. Captain Joseph Perium of Company K had a minié ball punch through the right side of his nose and exit behind his left ear. He would live for five days.

The First Minnesota, being a well-drilled and veteran regiment, no doubt started the charge as a perfect double-ranked line sweeping down the slope. The challenges to maintaining that formation were many: rifle and artillery fire, stepping over bodies and the occasional large stone that stuck up from the field, and negotiating still-standing fence posts and the unevenness of the ground. The line must have been still together but getting ragged by the time it reached the rebels. Private Daniel Sullivan of Company D, a twenty-one-year-old Irish farmer from near Minneapolis, wrote, "Our regt. [regiment] looked like scurmishers when chargeing." Sullivan probably was commenting not only on how few of them there were but also that they were spread out in a more open formation.[21]

From the lay of the land, and an oddly shaped fence line on the west side of the Plum Run ravine that may not have been completely taken down, Wilcox's brigade apparently moved forward faster on the left—the First Minnesota's right. It seems that the right of the First Minnesota reached the Confederate line before its left did.[22] Perhaps the First came into initial contact with a portion of Wilcox's Ninth Alabama Regiment, which was most likely ahead of the rest of the brigade in its attempt to take Rorty's battery on Cemetery Ridge. In any event, indications are that the Ninth Alabama was farther north (to the right) of the First Minnesota and probably did not come in direct contact with the regiment but fired into the flank and rear of the Minnesotans.

In a letter to his brother shortly after the battle, John Plummer of Company D, on the left flank of the regiment, wrote how they were halted halfway across the second field, which would have been the harvested wheat field just before the ravine. This may have been an attempt to keep the regimental alignment. Some men ran out in front and beckoned the others on to finish the charge and close with the rebels. The left of the regiment seems to have moved forward once more, then was ordered to halt again at the edge of the second field, the lip of the ravine.

Private Daniel Sullivan was also from Company D, and he mentioned the halt as well, "We started down the hill and they opened on us. We got the order to hault, and they give us hell . . . they was lotts of us hit. I got it when chargein and thought I would not stop. Keped on but it made [me] lame."[23] Sullivan was shot through the heel.

Whatever stopping and restarting the left wing of the regiment was doing, the shock value of the charge apparently did its job. Colonel Colvill gave the order "Charge!" when the regiment neared the front Confederate line. The men dropped their muskets off their shoulders and held them in the charge bayonet position: torso twisted to the right at the hips with rifle butt trailing at the level of the right thigh and bayonet pointing at the enemy's chest. The pent-up terror and energy could finally be released, and the men must have screamed and bellowed like banshees.

William Lochren wrote, "The men were never made who will stand against leveled bayonets coming with such momentum and evident desperation. The first line broke in our front as we reached it, and rushed back through the second line, stopping the whole advance."[24]

In the face of this intimidating sight, the Confederates probably had no idea how small a force the First Minnesota was. They only saw leveled bayonets and screaming men charging out of the dense smoke. Colvill roared "Fire!" and the regiment, possibly still on the run, delivered a volley.[25] The disordered Confederate troops had endured a fighting advance across the six hundred yards from the Emmitsburg Road.

Plum Run and its trees, rocks, and boulders had done much to break up their alignment and reduce their forward momentum as well. The shock of the First Minnesota's charge and volley was too much, and Wilcox's brigade came to a complete halt.

George Clark of Wilcox's Eleventh Alabama Regiment wrote about this moment after the war. He remembered that, by the time the Confederates had made it to the low ground along Plum Run, they were nearly a mob. The orders from both Barksdale and Wilcox were to keep the pressure on and the movement forward. According to Clark, "the brigades of Barksdale, Wilcox, Perry and Wright were in marked confusion, mixed up indiscriminately, officers apart from their men, men without officers, but all pushing forward notwithstanding."[26]

It was a situation that was nothing short of salvation for the men of the First Minnesota. Private Charles Muller of Company A recalled, "We kept on running as fast as we could so as not to give the enemy a chance to reload their rifles again. And we got there before they had loaded; we run up on to them to within 4 yards when we begin to fire our first shot, and then we went at them with our bayonets."[27]

Lieutenant Martin Maginnis of Company H, a twenty-one-year-old Irish immigrant from Red Wing, Minnesota, remembered the moment with, "But little ammunition was wasted at that volley. A perfect swath of men sink to the ground, and the living recoil back on their second and third lines. Their supporting lines, confused and excited, wildly commenced firing through the mass in front, slaughtering their own men by the hundreds and throwing the whole column into confusion, while their artillery from the rear fired on friend and foe alike."[28]

The ravine filled with smoke and the deafening roar of combat. The men of the First Minnesota took what cover they could find among the bushes, brush, boulders, and in some places the dry ditch of Plum Run. On the right and center of the regiment,

Lieutenant Martin Maginnis of Company H

there was hand-to-hand combat and crushing skulls with musket butts and bayoneting. The left might have had some luck pushing back the rebel line, probably in conjunction with the 111th New York of Willard's brigade, which was an unknown number of yards to the south. Colonel Colvill wrote, "The smoke lifted. A glance showed the First Minnesota a grand line, every man straining every nerve, loading and firing from amidst the rocks upon the rebels no longer a line, but broken into clumps. Their men being thinnest toward our left there we commenced pressing them backward up the slope."[29]

In his official battle report, General Wilcox, referring to the First Minnesota's line, wrote, "Three several times did this last of the enemy's lines attempt to drive my men back, and were as often repulsed."[30] Sergeant Alfred Carpenter of Company K, a twenty-six-year-old farmer from St. Charles, Minnesota, also indicated that the regiment was ordered back but then went forward again. From this it seems that there was some seesaw action, and amazingly enough the tiny First Minnesota kept coming back both to deliver and receive more punishment. "So they give the order to hault. I took ame [aim] and mi old gun mist fire [misfired]. I turned around and stuck it in the ground and went to the rear about 6 rods [roughly thirty-three yards] and got behind a big rock," remembered Private Daniel Sullivan of Company D.[31]

Colonel Colvill was hit twice, but there are conflicting accounts of exactly when it happened. Colvill's version of it should be more accurate than any other. Christopher Heffelfinger, in his 1915 memoir, wrote that Colvill fell before the regiment reached the Plum Run ravine, and he also asserted that Colvill gave the order for the regiment to retire when he fell. From his position on the far left of the regiment, it is very unlikely that Heffelfinger could have heard Colvill give any orders after the start of the charge.

Colvill himself claimed that he was in the ravine as the regiment was making its stand. He was in his appropriate place after the charge had ended, directly behind the regimental colors in the center of the regiment. He wrote of the moment, "I never saw cooler work done on either side, and the destruction was awful. One of the last things I remember was one of the color-guard turning to me as he was raising his weapon to fire, making some remark, with a smile on his face."[32] He continued,

"Owing to the blinding smoke, we could see distinctly only at intervals. There was a gleam of light, in which my glance took in the slope on my left. I saw numbers of our men lying upon it as they had fallen. Then came a shock like a sledge hammer on my back bone between the shoulders. It turned me partly around and made me 'see stars.'"[33]

Ellet Perkins, color sergeant during the Battle of Gettysburg, was shot down during the charge on July 2, and the flag passed successively to each remaining member of the color guard. In 1904, on his death bed, Perkins had the remaining rags of the flag brought to him and died with the colors in his arms.

Colvill had been struck by a minié ball, and, from the track of the wound, he must have been in a crouching position when hit. A burly six-feet, five-inches tall, he probably did the sensible thing and crouched to try and make himself a smaller target, as well as to attempt to see under the haze of smoke. The bullet entered at the top of his right shoulder and passed under the shoulder blade. It struck the spine, taking off a portion of a vertebrae, and finally lodged under his left shoulder blade. He put his right foot down to steady himself and promptly received a minié ball through the ankle joint.

Colvill spun half around, and in a display of stunning understatement Captain Henry Coates of Company A said, "Colonel, you are badly hurt." Colvill answered, "I don't know. Take care of the men," then pitched forward and hit the ground near a shallow gully that was "not more than two feet wide and less in depth." In his agony, he managed to roll himself into the gully for protection and spent the rest of the fight listening to bullets zipping across the ground above him.[34]

The regiment's adjutant, Lieutenant John Pellar, went down with a broken arm. Major Mark Downie was hit once in the left foot and twice in the right arm. Lieutenant Colonel Charles Powell Adams was wounded in the chest, hip, and leg. First Lieutenant (soon to be captain) Thomas Sinclair of Company B was smashed in the chest by what must have been a spent bullet. It flattened itself against his breast bone, only causing severe concussion trauma.

The First Minnesota fought on savagely. The "unknown sergeant" wrote of the stand on Plum Run, "Who that was an actor there, can give the order, or detail the changes of those eventful and exciting movements, when neither ball or shell was heard—and we could not see our comrades fall, when every faculty was absorbed in the one thought of whipping the enemy in front."[35]

Like Sinclair, Lieutenant Heffelfinger was struck in the chest by a minié ball. In one of many similar freak incidents in the war, the ball punched through his uniform coat, took a bite out of the edge of a small leather memo book in his breast pocket, shattered the small wooden pencil in the memo book, and penetrated his shirt. Miraculously, it did not enter his body. For several days Heffelfinger was badly bruised and sore from the concussion, but he remained on duty with the regiment.[36]

Amazingly, the regiment was holding its own against Wilcox's brigade.

The real slaughter began when the much wider Confederate line began to lap around the flanks of the First Minnesota. The worst encroachment came on the regiment's right. Company G on the far right flank refused its position, that is, bent itself back at a right angle to the rest of the line. The rebels started a merciless enfilading fire into the flank and back of the Minnesotans.

As the First Minnesota was fighting for its life along Plum Run, to the south the more equally matched brigade of Colonel George Willard was pummeling General William Barksdale's brigade of Mississippians, forcing them back toward the Emmitsburg Road. Willard's command took grim satisfaction in its opportunity to fight Barksdale, one of those responsible for the surrender of the New York brigade at Harpers Ferry. As their charge began, a cry echoed throughout the entire brigade: "Remember Harpers Ferry!"[37]

The 125th, 126th, and 111th New York Regiments of Willard's brigade had probably been engaging Barksdale's rebel brigade for about ten or fifteen minutes prior to the charge of the First Minnesota and had begun to dislodge them from the Plum Run swale as the Minnesotans slammed into Wilcox's brigade. When Hancock ordered the 111th New York to charge, the regiment moved to the right to clear the 126th New York, then left-faced and charged at the double-quick to catch up with the other two regiments. They hit somewhere in the vicinity of Barksdale's far left and Wilcox's far right. The fact that Wilcox's right did not envelop the First Minnesota the way his left did suggests that the 111th New York was keeping them busy.

Willard's men pushed the Mississippians back up the slope toward the Emmitsburg Road. As they emerged from the scrubby area along Plum Run, they were met by severe fire from rebel artillery, which had advanced to the Peach Orchard on their left. They also received rifle fire from the right, which, along with Barksdale's retreating men, was probably coming from Wilcox's right flank.[38] Wilcox had probably refused his line slightly to meet the attack of the 111th New York. This fallback may have been part of the response to the First Minnesota's attack as well and was probably what the men of the First Minnesota's left wing meant when they said Wilcox's right was forced back.

At least a portion of Willard's brigade pushed on for another couple of hundred yards toward the Emmitsburg Road.[39] A member of the 126th New York wrote that the other two regiments halted shortly after emerging from the swale, but that the 126th continued.[40] This makes sense, as it was unlikely the 111th simply would bypass Wilcox's right flank and allow itself to be enfiladed in its own right flank and rear. Confederate soldiers were dropping their weapons and lying on the ground in surrender, allowing Willard's advancing troops to march over them.[41] Squads of Willard's men, undoubtedly grateful for the opportunity, dropped out to round up the prisoners and march them back to the Union line on Cemetery Ridge.

Lead and iron finally bled the fight out of Confederate General Barksdale. He was shot in the lower left thigh, then later a cannonball nearly severed his left foot at the ankle. He finally was unhorsed when hit squarely in the right breast by a minié ball.[42] There are a number of claimants for the distinction of having put at least one minié ball into Barksdale—including an unknown man from the First Minnesota's Company F skirmish line and even one from Company G fighting down in the ravine with the regiment. However, it is probable he finally was dropped by fire from the 125th or 126th New York of Willard's brigade.[43] Barksdale was found alive just to the west of Plum Run's swale and taken to the Union Second Corps aid station on the Hummelbaugh farm on the Taneytown Road, where he died during the early morning of July 3.[44]

On the right of the First Minnesota, the situation was becoming worse and rapidly untenable. As the Confederate charge developed, the brigades to the left of Wilcox had followed the trip-hammer pattern and attacked. The brigade directly to the left of Wilcox was known as Perry's brigade, although it was commanded at Gettysburg by Colonel David Lang of the Eighth Florida. General Edward Perry was back in Virginia recovering from typhoid fever. By this point in the war, the brigade was composed of three undersized Florida regiments—the Second, Fifth, and Eighth—and capable of throwing a total of about 742 men into the assault.[45]

Lang's Floridians followed shortly behind Wilcox's advance and moved at the double-quick, probably both to catch up with Wilcox's left flank and to spend less time subjected to the murderous artillery and rifle fire of federal General Humphreys's guns.[46] They did a good deal to help collapse Humphreys's line, striking his right flank as Barksdale's men raked his left flank and Wilcox's brigade pummeled his center. As Humphreys withdrew, Lang moved his brigade into the broad trough of land between Wilcox's left and the Codori farm two hundred yards to the north.

Facing Lang now was the Nineteenth Maine, which like the First Minnesota earlier was lying on the ground for protection. According to Colonel Francis E. Heath of the Nineteenth Maine, when Humphreys's retreating troops were about 150 yards away, Humphreys—or an officer he took for Humphreys—rode up with part of his staff. The officer ordered Heath to have his men stop the retreating federals at the point of their bayonets. Heath told Humphreys—or whoever the officer was— that the retreating men were likely to carry his own regiment before them. He said his men would stay lying down, and the officer's troops could pass over and re-form behind his regiment.

After a heated exchange with Heath, Humphreys rode up and down behind the Nineteenth Maine's line ordering it to rise and fix bayonets. Colonel Heath followed along countermanding the order.[47] The refugees from the Third Corps passed over the Nineteenth Maine in the same way they had the First Minnesota. Private Silas Adams of Company F wrote:

> On they came like a great billow, rushing with an irresistible force that no troops could check in flight. They swept over us, they stepped on or between the men and even tumbled over us, having no regard to dignity or military order, or to pick out reasonable paths to walk in, as their only object seemed to be to get to the rear, out of the reach of their pursuers. There was neither order nor discipline in that broken mass of men, yet there were many brave spirits among the routed troops, and some would call out to us to "hang on and they would form in our rear," while others would tell us "we are whipped and to get out," and in passing to the rear they gave us lots of advice, but the Nineteenth hung on and not a man left the ranks.[48]

Colonel Heath wrote later that one of his officers counted thirteen flags passing over the Nineteenth Maine, one of which was a brigade flag. The other twelve flags would indicate that the colors, and remnants, of at least six regiments retreated over Heath's men. Heath said further that the retreating troops of Humphreys's command tried to form in his rear, "but only fifty or sixty files got in line [100 to 120 men] and it at once fell back."[49]

As the retreating troops of the Third Corps finished passing, the Nineteenth Maine rose up—nearly 440 strong—and delivered a volley into Lang's Confederates.[50] They dropped the color bearer of the Eighth Florida and brought Lang's troops to a standstill. A vicious firefight started on the open ground, neither force giving an inch as the bodies piled up.

Captain Isaac Starbird of Company F, on the far left flank, came to Colonel Heath at the center of the line. Starbird bore the distressing news that a large body of troops was deploying on the regiment's left flank. Heath quickly went to the left of the Nineteenth Maine where he saw, "A regiment formed in double columns in the act of deploying, it was formed so that when in line its left wing could have reached nearly to my colors [the middle of the Nineteenth Maine], and the two lines would not have been more than twenty yards apart."[51]

Fortunately for the Nineteenth, the Confederate regiment seemed to have other prey on its mind. It seems inconceivable that this unknown rebel regiment would have ignored the threat posed by the Nineteenth Maine. More than likely the smoke and confusion of battle were factors. The big question is, whose was this regiment? It seems unlikely it was part of Lang's force, since they were all fully occupied with the Nineteenth Maine, certainly to the extent of all three of Lang's small regiments knowing that the Maine regiment was directly in front of them.

Consequently, the regiment that Starbird saw was probably the Ninth Alabama of Wilcox's brigade. The First Minnesota's stand was holding up most of Wilcox's brigade, and Lang's force had moved past the stalled Alabamans by about one hundred yards. The Ninth Alabama probably could not move forward easily because of Lang's line. It might have formed into column of divisions, the double-column formation Heath mentioned, in which a regiment moves forward two companies abreast, forming a mass ten ranks deep.[52] This would have let them pass Lang, with the possible intention of wheeling left to deploy back into a battle line on the right and rear of the First Minnesota. It would also have provided a narrower target for the artillery battery that Wilcox had sent them forward to take, either Thomas's or Rorty's.

Colonel Heath indicated these troops were facing outward in relation to his own regiment, which means they were facing away, or starting to face away, from the Nineteenth Maine.[53] Heath ordered Starbird's company to refuse itself to the regimental line, and they put a deadly enfilading fire into the flank and back of these rebels.[54] This mystery regiment disintegrated and disappeared into the battle smoke.

It was now sometime between 6:45 and 7:15 or 7:20 P.M., and the sun was nearly down. Muzzle flashes became the primary illumination in the smoky chaos of twilight. The First Minnesota received some relief when the Nineteenth Maine broke up the troops on the Minnesotans' right flank and rear. Colonel Colvill stated that "a considerable 'jam' of Rebel troops had collected" in this area to the right of the regiment and had they been "properly commanded they would have taken the battery" (Evan Thomas's Battery C, Fourth U.S.).[55] Clearly this portion of the rebel line was collapsing into a mob, although at least part was able to maintain a brisk fire into the flank and rear of the First Minnesota.

The Confederate commanders realized that their forward momentum had been stymied and their men, and luck, were just about played out. Cadmus Wilcox said that he had sent to his division commander, Major General Richard Anderson, for reinforcements. He was told to hang on as things would surely turn around. No reinforcements were ever sent. Wilcox wrote that there was no support on either his right or left.[56] At this point that was essentially true: Barksdale's men, formerly on his right, already were pushed back across the Emmitsburg Road, and Lang's Floridians were one hundred yards or so farther advanced, making it appear to Wilcox as though no one was on his left either.

The last section of Confederate troops to attack was the brigade of Brigadier General Ambrose R. Wright and parts of Brigadier General Carnot Posey's brigade. For reasons never satisfactorily explained in any official report, the Confederate assault broke down after Posey's brigade, and no other Confederate units advanced.[57] Wright's and Posey's troops did, in fact, punch through the paper-thin federal line in the area where Pickett's Charge would strike less than twenty hours later. But the Confederates were fought out and too poorly supported. They could not hold and quickly were pushed back.

It must have been Wright's troops that prompted Lieutenant Colonel Henry W. Cunningham of the Nineteenth Maine to consult with Colonel Heath as Heath returned to the center of the regiment. The word was that the rebels had advanced past the Nineteenth's right flank, and it was potentially in danger of being cut off and surrounded. Heath promptly had the regiment withdraw farther up the crest of Cemetery Ridge, but "upon getting out of the smoke I could see nothing alarming and faced to the front and ordered a charge."[58] The Nineteenth Maine charged in conjunction with a number of other regiments, including portions of rallied Third Corps troops, that were advancing.[59]

Confederate Colonel David Lang paid an unintentional compliment to the First Minnesota in his official battle report. He wrote, "an aide from the right informed me that a heavy force had advanced upon General Wilcox's brigade, and was forcing it back."[60] The handful of Minnesotans could hardly be considered "a heavy force," but they were obviously having that effect.

Lang's report indicated that Wilcox was beginning to withdraw already, and "a heavy fire of musketry was poured upon my brigade from the woods fifty yards immediately in my front."[61] This musketry was from the Nineteenth Maine and likely from rallied pockets of Third Corps troops as well. Undoubtedly he was referring to the initial fire of the Nineteenth into the Floridians. By "woods," Lang was alluding to the spare stand of timber that extended south and west down the slope of the small land spur where the Nineteenth Maine was posted. Lang added that another aide from his right soon came to inform him that Wilcox had fallen back, and the federal infantry had moved far beyond his line on the right flank. Lang went to check for himself: "I discovered that the enemy had passed me more than 100 yards, and was attempting to surround me."[62]

It is hard to say if Lang was seeing the First Minnesota, which would have been about one hundred yards behind him on his right, or if he actually was seeing the portion of Willard's brigade that had moved out much farther toward the Emmitsburg Road. In either case, it was enough to make him decide to withdraw. He did not mention the charge of the Nineteenth Maine or of any other federal troops, but surely those lines of bellowing men and bristling bayonets helped speed his retreat.

To the south, Colonel Willard soon realized that his brigade was sticking out like a sore thumb. Part of it was halfway between the Plum Run swale and the Emmitsburg Road in pursuit of Barksdale's men. Confederate Colonel E. Porter Alexander, in command of all of Longstreet's artillery for the July 2 assault, had rushed his guns forward to the Peach Orchard as soon as the federals were driven out. From this vantage point, Alexander saw to his disappointment that the main Union line had not been broken. But he had the consolation of pulverizing the federal artillery and infantry with his sixty-two guns, recalling, "There was plenty to shoot at. One could take his choice and here my guns stood and fired until it was too dark to see anything more."[63]

Part of what he pulverized was Willard's brigade. Willard's men were being hit with artillery fire from the front, along the Emmitsburg Road, as well as on the left flank from the Peach Orchard. Willard had his men drag several abandoned federal artillery pieces back, about-facing his troops and marching them in quick-time back to Cemetery Ridge.[64] Willard and his command had made a splendid accounting of themselves, erasing any stigma created by the fiasco at Harpers Ferry.

Unfortunately for George Willard, there would be no opportunity for laurels. While he was moving his men across the scrubby Plum Run swale, an artillery shell exploded near him. A fragment tore off a portion of his face and head, "tearing the angle of his mouth and shattered his chin and shoulder."[65] As Willard sprawled lifelessly on the ground, his horse bolted at full gallop into the Confederate lines to the west.[66]

Elements of the Third Corps were still re-forming on Cemetery Ridge. It appears that sufficient men of this devastated corps formed a steady enough line to charge, and they plunged into the mass of rebels bunched up between the First Minnesota and the Nineteenth Maine. The First Division of the Twelfth Corps was sent from Culp's Hill on the far right of the federal line, where they established a position for a short time to the left of Willard's brigade as the New Yorkers fell back to Cemetery Ridge.

Colonel Colvill, lying stunned and bleeding in a ditch near Plum Run, gasped out the command for the First Minnesota to withdraw. The order made its way to the next ranking officer physically still able to lead, Captain Nathan Messick of Company G. Messick, a thirty-six-year-old cobbler from Faribault, Minnesota, passed along the word for the regiment to retire back to the ridge.

Apparently the right portion of the regiment, which was most directly engaged in hand-to-hand fighting and taking the worst punishment, disengaged and pulled back first. Lieutenant Heffelfinger of Company D, on the far left, did not notice the regimental colors going back until Sergeant Horace Martin pointed it out to him. Sergeant Henry Taylor of Company E, to the left center of the regiment, mentioned that he had to yell the order to fall back repeatedly to get most of the men to respond. For many, the real terror began now, when the time had come to disengage and withdraw. They had lasted up until now, and, like turning loose and jumping off a tiger, they feared their luck would not hold for the trip back to Cemetery Ridge.

Private John Plummer of Company D wrote, "We dreaded to go back for the danger of it, more than staying there. . . . We fell back, and it was then I had the first feeling of fear during the fight. I felt almost sure I would be hit, and I saw many wounded going back."[67] Plummer made it back unharmed. His comrade Daniel Sullivan still was huddled behind a large rock, nursing his wounded heel. Watching in agony, as retreating men zipped past him, Sullivan observed, "Pretty soon the Boys came back kiteing, but the Rebels did not come."[68]

Private Charles Muller of Company A, in the middle of the regimental line, said that the rebels had moved around so far on the flanks that there was only a space of about forty or fifty yards to go through for the retreat. The rebels kept up a hot fire, and Muller saw a Confederate soldier take deliberate aim at him. The ball hit Muller in the right thigh, but did not break the femur. He was able to pick himself up and continue running his zigzag pattern back up the slope. Muller took the time to offer some advice to a comrade during his run back to the top of Cemetery Ridge, "I kept on running up to the open field in a zikzak way and there was a man in front of me walking along in a furrow. I told him to not walk that way or else he may git a ball. He turned round and said,

'You look out for yourself,' and not five seconds after a ball struck him on the head but only scratched his skin."[69]

Private Isaac Taylor of Company E started falling back with the rest of the regiment. A shell burst above him, and fragments took off the back of his head, coursed down through his body, and cut his waist belt apart as they nearly cleaved him in half.[70]

It was dusk by this time; some accounts indicate it was completely dark. At Gettysburg the sun set on July 2, 1863, at 7:32 P.M. local time.[71] As was the norm during the Civil War, the fighting subsided as the light faded. Both sides pulled back and left the contested fields in the middle to the dead, the dying, and the ravenous hogs. These huge farm hogs, unpenned during the fighting, devoured some of the dead and tried for some of the living during the night.[72]

What was left of the regiment regrouped on the crest of Cemetery Ridge. A preliminary count showed forty-seven men were still on their feet. While this count probably was correct, taking a count at five-minute intervals for a couple of hours after sunset probably would have given a different tally each time. John Plummer of Company D wrote within a few weeks of the battle, "When we got back to the colors, where we rallied, scarce twenty-five men were to be found."[73] Men were helping comrades to hospitals and to the Hummelbaugh farm aid station, and some already were making their way back onto the charge field and the area of the Plum Run stand to help bring back wounded.

About four hundred of the Confederates who had advanced to out-flank the First Minnesota had been cut off from Wilcox's and Lang's re-treat and were taken prisoner.[74] They were rounded up by men of the First Minnesota and the Nineteenth Maine, as well as rallied troops from the Third Corps. The men must have been functioning on pure army discipline and the instinct to get the job done and the area se-cured. Adrenaline was still flowing, hearts were still surging, ears were ringing from the rapidly ebbing roar of battle. It is not hard to imagine that nearly every man was in glassy-eyed shock.

The "unknown sergeant," whose letter was published in the *Saint Paul Pioneer* a little over a month after the battle, wrote of what must have pierced through the shock and into the heart of every Minnesotan who made it back to Cemetery Ridge at sunset on July 2, 1863: "But, good God! Where was the First Minnesota? Our flag was carried back to the battery [Thomas's Battery C], and seventy men, scarce one of them unmarked by scratches and bullet holes through their clothing, are all that formed around it; the other two hundred, alas, lay bleeding under it."[75]

— 7 —

Dead men and horses lying all around me

THE DESTRUCTION within the First Minnesota was astonishing. The entire episode, from the charge to the retreat back to the top of Cemetery Ridge, had lasted at most fifteen or twenty minutes.[1] Nearly two-thirds of those in the charge were sprawled, bleeding, where they fell, from the pasture down to and along Plum Run. Many were making their way to the Second Corps Hospital or the Hummelbaugh farm aid station on the Taneytown Road. "It cannot, perhaps, be claimed that July 2nd was a Union success, but it certainly was a Confederate failure—if their effort was to take the ridge—and all present agree that they *were* trying, all right," mused Orderly Sergeant James Wright of Company F.[2]

The fight on Plum Run would keep Regimental Quartermaster Francis Baasen busy requisitioning new uniforms in the days to come. After the battle Baasen wrote, "Every man, without exception, had his clothing riddled—some of them all to rags."[3]

In a letter written at the end of July, Alfred Carpenter of Company K related, "The ground was strewed with dead and dying, whose groans and prayers and cries for help and water rent the air. The sun had gone down and in the darkness we hurried, stumbled over the field in search of our fallen companions."[4]

The initial race back down the field to help the wounded, under the cover of darkness, was not very well organized. The situation was still chaotic, and men ventured out individually and in groups to do what they could for their comrades. Edward Bassett, William Ramsey, and Cal Jackson, three privates in Company G, went together.[5]

Lieutenant Heffelfinger approached Captain Messick, now in charge of the regiment, and asked permission, which was granted, to take a few men and gather the regiment's wounded. His group probably included Sergeant Henry Taylor and some other men of Company E. In any case, whether with Heffelfinger or not, Taylor and a small group from Company E also went. Second Lieutenant Lochren, who now commanded Company K as well as being the acting adjutant, asked Heffelfinger if he would look after his company's wounded, too.[6]

Those who could were fending for themselves. On hands and knees, Mat Marvin had crawled back to the regiment's position next to Thomas's artillery battery. He could not walk, so the slightly wounded Charlie North from his company helped him. Together they made their way back to the Second Corps, Second Division hospital in the fields along the Granite Schoolhouse Road just off the Taneytown Road.[7]

The end of his zigzag run brought Charles Muller to the handful of First Minnesota men forming on Cemetery Ridge. His company captain, Henry Coates, asked thirty-three-year-old Austrian Private Jacob Fegar to help him back to the hospital. There Muller sat on a rock and

The ambitious Lieutenant Colonel Charles Powell Adams of the First Minnesota

cut away his blood-soaked trouser leg. Fegar brought him a pail of water and a piece of cloth fifteen inches long, obviously the only thing he could find. In the dim light of the rising moon, Charles Muller washed and bandaged his own gunshot wound.[8]

By 8:00 P.M. Lieutenant Jasper N. Searles had the division's ambulance corps fanning out on the field with stretchers. Searles found and personally helped to evacuate the First Minnesota's lieutenant colonel, Charles Powell Adams.[9] Adams had been shot through the left side of his chest, the bullet exiting near the spine. He was also hit in the groin, the bullet passing through his leg, and had taken another minié ball in that same leg, which lodged just above the knee.[10] He was not expected to live.

The July 2, 1863, diary entry of Sergeant Henry Taylor, Company E, would tell the story of the regiment for this day: "I find I am left in command of our company, though a sergeant. Out of 36 officers and men, 15 minutes has reduced us to nine men; not any missing but all killed or wounded. List of killed, Capt. Louis Muller, 1st Sgt. J. G. Trevor, Privates J. W. Davis, Norman Fowler, Israel Jackins and Isaac L. Taylor."[11]

Undoubtedly Taylor added to, or wrote, this entry after July 2. He probably lacked the time and energy to write it that night, and he did not know his brother's fate until the next morning. Taylor thought he had seen Isaac go down during the charge but was told by Corporal Edward Austin that Isaac had fallen back with the rest of Company E during the retreat from Plum Run. Henry Taylor looked for his brother until 9:00 P.M., knowing Isaac was dead or wounded since he was not with the company. He then rejoined the remnants of the First Minnesota about 10:00 P.M. to have a short and fitful night's sleep among the dead scattered along Cemetery Ridge.[12]

Company F was taking stock of its own day's battle. Its casualties were considerably more manageable than the rest of the regiment's. Corporal Marion Abbott's right arm was shattered, probably by a minié ball. James F. Bachelor was shot in the foot, and Levi King was hit in the face, fracturing his jaw.

Jonas P. Davis, whom Captain Ball had sent back to report to and receive further orders from Colonel Colvill, had not returned, and his fate was unknown. The twenty-three-year-old Davis did not appear on any of the casualty lists, and he survived the war. He could have reached the regiment too late to participate in the charge, or perhaps he was in the charge and returned unscathed.

Ball had been placed in position and told to stay, despite having asked permission to go immediately to find his regiment. He was told he could go in the morning. He sent Sergeant Philip Hamlin back to where the First Minnesota was last posted, about a quarter of a mile north. Hamlin was to report the situation and casualties of Company F, then receive orders and return.

As the army struggled to recover, sort itself out, and get some much needed sleep, more fighting began to rage on the far right of the federal line. John Plummer of Company D did not know what to make of it but feared the worst: "Musketry was heard very plain, seemingly scarce half a mile off, and completely in our rear; in fact, some of the bullets whistled over our heads. Now we were sure the battle was gone up for us, for the fighting continued fierce, and seemed growing nearer all the time. We made up our minds that we were whipped, and expected before morning to see the whole Army routed, flying for Baltimore."[13]

The fighting continued for a time but eventually died down. It was Confederate General Richard Ewell's Second Corps on the Confederate left making a last-ditch effort to take Culp's Hill. In the dark they succeeded in driving some federals out of their first line of breastworks and taking over some works abandoned by the Twelfth Corps division that had been sent to support the Union left. Thus the rebels took, somewhat by default, the "barb" of the Union army's fishhook-shaped battle line.

That was the only point of the main federal line that was given up on this terrible day. Daniel Sickles's Third Corps had done its unintended work as a breakwater. The Confederates found what ground they could, not covered with dead bodies or horse carcasses, and lay down to sleep along Sickles's former advanced-line position. The area between the Emmitsburg Road and the federal line on Cemetery Ridge was a no-man's land of death, wailing wounded, and men with stretchers moving quickly and silently among them.

Philip Hamlin returned to Company F with news worse than anyone could have expected. He told Captain Ball that he could only find a few men of the regiment, and it was assumed by all that the rest were dead or wounded. Despite the entreaties of some of the men to go immediately to the regiment for news, Ball said that he had been ordered to stay there for the night and that his name, company, and regiment had been taken down. They would stay there for the night.

The tattered remains of the First Minnesota were gathered and formed by Captain Messick and marched to their assigned spot on the battle line, between 350 and 400 yards north along Cemetery Ridge, roughly due west of the reserve position they held earlier in the day.

John Plummer wrote that he, and most others, lay down to sleep, "with our equipment on and guns by our sides, and I here say I never slept better and had more pleasant dreams in my life than I had on the battle field of Gettysburg, with dead men and horses lying all around me."[14]

It was a well-earned sleep that Plummer and the others would need when morning came.

— 8 —

We just rushed in like wild beasts

ORDERLY SERGEANT JAMES WRIGHT had been lulled to sleep by rifle fire. Now, only a few hours later, he was awakened by it. The rattle of musketry rose to a fierce crescendo in the area behind and to the right of the First Minnesota. The Twelfth Corps was busy at daybreak trying to drive the rebels out of the federal entrenchment along Culp's Hill. The seesaw combat lasted until ten in the morning, when the rebels were finally dislodged and pushed back. For those Confederates who had not achieved eternal sleep this morning or the night before, their fighting earned them only a short night's rest in the Union breastworks.

Captain Ball of Company F, First Minnesota, had spent most of the night pacing. He heard twice more from the regiment, confirming the worst. He ordered the bleary-eyed Wright to form the men and rapidly marched them to the First Minnesota's position on the line. Wright wrote of the reunion, "We had not been separated far, or long, but the greetings were as sincere and earnest as if oceans had divided us and years had elapsed. There was a flood of inquiries about the missing ones, and the answers left no doubts in our minds of the awful calamity that [had] befallen the regiment."[1]

Company F added little more than twenty men to the regiment's tattered ranks. It probably brought the number to something over one hundred men. Wright made note of the fact: "Under ordinary circumstances an organization that had suffered one half the loss that we had

82

would have been sent to the rear instead of the firing-line–but this was no ordinary occasion."[2]

Sergeant Henry Taylor found time to take out his diary and pencil and write, "Friday, July 3: Enemy feel of us at daylight–fighting on our right. At 8:30 A.M. Mr. Snow tells me he saw my brother dead a little to our left and rear."[3] In a letter to his parents three days later, Taylor told, in rather grisly detail, of the death of his brother Isaac. He offered the solace that Isaac would have been killed instantly, given the nature of his wounds. "I cannot express to you my sorrow at his loss. I feel as though I was all alone," he wrote.[4]

He unburdened himself in a detailed letter to his sister dated July 19, 1863, from the regiment's camp near Snickers Gap, Virginia. Taylor told of what must have been the most harrowing experience of his life:

> I looked for Isaac till about 9 P.M. but could not find him. . . . I slept a little. . . . July 3rd, half past eight, a man of Company G (Snow) was coming up with coffee for some of the officers, and saw Isaac lying dead–he told me he thought he saw my brother–killed.[5] I went with him to the spot and found it but too true, secured his things–knapsack, haversack, and canteen were gone, he probably threw them off when he went into action. I found a spade and took William E. Cundy and James L. Brown of Co. E and went and dug his grave. We laid him down with all his clothes on, as he fell, and spread a shelter tent over him. As we laid him down, I remarked, "Well Isaac, all I can give you is a soldier's grave." I then sat down on a stone while the two comrades buried him. I was the only one to weep over his grave–his Father, Mother, brothers and sisters were all ignorant of his death.[6]

While the morning fighting raged around Culp's Hill on the far right, the Union center was relatively quiet except for periodic exchanges of fire by pickets or sharpshooters and the occasional artillery round. About 11:00 A.M. a fierce duel began between artillery of Confederate General A. P. Hill and some of General Hancock's batteries near the First Minnesota's position. It lasted about ten or fifteen minutes, then the field became quiet again.[7] "What a pitiable picture we would have made that morning. The stains of powder and dirt, gathered in the marching and the fighting of the two previous days, still covered our hands, faces and clothing, and physical weariness and mental depression and suffering was written on every countenance," reported Sergeant Wright.[8]

The men began to build a barricade of fence rails, sticks, brush, and rocks. They dug up dirt and gravel with their bayonets, tin plates, and cups, filling their knapsacks and blankets and adding them to their meager defensive line. Parties went out with canteens to bring water. Then they built fires and made coffee. James Wright noted, "No man can fully and rightly appreciate the value of a cup of coffee until he had partaken of one under some similar circumstances. After an examination of our rifles and ammunition, we laid down behind the little shelters we had made and went to sleep."[9]

The day dragged on, and many of the men slept despite the conditions and the heat. The occasional shot from the rebel sharpshooters usually struck the flimsy barricade, but at least one found flesh. Twenty-three-year-old Private Romulus E. Jacobs of Company F was hit in the shoulder. The impact made such a loud noise that his comrades thought he had been hit with one of the more hideous innovations of the Civil War, the exploding bullet. Inspection of the wound showed that a normal minié ball actually had slapped through numerous folds of Jacobs's rubber "gum" blanket on entry and exit.[10]

Shortly after noon a lunch was served at General John Gibbon's headquarters, at the Peter Frey farm just south of Meade's headquarters. General Meade was present, as were General Hancock and several others. Gibbon's orderlies had produced a number of tough old roosters to go in the stew pot, and Gibbon chose not to ask where they got them.[11]

On the night of July 2 Meade told Gibbon that, if the rebels attacked on July 3, it would be on his front. Meade felt that after having made attacks on both flanks Lee would make a final stab at the Union center, Gibbon's division of the Second Corps. Over their stewed rooster, Meade told Gibbon that he wanted all of the provost guard relieved and sent back to their regiments to add needed manpower to the battle line. "General Gibbon called up Captain Wilson Farrell, 1st Minnesota, who commanded the provost guard of his division, and directed him for that day to join the regiment. 'Very well, sir,' said the Captain as he touched his hat and turned away. He was a quiet, excellent gentleman and a thorough soldier. I knew him well and esteemed him. I never saw him again," remembered Lieutenant Frank A. Haskell of General Gibbon's Staff.[12]

The warm, muggy day continued. The temperature reached eighty-seven degrees for the wool-clad soldiers lying in the sun. The men dozed, wrote in their diaries, and listened to the occasional bullet thud into their dirt-filled knapsacks. At 12:30 P.M. John Plummer and others gathered around one of the First Minnesota's lieutenants, who had acquired a copy of the July 2 *Baltimore Clipper* newspaper and was reading it aloud. Time passed. It was around one P.M.[13]

"Not a piece of artillery was fired, and even the skirmishers scarcely got off a shot. The silence seemed to grow more and more intense. Bang! Bang!! Two signal guns sent shot into our lines. How can mortal pen write or mortal tongue or mortal mind conceive what followed! Along a whole front, especially in front of our Corps on the left-center, a hundred and forty-five 'war dogs' opened their bronzen throats, and fired in volley not as artillery but as the continual rattle of musketry with all the weight and sound and metal from a ten-pound Parrot to a 32-pound howitzer," recalled Private Daniel Bond of Company F.[14]

The exact number of cannon engaged has been a disputed point. In this case, however, Bond was about right. Both sides necessarily maintained an artillery reserve, and a count of the batteries actually engaged at the beginning of this cannonade shows about 142 Confederate cannon and 103 Union cannon were firing at the height of this vicious artillery duel.[15] Miles away, in farmyards and villages all over southern Pennsylvania and northern Maryland, villagers and farm folk could see the expanding column of white smoke rising in the air. The rumble of the cannonade was reported in towns as far as 150 miles away.[16]

The Confederate artillery was pouring shot and shell into the Union position like a hailstorm. Federal batteries on Cemetery Hill, Cemetery Ridge, and Little Round Top opened on the Confederate batteries. There are multiple arguments about where, or whom, the first "signal" shot struck. One claim comes from William Harmon of the First Minnesota's Company C, a twenty-five-year-old lieutenant from Minneapolis. As part of the division's provost guard, Harmon was at division headquarters. He declared that the first shot decapitated one of General John Gibbon's orderlies.[17]

The newspaper "read-aloud" stopped abruptly, and Plummer and the others quickly returned to their places in the line. "There was an incessant, discordant flight of shells, seemingly in and from all directions: howling, shrieking, striking, exploding, tearing, smashing and destroying. The ground was torn-up, fences and trees knocked to splinters, rocks and small stones were flying in the air, ammunition boxes and caissons were exploded; guns were dismounted and men and horses were torn to pieces. We commended our soul to God, shut our teeth hard and lay flat on the ground, expecting every minute to be blown to atoms," wrote Sergeant James Wright.[18]

An unknown sergeant of the First recalled that, "The roar was terrific and deafening, and cannon balls, bursting shells, grape, canister, shrapnel, railroad iron and Whitworth bolts from England, and even sledges, caisson bolts and spikes—iron in every imaginable shape, was tearing up the ground and flying with horrible screeches as of invisible demons through the air. An ammunition caisson would explode, scattering fragments of timber, wheels, clothing and bodies high into the air."[19]

The Confederate gunners were shooting a little high, and while some of the shots landed among the federal troops, most landed in the rear area. The First Minnesota had the good fortune to be lying on seemingly "blessed" ground. Shells fell into regiments to the left and right of the Minnesotans, pulverized the ridge behind them, and smacked into the ridge in front of them and bounced over their heads. Few rounds entered the ranks of the First Minnesota, and no one was killed or wounded.

Lieutenant Heffelfinger of Company D did have a close call, along with another soldier: "A solid-shot, fired from the enemy's artillery, struck the ground some distance in front and tore up the ground between me and one of the soldiers of my company and threw dirt and sand over us. When this shot passed, one of the boys said, 'Never mind, Lieutenant, lightning never strikes twice in the same place.'"[20]

The small Leister farmhouse, used as Meade's headquarters, was hit, and the surrounding farmyard was riddled. Sixteen horses hitched in front of the house were disemboweled and chopped to pieces by the murderous rain of solid shot and exploding shell. In what must have been hyperbole induced by the experience, a reporter for the *New York Times* estimated that the shells dropped at a rate of six per second and at no time fewer than two per second.[21]

The field hospitals in the rear became a nightmare of chaos and panic. "It caused some skedadling among those that could walk and some holloring and groaning among those that could not walk. I thought that if the Rebs had a shell for me that it could not kill me any younger, and that they can't do it but once," Sergeant Mat Marvin of Company K asserted.[22]

Marvin moved himself and his wounded captain, thirty-year-old Joseph Perium of Winona, behind an apple tree. The exploding shells sent a constant shower of tree limbs and splinters raining down on them. Marvin confided to his diary, "I was laying by the side of my Captain, who was wounded in the head, the ball entering at the nose and came out back of the left ear. In taking care of him I got pretty well covered with blood, as he bled a good deal. He wanted to go back to the front, so I had to hold him most of the time."[23] Ambulances began moving the wounded to a new field hospital two miles farther behind the lines.

The ordeal continued for the men on the battle line. Daniel Bond wrote of the incessant rain of shells:

> As we lay flat on our faces they would strike the ground in front of us and, bounding over our heads, would go on their way growling in an anger too terrible for conception. Again they would explode in our front and the ugly missles would come down with a sound unpleasant to the ears. Each fell with a proximity that in hours of less excitement would cause the bravest to think of the uncertainty of human life.
>
> Again they would sing in wrath so very close that we would involuntarily cling more closely to Mother Earth. Here they would strike in a cassion, and high in the air would go a cloud of smoke and wide and far the scattered fragments of shells and timbers would fill the air.[24]

John Plummer of Company D remembered, "Caisson after caisson blowed up, and still the Rebels' fire was fierce and rapid as ever. I kept thinking surely they cannot fire much longer, their guns will get so hot they will have to stop, and they cannot afford, so far from their base, to waste so much ammunition. It was awful hot where we lay, with the sun shining down on us and we so close to the ground that not a breath of air could reach us."[25]

Out of the smoke, fire, thundering explosions, and roaring artillery appeared a tall man on a large horse. It was a memory that men of the

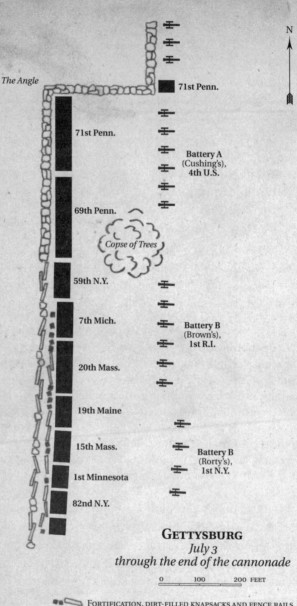

N

The Angle

71st Penn.

71st Penn.

Battery A
(Cushing's),
4th U.S.

69th Penn.

Copse of Trees

59th N.Y.

7th Mich.

Battery B
(Brown's),
1st R.I.

20th Mass.

19th Maine

15th Mass.

Battery B
(Rorty's),
1st N.Y.

1st Minnesota

82nd N.Y.

GETTYSBURG
July 3
through the end of the cannonade

0   100   200 FEET

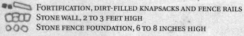

UNION
UNION ARTILLERY

 FORTIFICATION, DIRT-FILLED KNAPSACKS AND FENCE RAILS
STONE WALL, 2 TO 3 FEET HIGH
STONE FENCE FOUNDATION, 6 TO 8 INCHES HIGH

Second Corps carried for the rest of their lives: Hancock's Ride. Starting on the far left flank of his corps and riding slowly its entire length north to Ziegler's Grove, General Winfield Scott Hancock provided inspiration to help his men bear the hellish cannonade. Smiling at the men, doffing his hat, and maintaining a cool indifference to the chaos around him, Hancock was implored by a captain to dismount, but replied, "There are times when a corps commander's life doesn't count."[26]

No one seemed to be certain how long the Confederate bombardment lasted. Estimates ranged from thirty minutes to two hours or more.[27] General John Gibbon observed, "How long did the pandemonium last? Measured by our feelings it might have been an age. In point of fact it may have been an hour or three or five. The measurement of time under such circumstances, regular as it is by the watch, is exceedingly uncertain by the watchers."[28]

According to the Confederate artillery commander of the bombardment, Colonel E. Porter Alexander, it lasted about forty-five to fifty minutes. As indicated by Gibbon, it must have seemed an eternity to the men lying beneath it. Some of the exhausted Minnesota troops actually were lulled to sleep as they hugged the ground for protection.[29] Eventually the federal guns quit firing, not only to save ammunition but to coax the Confederates to stop the shelling and bring on the inevitable. "The Confederate fire ceased. We got onto our feet and pulled ourselves together for what we felt certain was coming. Soon it was said, 'they are coming,' and we stood and, eagerly watching, saw a long line of men coming out of the woods on Seminary Ridge. It was followed by others on either flank," Sergeant James Wright recalled.[30]

Lee had assembled between ten and eleven thousand men for the assault, led by General George Pickett's fresh division of General James Longstreet's First Corps.[31] The rebels dressed ranks and presented a front nearly a mile wide. They had almost a mile of open fields to cross in order to reach the Union troops on Cemetery Ridge. There were several lines of fences they would have to contend with as they traversed the fields under constant fire. "It was a magnificent spectacle. A rising tide of armed men rolling towards us in steel crested billows. The tense inaction of hours was ended and we hastily made preparations to meet this avalanche of bayonets that was being projected against us. Command was given not to fire until ordered—and then to fire at their feet. This was to correct, as far as was possible, the tendency to overshoot," Sergeant Wright explained.[32]

"Almost instantly our whole line bristled with fresh artillery which opened upon the enemy, making terrible havoc in their ranks. Wide gaps were opened but were immediately closed and the line came on in splendid order, down the slope, across the plain, over the ravine and are now half way up the hill towards us," Sergeant Alfred Carpenter of Company K remembered.[33] The federal artillery tracked the rebels across the entire field, cutting the ranks apart with solid shot, shell, and spherical-case. Now, as the Confederates approached within a few hundred yards, the artillery opened up on them with canister and then double-canister, scything down the advancing gray wall. Private Daniel Bond of Company F and others in the line took a couple of steps forward from their meager, cobbled-together breastwork.

Bond and the rest must have had an especially skimpy defensive breastwork to leave it for the shattered rail fence in front of them. The fence was built upon a low stone foundation that rose only a few inches above the ground. Bond set his extra cartridges on that stone ledge and waited with his rifle across a fence rail, later recalling the moment:

> Never in my life have I felt so strong as I did at that minute as I looked along our lines and saw that the whole fence was bristling with guns. And that all the soldiers were calmly waiting the onset. I stole a glance at the countenances of those who were nearest to me. I saw there nothing but a determination to do or to die.
>
> Here was the old 2nd Corps, not over 7,000 strong, waiting patiently the approach of 30,000 of the best troops in the rebel army and as good soldiers as the world ever saw.[34] But we had the advantage of position. When they had reached a point about 300 yards distant one of our boys fired at them. Lieutenant Ball spoke out, commanding us not to fire yet, "They are not close enough."[35] I took a look at them and turned to the lieutenant and said we can throw our balls through their ranks every shot from here. "Fire away, then." It seemed that the whole Corps had come to the same conclusion for the entire line fired at once.[36]

Sergeant Alfred Carpenter of Company K wrote, "They are now within musket range and our infantry open; men stagger from their ranks by the scores, hundreds, thousands, but on they come like an in-rolling wave of the sea."[37] Federal soldiers, loading and firing as fast as they could, began to chant, "Fredericksburg! Fredericksburg! Fredericksburg!" taunting the rebels with grim satisfaction.[38] The bloody boot was on the other foot. The Confederates funneled toward the assigned focal point of their charge, a small copse of trees at the Union center that was about 150 yards north of the First Minnesota's position.

General Hancock saw an opportunity. He ordered the Sixteenth and Thirteenth Vermont Regiments to swing down Cemetery Ridge on the left. Farther north, on the right of the Second Corps line, other regiments were given similar orders. Outflanked on both sides, the rebels were forced into a funnel of enfilading rifle fire from both sides and murderous rifle and artillery fire from the front. They were caught in a worse cross fire than the First Minnesota had endured the day before.

Soon after ordering the flank movement, Hancock was wounded by a minié ball in the right thigh, near the groin, and was helped down from his horse. Despite the insistence of his aides that he leave the field, he refused to be carried off until he was sure the rebels were repulsed.[39]

General Gibbon became a casualty about the same time as Hancock. Gibbon was behind the Nineteenth Maine, trying to induce it into a flanking movement while Hancock was getting the Vermonters into motion.[40] A minié ball hit his left shoulder and exited out the back, clipping the edge of his shoulder blade. As blood trickled down his arm and off his left hand, a faint and woozy Gibbon finally sent an aide to turn over command of the division to General William Harrow. Another aide helped Gibbon off the field toward an ambulance to take him to a field hospital.[41] A surgeon informed Gibbon later that he would be dead if the bullet had passed a quarter of an inch farther to the left. Gibbon responded with a dry, "Ah, the quarter-inches are in the hands of God."[42]

Sergeant Alfred Carpenter of Company K, reliving the fiercest of the fighting, wrote that "Men fell about us unheeded, unnoticed; we scarcely knew they were falling, so great was the intensity of attention to the approaching foe. Our muskets became so heated we could no longer handle them. We dropped them and picked up those of the wounded. Our cartridges gave out. We rifled the boxes of the dead. Artillerymen from the disabled pieces in our rear sprang forward, and

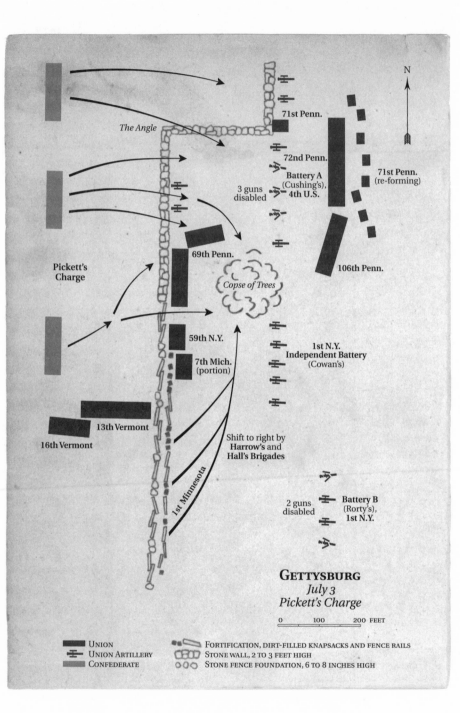

N

71st Penn.

The Angle

71st Penn.
(re-forming)

72nd Penn.

Battery A
(Cushing's),
4th U.S.

3 guns
disabled

106th Penn.

Pickett's
Charge

69th Penn.

Copse of Trees

59th N.Y.

7th Mich.
(portion)

1st N.Y.
Independent Battery
(Cowan's)

13th Vermont

16th Vermont

Shift to right by
Harrow's and
Hall's Brigades

2 guns
disabled

Battery B
(Rorty's),
1st N.Y.

1st Minnesota

GETTYSBURG
July 3
Pickett's Charge

0   100   200 FEET

▬	UNION
⚓	UNION ARTILLERY
▬	CONFEDERATE

FORTIFICATION, DIRT-FILLED KNAPSACKS AND FENCE RAILS
STONE WALL, 2 TO 3 FEET HIGH
STONE FENCE FOUNDATION, 6 TO 8 INCHES HIGH

seizing guns and cartridges from the wounded, fought by our side as infantrymen."[43] The remains of Pickett's Charge smashed into the Union line and hand-to-hand combat ensued.[44] The rebels punched through at one point only, a right angle in a stone fence about four hundred feet northwest of the copse of trees. The First Minnesota and the rest of its brigade shifted to the right, on the run, to meet the crisis. "It was a grand rush to get there in the quickest time, without much regard to the manner of it. Just then I was conscious of coming in contact with something. I was partly turned aside, staggered, confused and half blinded; but it was only for an instant, then my vision cleared and I braced up and ran on again," Sergeant James Wright remembered.[45]

The First Minnesota's casualties continued to mount. During this rush to the right, Captain Nathan Messick was killed. Messick had received two slight wounds during the charge the day before. Now he was hit by a shell fragment that entered just above the outside corner of his right eye, ranging downward and exiting behind his right ear, killing him instantly.[46] Messick had commanded the regiment for less than twenty-four hours.

Captain Nathan Messick, Company G, took command on the evening of July 2 after all field and staff offices had fallen. About twenty hours later he was killed in Pickett's Charge.

Henry O'Brien earned the Medal of Honor for his courageous charge with the regimental colors in the repulse of Pickett's Charge.

Corporal John Dehn, a twenty-seven-year-old German farmer from near St. Paul, was the last member of the color guard still on his feet. A minié ball ripped through his hand, and as he dropped the flag Corporal Henry O'Brien of Company E grabbed it. The impetuous twenty-one-year-old miller from St. Anthony, Minnesota, held the flag high and raced ahead of the regiment toward the rebels. Lieutenant Lochren later wrote, "My feeling at the instant blamed his rashness in so risking its capture. But the effect was electrical. Every man of the 1st Minnesota sprang to protect its flag, and the rest rushed with them upon the enemy."[47] Corporal O'Brien was shot twice after he took up the colors, the first minié ball striking his head. It must have been a grazing flesh wound or a spent bullet because O'Brien stayed on his feet and kept running forward. The second ball punched through his hand and cut the flagstaff in half.[48]

Wright described the chaotic combat, "Closing in on them with a rush and a cheer, there was shooting, stabbing, and clubbing—for there was not time to reload."[49] William Lochren remembered how, "The bayonet was used for a few minutes, and cobble stones, with which the ground was well covered, filled the air, being thrown by those in the rear over the heads of their comrades."[50]

Captain Wilson Farrell of Company C, a thirty-three-year-old clerk from St. Paul, was wounded mortally as he ran into the fight with his company. He would die the next evening.[51] According to the June 28, 1863, muster roll, Company C added sixty-two more officers and men to the battle line of the First Minnesota, although the mass of brawling men around the small copse of trees hardly constituted a "battle line" at that time. However, Private Rufus M. Eastman of Company C wrote that only about fifty officers and men were present in the company at that time, and only twenty-seven of those "went to the front." It is assumed that the others decided, or received undocumented last-minute orders, to stay and gather the enormous number of rebel prisoners who were sent, unarmed, to the rear of the Union line.[52]

Forty-one-year-old Private Marshall Sherman, a St. Paul house painter in Company C, pushed his way to the stone wall in front of the copse of trees, firing into the gray mass. He was facing the remnants of Confederate Brigadier General Richard Garnett's brigade of Virginians. The Twenty-eighth Virginia Regiment was moving directly toward Sherman. He saw a Confederate lieutenant, waving a rebel battle flag, advance ahead of the troops. While Sherman could not hear the lieutenant over the roar of battle, it was obvious he was trying to rally and inspire the rebels to push on to the stone wall.

At the same moment, not far to Sherman's left, Daniel Bond spied the same lieutenant and the same flag. Bond was determined to have that flag and was desperately trying to ram a minié ball down the overheated and fouled bore of his rifle-musket. He was dancing around, jabbing with the ramrod, and only succeeding in getting the ball halfway down. Corporal Caleb Jackson of Company G shouted at Bond, asking why didn't he fire? When told he could not get the ball seated in the bore, Jackson yelled back, "Well, lay down then, don't stand there and let them shoot at you!"

Of this Bond wrote:

> This was sound advice, but I was too much interested in securing a flag to heed it. I pushed on and reached the wall just a little to the left of where the flag was. I really believe there was twenty rebels jumped up without their guns, hollering "Don't shoot!" Do not take this that I mean to say that twenty men surrendered to me, (I am not that kind of a hero, and God forbid that I ever should be), but I was on this occasion the first one to the wall and the rebels knew when I appeared that our men would not fire on them, should they spring up and surrender.
>
> We never attempted to guard them to the rear, but just told them to run back, leaving the duty of collecting for the provost guards. But to the right of the flags the rebels were still fighting and I saw one loading his gun with his eye fixed on the particular flag which was nearest to me. And I stopped, put my ramrod against the stone wall and pushed the bullet home, capped my gun and raised my eyes. The rebels to the right of the flag were all passing through our lines minus their guns, and Marshall Sherman of Company "C" had my prize.[53]

Sherman had watched the Confederate lieutenant advance with the flag until he was fifty feet in front of his men and about a hundred feet from Sherman and the federal troops. Sherman knew well the inspiration and impetus to attack that a battle flag represented for men in combat. Whether by instinct and passion in the heat of battle, or calculated design, Marshall Sherman was determined that the battle flag of the Twenty-eighth Virginia would come down.

He dropped his rifle into bayonet-charge position and ran for the lieutenant. The rebel officer did not seem to notice Sherman in the smoke and confusion until the Minnesotan was right on top of him. The officer could not hear Sherman's bellowed command to drop the flag, but the menacing bayonet at his chest and Sherman cocking the hammer of his rifle said more than words could. The rebel dropped the flag into the dust. Sherman picked it up and dragged it along as he quickly muscled the rebel lieutenant back through the cheering federal line.[54]

For their valor in the face of the enemy, both Henry O'Brien and Marshall Sherman received a decoration that had been established by Congress just one year before: the Medal of Honor.[55] "Say! but there was fighting for you. If men ever become devils that was one of the times. We were crazy with the excitement of the fight. We just rushed in like wild beasts. Men swore and cursed and struggled and fought, grappled in hand-to-hand fight, threw stones, clubbed their muskets, kicked and yelled and hurrahed," described Lieutenant William Harmon of Company C.[56]

The overpowered Confederates continued to throw down their weapons and surrender. Others began pouring back across the fields toward the Confederate lines on Seminary Ridge. The firing began to decrease. Wright noted that "As soon as the smoke lifted sufficiently to permit us to see, all that could be seen of the mighty force that had been driven so furiously

Private Marshall Sherman, Company C, First Minnesota, posed with his Gettysburg prize—the colors of the Twenty-eighth Virginia. Sherman reenlisted in spring 1864. A little more than a year after Gettysburg, he lost a leg at the Battle of Deep Bottom during the siege of Petersburg, Virginia.

against us was scattered and running to the rear—that is, all that were able to run. The bodies of many unfortunate victims marked the course of the assault."[57]

Given the frantic state of the combat, the killing frenzy continued for many men. While the rifle fire had tapered off, several still loaded and fired as fast as they could at anything gray. Lieutenant William Harmon observed General Alexander Hays, who commanded the Second Corps' Third Division, trying to gain control of the men: "General Hayes rode along the line swearing like a pirate, as the best of men sometimes will in battle. He was trailing a confederate flag in the dust behind his horse and was shouting, 'Stop firing, you—fools; don't you know enough to stop firing; it's all over—stop! stop! stop!"[58]

The Battle of Gettysburg was over.

As a roaring cheer arose from the Union line on Cemetery Ridge, pain began to well up from Orderly Sergeant James Wright's face, neck, and chest. Wright recalled, "I observed that my neck and face were bleeding. I then found that the left shoulder, breast and sleeve of my blouse were ornamented with shreds of lead and splinters of wood, and several of the latter were driven into the side of my face and neck."[59] He also discovered several large pieces of lead driven into his shoulder and upper chest and realized what had hit him earlier. A bullet had apparently shattered someone's gun stock, and the blast had peppered him with fragments of wood and lead.

Corporal Newell Irvine of Company D, a thirty-four-year-old farmer from Monticello, Minnesota, had taken up the regimental flag when Henry O'Brien was shot down.[60] The lower piece of the severed staff had been lost in the fighting, so the men broke the staff of the captured Confederate flag in two and shaped the ends with a pocket knife and nailed and reinforced them with a strap from a knapsack. The symbolism of the two united pieces, and the way they were joined, was not lost on the men.[61] As the veterans of the regiment stated in the 1916 regimental history:

> Somebody brought a piece of Confederate flagstaff that belonged to a captured flag, and Irvine said: "We can use this all right enough, for it has been captured from the rebs and is now a Union stick." And so the Union piece and the Confederate piece were spliced and formed an

indissoluble union, and thus united held aloft the Union colors thereafter, and still hold them in their place of honor in Minnesota's new
Capitol. And this splicing of the pieces of flagstaff fore-shadowed the
time when Union and Confederate should unite in upholding the colors of the old Union forever.[62]

*Corporal Newell Irvine was the last man
to take up the regimental colors at Gettysburg
and the only one not to be shot for it, although
he was killed later in the war. He is holding
the tattered remains of the regiment's national
colors and the shot-in-half flagstaff.*

*The spliced flagstaff of the
First Minnesota,
still held together by
he original brass nails
and leather strap from
a soldier's knapsack*

— 9 —

The funeral of our regiment

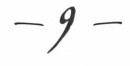

IN THREE DAYS OF COMBAT, the two armies had used 569 tons of ammunition. Nearly 164,000 men had been engaged; almost 8,000 lay dead on the field; 27,000 were wounded; 11,000 were captured or missing in action (many of the missing were, in fact, dead but either not found or not identified); more than 5,000 dead horses and mules littered the battlefield.[1]

While the battle was abating, General Hancock allowed himself to be removed by ambulance. But he ordered the driver to stop directly behind the lines, on the Taneytown Road, so he could dictate a dispatch. With occasional artillery rounds exploding around the ambulance, the nervous driver informed Hancock that the rebels were enfilading the road, and it would be best to move on. Hancock roared back, "We've enfiladed them, damn them!" The ambulance stayed in place until Hancock had finished his dispatch to Meade and sent it off by way of a medical officer.[2] True to form, Hancock suggested pressing the rebels hard: "I have never seen a more formidable attack, and if the Sixth and Fifth Corps have pressed up, the enemy will be destroyed. The enemy must be short of ammunition, as I was shot with a tenpenny nail."[3]

The rebel army was in need of supplies and ammunition but was not yet to the point of shooting nails from their muskets, as Hancock thought. Dr. Alexander N. Dougherty, the Second Corps medical director, had pulled the nail from Hancock's wound shortly after he was taken from his horse. The rebel bullet had passed first through the saddle pommel, carrying bits of leather, wood, and the nail into the wound near Hancock's groin.[4]

The battle was over, but neither side knew it yet. We can only speculate what would have happened if Hancock had not been wounded severely and taken from the field. Lee's army regrouped itself as best it could for an anticipated counterattack. The stunned and bloodied Union troops were in no condition to press one immediately.

The First Minnesota, like every other unit, started sorting through the chaos to gather its wounded and secure prisoners. Every man was accounted for but Private Michael Devlin of Company A, a twenty-three-year-old Irish farmer from near St. Paul. Devlin had been wounded seriously in the melee and inadvertently taken to another division's hospital.[5] Company C was sent into the field to gather as many rebels as they could. Lieutenant Harmon led the company as far as the Emmitsburg Road, ordering the prisoners back toward the federal line.

Some of the dead at Gettysburg,
photographed on July 4 by Alexander Gardner

Passions still ran high, and it was dangerous duty for the Union soldiers, mingling in the open fields with the still-armed rebels. Harmon had a close call: "A straggler lying in a fence corner drew a bead on me, and was about to shoot, when I covered him with my revolver and told him to drop his gun. He did, too, and it was all I could do to keep the boys from killing him."[6]

A 1905 account by Rufus M. Eastman, a thirty-year-old private in Company C during the battle, stated that a handful of Company C men went out to gather prisoners but that Sergeant John Cole formed and commanded the company, "he being, I think, the ranking officer [noncommissioned] in sight, and uninjured." No mention was made of Lieutenant William Harmon. Eastman wrote that the group consisted of himself, Cole, Charles I. Clark, John Brown, and Marshall Sherman. Sergeant Cole rounded up fifty rebels and conducted them back to the federal line while ordering the rest of the men forward to gather what they could. The men collected a few more as they approached the Emmitsburg Road, but then:

> Soon discovered what seemed a full line of battle behind, or between, the fences, and called to them to drop their guns and come in. They feared our batteries would open on them. We told them there was no danger, if they dropped their guns. They did so, and came over the fence in a body, upon which the rebs opened a battery, firing over us. The prisoners objected to advancing, as they were, by front. Eastman being on their right, led them by right-oblique into and up a ravine to a notch in the stone wall. The prisoners filed through, and we returned to find a few more.[7]

The artillery discharges that so unnerved Hancock's ambulance driver and Eastman's prisoners was cover fire from Longstreet's guns. Upon seeing the federal skirmish lines advancing, along with the men gathering prisoners, Longstreet assumed a counterattack was under way. He soon realized that the Union troops were simply sending out "feelers."[8]

Due both to the chaos of the moment and the subsequent incompleteness of Confederate records, it is difficult to determine the number of rebel prisoners taken after Pickett's Charge. They quickly were hustled behind the lines to mingle with other prisoners in holding areas and hospitals. A best guess, from a tabulation of reports from Union commanders, is that 3,750 prisoners resulted from Pickett's Charge. Roughly 62 percent of those taking part in the charge itself were killed, wounded, missing, or taken prisoner. All Union units combined lost about 25 percent. General Gibbon's division of the Second Corps, of which the First Minnesota was part, lost nearly 40 percent.[9]

The casualty list for the First Minnesota had grown substantially within a couple of hours. Private Romulus E. Jacobs of Company F had been shot by a rebel sharpshooter before the cannonade, and thirty-four men were wounded and another fifteen were killed or died of wounds as a result of the action. Of these, three more officers were among the dead or would die of their wounds, and three other officers were wounded but would recover. These numbers included killed and wounded from all ten of the regiment's companies plus Company L—the sharpshooters—which sustained two casualties on July 3.

Filthy, stunned, ragged, and ears ringing from the cacophony of two intense days of close combat, the First Minnesota drew itself together and counted somewhere between seventy-five and ninety officers and men still armed and able to walk upright, not including Companies C or L. Some, like Orderly Sergeant James Wright, undoubtedly were walking wounded, bloodied but not incapacitated. Sergeant Wright wrote of the moment when he realized the crisis was ended:

> Now that the critical part of the struggle was apparently over, the intense feelings that had carried us through it subsided rapidly and the usual relaxation following such high-pressure emotions followed. For about 65 hours we had been under almost constant physical or mental strain—or both—and had pretty nearly reached the limit of both, and, as soon as the need for further exercise of muscles or will ceased to be imperative, most of the men realized that they were bordering upon a condition of collapse."[10]

The battlefield was surreal in its destruction and carnage. One federal private from the Fifth Corps left a description of sights along the edge of the Wheat Field that aptly could apply to many areas of the battlefield:

> Corpses strewed the ground at every step. Arms, legs, heads, and parts of dismembered bodies were scattered all about, and sticking among

the rocks, and against the trunks of trees, hair, brains, entrails, and shreds of human flesh still hung, a disgusting, sickening, heartrending spectacle to our young minds. One man has as many as twenty canister or case shots through different parts of his body, though none through a vital organ, and he was still gasping and twitching with a slight motion of the muscles, and vibrations of the pulse, although utterly unconscious of approaching death."[11]

Captains Coates and Chase made it back to the regiment roughly an hour after the fighting had subsided. Being with the men at the field hospital, they probably were engaged in helping evacuate the hospital farther to the rear after the cannonade began.[12] It must have been a shock to Coates to discover the extent of further casualties in the regiment, as well as being informed he was now in command.

Private Edward Bassett and several others of Company G helped carry Captain Messick's body off the field. The group was led by Private George A. Williams of Company G, who had been serving as cook for Messick. Williams sat with the body until 3:00 A.M. on the morning of July 4 when Lieutenant Jasper Searles was able to provide an ambulance to transport the body farther to the rear.

Around 6:00 P.M. on July 3, the gathering clouds finally broke loose with a short thunderstorm. Dr. Michael Jacobs, a professor at Gettysburg College, noted in his meteorological journal that, "The thunder seemed tame, after the artillery firing of the afternoon."[13] It rained intermittently the evening and night of July 3, the start of a three-week period of almost daily showers and deluges. The morning of July 4 found the two armies sitting in the mud, staring at each other across the fields.

Reconnaissance parties from the Twelfth, Eleventh, and Fifth Corps were sent out to determine the position of the rebel battle line. It was found that they had withdrawn from the Cemetery and Culp's Hills areas on the federal right and had pulled back and refused their right flank on the federal left. Union forces entered the town, allowing many soldiers and officers who had been in hiding since the retreat of July 1 finally to come out of basements and attics. Rebel and federal skirmishers out on advanced lines continued to take shots at one another. A few artillery batteries on each side also exchanged sporadic fire, but no one seemed anxious to bring on a resumption of the battle.

Robert E. Lee knew that it was over, and there was nothing left to do but collect what he could of his wounded and try to make it back to Virginia with the remainder of his army. He began issuing orders the night of July 3 to prepare for a withdrawal. Brigadier General John Imboden, commanding an independent cavalry brigade that had not participated directly in the battle, was given the daunting task of getting the rebel wounded back to Virginia.

On Independence Day, 1863, Captain Nathan S. Messick was laid to rest on the banks of Rock Creek to the east of Cemetery Ridge. He was bound in a shelter tent, his face carefully wrapped with towels, and his body completely covered with fresh boughs from a tree. The regimental chaplain, F. A. Conwell, read a funeral service before the grave was filled in. A carved headboard nailed to an oak tree above his grave ensured that the family would later be able to identify and remove the body. The chaplain wrote to Messick's widow, saying, "We had a religious service, and not an eye or heart but was melted. It appeared like the funeral of our regiment."[14]

That same Saturday morning, a detail of the First Minnesota was sent to bury the dead from the charge of July 2. They made crude headboards, but in the current combat conditions, lack of time and supplies dictated shortcuts for the care of the bodies of even the best of friends. The headboards, made from scrap wood and pieces of ammunition boxes and hardtack boxes, were marked with pencil. The weathering of time effaced some of them enough that twenty-two bodies now lie in the Minnesota plot of the Gettysburg National Cemetery with nothing but "Unknown. Regt. 1" on their stones.[15]

In a postwar article, Jasper Searles wrote, "The burial of the dead in one common grave by the survivors on the following day [July 4] was at once the saddest and most glorious of all the duties that ever fell to the lot of this regiment to perform."[16] Given that more than two-thirds of the dead in the Minnesota plot at the National Cemetery were identified, Searles was probably referring to a burial trench, as opposed to a common hole in which all the bodies were piled. This method was employed with Confederate dead—as it was by the Confederates when burying Union dead—but it is highly unlikely that the men of the regiment, regardless of time constraints, would have buried their comrades in a common pit with the bodies jumbled together or stacked like cordwood. The individual headboards probably were placed at the head of each body laid out in a trench.[17]

The regiment was also among the many assigned to collect all serviceable weapons and equipment scattered over the field. This was a widespread practice and common sense after a battle, not only for the economics of it but also to keep weapons and equipment out of the hands of rebels and civilians. The First Minnesota's brigade alone collected 1,740 muskets.[18] The process involved sticking the weapon, bayonet down, into the ground so it could be seen clearly and later gathered by ordnance details. In a short time the entire battlefield was dotted with "acres of muskets as thick as young trees in a nursery."[19]

James Wright recalled the overwhelming amount of destruction and misery:

> It is true we were no longer the sensitive, sentimental youngsters we were when we left our northern homes. Mere sentiment had been knocked out of us by the actual experiences of years of active war; military training and every-day surroundings had tended to repress expressions of feeling and had changed us to seasoned soldiers; but no one, though but moderately endowed with common sense and no more than the ordinary amount of compassion in his make-up, could fail to sympathize, deeply, with the overwhelming amount of suffering that existed and which they were powerless to relieve. Tens of thousands were suffering from wounds, many were dying every hour; and many still living considered those already dead more fortunate than themselves.[20]

Also on July 4, Lieutenant Christopher Heffelfinger visited the Second Corps hospital, southeast of the battlefield along Rock Creek. He checked on some of the men and then found Colonel Colvill and Captain Perium, who mercifully was unconscious. Perium would live for three more days. Heffelfinger, undoubtedly putting the best face on the situation for his memoir, said that, despite being severely wounded, Colvill, "seemed to be cheerful."[21]

The specifics of Colonel Colvill's care and location after his wounding are somewhat confusing. He was probably first taken to the aid station on the Hummelbaugh farm from the Plum Run ravine on the night of July 2. There his wounds would have been examined after his uniform coat, shirt, and probably the lower portion of the right trouser leg had been cut off. Bleeding would have been stanched and the wounds lightly dressed. He would have then been sent to his division's hospital, located along the Granite School House Road until it was moved during the cannonade on July 3.

However, Colvill seems to have two women vying, in a historical sense, for his body. There are two opposing stories about where he was and who cared for him, beginning shortly after the battle, and both from sources that seem to have no vested interest in making up a story.

Miss Cornelia Hancock—no relation to the general—arrived on the battlefield three days after the close of the fighting. She was a twenty-three-year-old Quaker volunteer nurse from the tiny village of Hancock's Bridge in New Jersey. Miss Hancock accompanied her brother-in-law, Dr. Henry T. Child of Philadelphia, to help in the Second Corps hospitals. A compilation of her letters published in 1937 includes one dated July 8, 1863, in which she said, "The First Minnesota Regiment bears the first honors here for loss in the late battle. . . . The Colonel I know well; he is a very fine man."[22]

By August many of the corps hospitals had been closed and the patients moved to the General Hospital, a tent city known as Camp Letterman, on the York Pike northeast of town. In a letter of August 6, 1863, Miss Hancock mentioned that Colvill was "getting better" and was expecting a visit from Dr. Child. In a letter dated "Philadelphia, Sunday, Sept. [no day], 1863," Miss Hancock stated that she accompanied Colvill to an army hospital in Harrisburg, Pennsylvania.

Colvill was transported in either a railroad cattle car or a freight car; his stretcher was suspended from the ceiling by large rubber ropes to give him a smoother and less traumatizing ride. Miss Hancock and others took turns keeping the stretcher steady throughout the trip. She mentioned that she wished all the wounded could be transported with such care, "but the one great fact ever before ones eyes in the army—he is an officer."[23]

In opposition is the tale of Matilda (Tillie) Pierce, a fifteen-year-old girl who lived in Gettysburg at the time of the battle. A quarter century after the battle, she wrote a small book that told her story of the town, the battle, and the events following the battle. Time cannot be a factor in judging the veracity of her story concerning Colonel Colvill. Although the account is twenty-six years after the fact—in contrast to Hancock's letters written at the time—the detail and specificity are too great for it to be fabricated or misremembered.

Tillie Pierce Alleman—she was married by the time of publication—declared that "a few days after the battle" several soldiers came and talked with her mother about a room for their wounded colonel. She correctly described Colvill as being "very tall," even by today's standards at six feet, five inches, and accurately described the nature of his wounds. According to Alleman the surgeons had wanted to amputate Colvill's severely wounded foot, saying it was necessary to save his life.[24] Colvill is supposed to have told them no, "that if his foot must go he would go too."[25]

Over the course of "several months," Alleman's mother, two soldiers from the First Minnesota, identified as Milton L. Bevans, a musician of Company F, and Private Walter S. Reed of Company G, assigned to nurse Colvill, and finally Colvill's own sister administered to this suffering, incapacitated bear of a man.[26] Under the circumstances, the family and Colvill naturally became quite close. He is reported to have visited them the year after the war when he was in Gettysburg to tour the battlefield. Alleman maintained that he left on crutches at the end of his "several month" stay in their house and returned "to his home in St. Paul." Bevans and Reed were said to be with him still.

Mrs. Alleman's story seems as authentic as Miss Hancock's, and neither woman had any reason to fabricate. There also seems to be no special logic in either of them choosing Colvill as the subject of a concocted story. Despite the special status of Colvill and the First Minnesota, there were many heroes and heroic regiments from the battle. Miss Hancock was writing her letters at a time before word of the regiment's story really had spread widely. Both women must have known Colvill, or people who knew him well, to have written the things they did.

The only part of Mrs. Alleman's story that seems unusual is that two men would be detached for "several months" to nurse their colonel. There were army and volunteer nurses to do that if Colvill was staying in an army hospital. However, Bevans was Colvill's orderly, so there is some logic in his being with the colonel. Reed, on the other hand, was himself wounded, shot in the shoulder during the charge on July 2. It seems unlikely, needing nursing himself, that he was in any condition to help Colvill, unless his own wound was very slight. In addition, Colvill attended a banquet given for the First Minnesota in Washington, D.C., on February 6, 1864, eight months after his wounding. Colvill was carried into the banquet hall by Captain Thomas Sinclair and Sergeant John Merritt.[27] Obviously he was unable to stand and walk at that time, making Mrs. Alleman's assertion that he left her home on crutches suspect.[28]

Cornelia Hancock's observation of the difference between the treatment of officers and enlisted men can certainly be confirmed by the stories of other men of the First Minnesota. But it is easy to understand how overwhelming the situation was for all involved. Civilian and military doctors came swarming to the small town of Gettysburg, but the level of suffering in the first few days after the battle must have been numbing to contemplate. No one in either army, and certainly not in the town, was prepared to deal with the phenomenal number of dead and wounded.

A warm, damp shroud of fetid air blanketed the entire area: rotting bodies, decaying horses, excrement and urine from men unable to care for themselves, and festering wounds that soon became covered with maggots from the hordes of blow-flies that descended on the battlefield. The scene

Leg brace used on Colonel William Colvill after his severe wounding at Gettysburg. It was probably fabricated at the field hospital from empty ammunition or hardtack boxes. Note the downward slope of the foot rest, which corresponds to the position Colvill had to keep his foot in for the rest of his life, due to the shattered ankle joint.

was a horror-filled assault on the senses of anyone unfortunate enough to have to be there, kind enough to travel there to help, or callous enough to come and gawk. The citizenry of Gettysburg was by turns grateful, shocked, indignant, and outraged by it all.

There are numerous stories of callousness and opportunism displayed by townspeople, as well as those who traveled to the area ostensibly to help. Sergeant Mat Marvin of Company K, suffering with his foot wound in the Second Corps hospital along Rock Creek, noted on July 5, "There has been a continual line of ambulances bringing in wounded Rebs. We have had to lay here all day in the mud with clothes and blankets soaking wet. There is a horrible stink rising from so many wounded. There is no citizen [to] offer a word of consolation, but charge $2 per bushel for corn, $1 per loaf of bread, 2¢ per quart of milk. We had no dish to get grub in and they charged our nurse 50¢ for an old bucket."[29]

At a time when a private in the army made thirteen dollars a month, the prices were more than a little inflated. Private Charles Muller of Company A told of the resourcefulness of some soldiers in their trying situation: "On the night from 4 to 5 July my neighbor, Henry Nikel, dit use his shoes as a privie and next day he dit use mine and then dit throw those down the hill so both our shoes were gone."[30] Henry Nickell's creative use of his and Muller's footwear probably was not unique. Given that both men were wounded in the thigh, they would not be using the shoes any time soon anyway. In fact, Nickell would die from his wound five weeks later.

Charles Muller endured a number of experiences that were common among wounded men, especially at Gettysburg. On July 5 and 6, Muller and all others in the Second Corps hospital were moved once again, this time across an s-shaped bend in Rock Creek to higher and drier ground. Writing of his new hospital accommodations, Muller recalled, "It happened I was placed in a tent opposite the surgical tent where I could see all the operations of 4 doctors. There were two long tables in that tent and a doctor was working on each end of them tables, cutting off hands and feet all day from morning til night. And every day about 8 o'clock a detail of men came around whit stretchers to carry off the hands and feet to be buried."[31]

An incident on July 7 is stunning for its insensitivity and outright cruelty. Muller noted that he watched with interest as a number of men appeared near his tent, measuring and cutting boards, pounding some into the ground, and nailing on cross pieces to the uprights. Others set and nailed flat boards on top:

> In a few minutes there were a row of tables about 40 or 50 feet long. Then some other men come along wit some baskets filled and covered wit table cloths. Then some ladies come and covered those tables [with] linen cloth and plates, saucers and cups, while others were cutting up some hams and roasted chickens and bread. And I dit see some nice cakes, even dishes wit candy and preserves, and from all appearance the men around the table were all preachers. And I did begin to figure out how long it will be before they will rush men over there [and] begin to distribute—but how much a man can be mistaken in his figurings.
>
> When everything was ready, then the whole cluck of preachers, their wives, sisters and daughters sat down around that table and had a good meal. And they were telling stories as if they were on a picnic ground, and not even a single one would look around to ask if we wanted something or not. Then towards 12 o'clock a girl of 19 or 20 came around and had [a] cup of coffee and ask me if [I] want a cup of coffee. I said yes and when she give it to me she said "now hurry up because I haven't much time to wait on you." I told her I dit [not] call on her to wait on me at all. Then she wanted to take the cup away of me again, but that was more than I would stand, and I told her to keep away or else I would knock her down. And I took a dislike against all the preachers in the world and have not got over that yet.[32]

Communication to and from family and friends in Minnesota was a matter of days, sometimes weeks. Probably the first relative to receive information about the fate of a loved one in the regiment was the father of Christopher Heffelfinger. Lieutenant Heffelfinger's father and several members of his family were living in Shippensburg, Pennsylvania, about twenty miles northwest of Gettysburg, and the elder Heffelfinger knew his son's regiment had been in the fight.

The Confederate army had occupied Shippensburg prior to the battle, and in anticipation, all local livestock had been driven farther north to save it from rebel requisition. With no transportation available, the elder Heffelfinger started walking early on the morning of July 5 and made it to Gettysburg by late afternoon. Heffelfinger's father was cruelly disappointed to discover he had missed the regiment's departure from Gettysburg by about an hour. He was directed to the hospital of the Second Corps, Second Division, and learned from the regimental surgeon, Dr. John B. LeBlond, that his son was still alive and was on the march with the regiment.[33]

The bulk of information was moved by mail, but some general news was transmitted by telegraph. The earliest came by way of a personal missive dated "9:00 P.M. July 3, 1863," sent by Lieutenant Edgar L. Sproat of Company A. Sproat, a twenty-nine-year-old clerk from St. Paul, certainly knew the letter would arrive in Washington much sooner than Minnesota, so he sent the letter to Minnesota Senator Morton S. Wilkinson, perhaps assuming Wilkinson would telegraph the information to Governor Ramsey or the newspapers in Minnesota.[34]

It is hard to discern exactly what happened then, because the letter to Governor Ramsey, sent by Wilkinson, was dated "Washington July 8, 1863," but appeared in the *St. Paul Pioneer* newspaper the next day. There certainly was no "next day delivery" service from Washington, D.C., to St. Paul in 1863. The letter looks like just that—a letter—but it could be a copy of a telegraph message that was sent to Ramsey. The penmanship shows the relative clarity and generic, open, looping writing of copy clerks of the period.

This first eyewitness report about the regiment at Gettysburg is an example of most early battle reports, regardless of the mode of communication. It is a balancing act between wanting to inform quickly and the very real need and desire to get the information correct. We have to wonder how inaccurate Sproat's original and hastily written letter was and how many of the inaccuracies came from Wilkinson's misreading of it or inability to decipher names and other information from Sproat's handwriting. If the letter was a telegraph message, there is the possibility that the operator made mistakes in taking down the message or in copying it out for delivery.

Wilkinson's original letter to Governor Ramsey—or the telegraph copy as the case may be—indicated that a Captain "Bugress" was killed. There was no such officer in the regiment, nor any with a name that could be confused or misspelled to resemble "Bugress"; it also referred to a "Lt. Polar"—wounded adjutant Lieutenant John Pellar; it called Colonel Colvill "Colonel Calvin," and it stated that Lieutenant William Lochren was dead, when Lochren had not even been wounded.[35]

In the version published July 9, some of the names were corrected, but Lieutenant Waldo Farrar's name was printed as "Tanner"—an obvious misreading of the handwriting in the Wilkinson telegraph copy original— and the incorrect information about Lochren being killed was printed. The original letter from Sproat to Wilkinson was printed with a story in the *New York Tribune*, datelined "Washington, July 7, 1863," and reprinted in a Minneapolis paper, the *State Atlas*,

William Lochren, shown while in the Minnesota Senate, seven years after Gettysburg. Second Lieutenant Lochren found himself in command of his company, as well as being assigned as regimental adjutant, by early evening of July 3.

on July 22, 1863. This contained the misinformation about Lochren's death, mentioned the death of the nonexistent Captain Bugress— spelled "Burgess" this time—and indicated that 220 men "went into the fight," a figure that was too low by at least one hundred.

Lochren's case was the sort that must have been particularly maddening and distressing. Newspapers of the time regularly reprinted items verbatim from other newspapers, with or without attribution, and the news of Lochren's death spread quickly. Lochren, in the meantime, was unharmed and working diligently to gather accurate information about the wounded and to relay it back to Minnesota newspapers and families. He received a letter from a friend, mentioning the incident of his "death":

Buffalo, N.Y. August 9th, 1863
My Dearest Friend Lock: You can imagine how very much astonished I am to find you hailing from this side of "Kingdom Come" as your letter sent to Warrham gives certain evidence of the fact. The Tribune does lie occasionally it seems, but it looked *awfully* true to me. I only arrived here last week and stopped on my way to see Jim, who is on a visit at his

fathers in Connecticut. I told him that you were killed at Gettysburg and the big tears dropped down his face, belieing your statement that no eyes would overflow at your loss. I must confess at feeling a big lump get in my throat when I thought I had seen and heard the last of "Lock."

Your Friend, M. J. Holmes[36]

On July 18, 1863, the *St. Paul Pioneer* printed a "complete" casualty list of the First Minnesota at Gettysburg, saying, incorrectly, Lieutenant Colonel Adams had died, misspelling some names beyond recognition, duplicating some names by adding different initials, with consequent variations of the same wounds, and leaving some names off while adding others who had not been wounded or at least never appeared on any official casualty list.

Letters found their way to William Lochren in his capacity as acting adjutant for the regiment as well as acting commander of Company K. He was deluged with inquiries and kept many of the letters his entire life.

Maurice Smith wrote:

July 20th, 1863. Commander of Company K, 1st Regiment Minnesota Volunteers

Dear Sir: I have a brother in your company and as I have not been able to hear from him since the late battle in Pennsylvania, I should be much obliged to you if you would write and let me know if he is killed or taken prisoner. His name is Augustus Smith.

Maurice Smith

Twenty-four-year-old Private Augustus Smith, a German immigrant farmer from Minnetrista, Minnesota, was killed in the charge on July 2.

An inquiry from William Tenney stated:

Little Valley, Olmsted County, Minnesota

Dear Sir: I saw in the Winona Republican an account of my sons being wounded at Gettysburg. You will do me a great favor to inform me the extent of his wound and your opinion in regard to his recovery. If you feel disposed, have the goodness to tell me what part he is wounded in. The person I allude to is Samuel S. Tenney. Do have the goodness to write soon.

Yours in haste, William P. Tenney, July the 17th

P.S. What hospital is he in?

Nineteen-year-old Private Sam Tenney was shot through the leg during the charge on July 2. He survived and recovered.

An anguished brother inquired:

Dear Sir: With grief have I noticed your dispatch to the Winona Republican dated July 4th, 1863 wherein you have found cause to place my brother Jacob Geisreiter among the killed. You will oblige his mourning relatives by writing to me the cause of his death and some of the details concerning the same. Should you have anything in your care that has once been the property of my beloved and deeply mourned brother, you will do us the kindness of forwarding the same to his brother.
    S. Geisreiter

Private Jacob Geisreiter, a twenty-five-year-old German immigrant, was killed repelling Pickett's Charge on July 3.

W. P. Horton, a concerned uncle, asked:

Cleveland, Ohio—July 14th, 1863
Dear Sir: I have in your regiment a nephew belonging to Company D, Charles H. Rines, whose mother is at my house visiting. Since the fight she has heard nothing from [him], and of course feels as any mother would under the circumstances. Will you please inform me at your earliest convenience of his fate? Is he alive and well or otherwise? I am, dear sir,
    Yours truly, W. P. Horton

Twenty-one-year-old farmer Private Charles Rines had five wounds in his side from the charge on July 2, probably from artillery shell fragments. He also survived and recovered.

A friend sought information on behalf of a new widow:

St. Charles, Mn. Sept. 6th, 1863. Lt. William Lochren, 1st Mn. Volunteers
    Sir: I am requested by the widow of Israel Durr, late of your company, to obtain for her the following information in order that she might apply for his pension and bounty, to wit: the time he received the wounds of which he died; what part of the body he was wounded; and by what he was wounded, whether ball, shell or bayonet. Also evidence of death by knowing witness. Yours respecfully, Samuel W. Burgess

Private Israel Durr had been shot through the side during the charge on July 2, the bullet puncturing his lung. The twenty-three-year-old soldier from Winona, Minnesota, died two days later, on July 4.

A sister wrote concerning the burial of her brother:

Blue Island, Illinois July 29th, 1863. Lt. Lochren
Dear Sir: I received your kind letter four days since, for which I should have thanked you immediately, but my husband as executor of my poor dear brother's will was in Minnesota, where he went to prove the will. I did not know whether he would think it prudent to remove the remains of my beloved brother at present, and I did not know what to tell you about his effects.

Consulting with my only remaining brother, it is thought best to wait until cold weather before removing the remains.

He had passed unharmed through so many battles we felt confident his precious life would be spared to us. His terrible death has made a great blank in the world that we feel can never be filled. This war is causing many desolate homes and broken hearts.

With much respect, yours truly, Mrs. Bery Sanders [the sister of Captain Joseph Perium].

Apparently Perium's sister and brother changed their minds about removing his body from the battlefield. Perhaps, after the establishment of the National Cemetery at Gettysburg in November 1863, they decided that it was the most fitting place for him, among his fallen comrades. Joseph Perium, captain of Company K, was buried in grave number 9, section B, of the Minnesota plot at the Gettysburg National Cemetery.

In the intervening weeks, Lochren received letters that surely cheered him in his grim work as body-counter and writer of condolence letters.

Gen Hospital—Brawd and Chery [Broad and Cherry]. Philadelphia, Penn.
July 16th, 1863
Lt. William Lochren, Sir: I have the honor to inform you that I still exist. My wound appears to be doing well, though today it is *most dam painfull*. . . . Sergt. Perkins is in the next bunk to me and says that he has a peculiar disgust for hard-bread soldiers. His leg is doing first rate. Please give my best respects to the Old Vets of the company. Please accept this from your old companion in the army.

Sgt. M. Marvin.

Hastings, Mn. Sept. 8th, 1863.
I arrived home on the first of this month after a weary, tedious journey. My wounds are all doing unusually well, but still I suffer very much from them at times. Especially is this true of the wound in the lung and

the one in my leg just above the knee. From the latter wound the ball has not been extracted.

The surgeons have so far been unable to find the ball. I expect to suffer from this wound, more or less, all my life.

I am growing restive from my forced absence from you, and shall rejoin the Regiment just as soon as I can mount a horse. My heart and my thoughts are ever with it, and it is now, and ever will be, the proudest boast of my life that my name was found among its roll of members, whose deeds by its more than Spartan courage, will live in undying colors until men shall cease to admire courage or love liberty. Oh! that I can soon be with you once again.

Major Downie will rejoin you in the course of 8 or 10 days. His wounds are almost well.

Give my love to Captain Coates, and all my brother officers, especially to the noble hearted Lt. Searles, for it was he who saved my life. I am, dear sir,

Most respectfully, Your Obedient Servant, [Lieutenant Colonel] Charles P. Adams

Lochren was not the only man in the regiment to perform the heartwrenching task of informing a wife, a brother or sister, a mother or father of the worst news they would ever receive.

Bivouack, 1st Minnesota—July 6th, 1863. Mr. Hamlin
Dear Sir: It becomes my melancholy duty to write to you concerning your brave boy who has fallen.
Sergt. Hamlin, of Co. F, was killed in the fighting near Gettysburg, Pa., on the 3rd instant about 5 o'clock in the afternoon. He was hit in four places at the same instant almost. One shot shattered his left leg, another passed through his thigh, a third through his neck on the right side, and a fourth almost directly through his heart. Sergeant Hamlin was beloved by us all and with you we mourn his early death. Long association has made me love him as a brother, and I miss him badly.

We buried him by moonlight near where he fell, under a walnut tree. I marked his grave, sodded it over, and enclosed it with rails. Philip was an earnest, and consistent Christian and I doubt not he is in the "better land." We often talked on the subject of death and I know he was prepared. I took a lock of his hair, thinking you would like it. I know his mother will. Also a bit of our tattered flag, which he loved so well.

I know of how little consequence words are to the bereaved, but tender you the condolence and sympathy of his comrades in arms.

Feeling for you in this severe affliction, and praying God to comfort you, I am sincerely yours,

James A. Wright, Orderly Sergt., Co. F, 1st Minnesota[37]

The Civil War was not finished with the Hamlin family. A year and a half after his death at Gettysburg, Philip's brother, Jacob Hamlin of Company G, Seventh Minnesota Regiment, was killed at the Battle of Nashville.

Two mothers in Minnesota would receive wonderful news, compared to what many others were receiving.

Division Hospital near Gettysburg, Pennsylvania. July 4th, 1863
Dear Mother: We have engaged the enemy again, but this time in a free country, and our company as well as the regiment has suffered very much. Ely and myself are both wounded; Ely through the side and myself through the leg and shoulder. I am not dangerously wounded, feel first rate and I would [ask] you to give yourself no uneasiness on my ac-

The U.S. Army General Hospital at the corner of Broad and Cherry Streets in Philadelphia. Many of the men from the First Minnesota recovered here, including Mat Marvin, Color Sergeant Ellet Perkins, Charley Goddard, and Charles Ely.

count, nor do I think there is any need of Mrs. Ely worrying about her son. Well mother, goodbye. Don't be so foolish as to come down here and worry about me for I am getting along fine.

Charles E. Goddard[38]

While they surely lamented the agony their sons were in, the two women at least knew they were alive and being treated in a hospital. The mothers of Charley Goddard and Charlie Ely finally traced their boys to a Philadelphia hospital. On July 22 the women arrived to take care of their sons and to distribute cakes, jellies, and other treats to the wounded of the First Minnesota. Both seventeen-year-old Goddard and eighteen-year-old Ely survived the war.

In midst of the letters filled with agony, mourning, or relief, the mundane matters of day-to-day living continued, prompted by the results of the battle. One soldier asked for assistance in a personal matter.

Jarvis Hospital, Baltimore, MD. July 20th '63
Captain Coates: Dear Sir, I have a note of fifty dollars against the late Captain Muller and want your advice what I shall do with. If you think you can collect it, I will send it to you. I wish you would advise me what to do. The note is for money loaned to him. Please answer soon and oblige.

Yours with respect, James Breakey, Co. E. Direct 'Jarvis U.S. and General Hospital, Baltimore, MD., Ward 8'[39]

Regimental business needed to be handled in the aftermath.

Special Order No. 58. Headquarters 1st Regt. Minn. Vols. Near Sandy Hook July 17, 1863. A board of Survey to consist of Captain Wilbur F. Duffy, Captain John Ball, and 2nd Lieutenant Mahlon Black will convene at this camp at nine o'clock A.M. of this day for the purpose of making inventories and reporting upon the condition of public property in the possession of Captains Nathan S. Messick; Wilson B. Farrell; Louis Muller and Joseph Perium late of this Regiment deceased, at the time of their deaths respectively, in accordance with Paragraph 1019. Revised Army Regulations. By Order of Capt. H. C. Coates. Comd.g 1st Regt. Minn. Vols. Wm. Lochren Act. Adj.

Letter writing probably was not uppermost in the minds of the majority of the Confederates at this time. For protection against an anticipated federal assault, the rebel army had taken the time and the energy to entrench their position along Seminary Ridge. Save for a few hours of desperately needed sleep during the night and early morning of July 3 to 4, most in the rebel camp were preparing for withdrawal. General John Imboden received his written orders from Lee and spent the day assembling the wagon train of wounded, along with artillery and cavalry escorts.

At noon, as Imboden described it, "the very windows of heaven seemed to have opened. The rain fell in blinding sheets; the meadows were soon overflowed, and fences gave way before the raging streams."[40] The ferocity of the storm added greatly to the misery of the rebel wounded and to the difficulty of the task of organizing and moving wagons and artillery.

It caused more concern among the wounded rebels in the Union Second Corps hospital along Rock Creek, east of the Taneytown Road. The Confederates had been gathered on some of the lowest ground in the area near the bank of the creek. The downpour caused it to rise so rapidly that soon the disabled southerners were in danger of drowning. Undoubtedly some did, as the federal hospital personnel worked frantically to drag the prisoner-patients up the slope to higher ground.[41]

Imboden finally got his wagon train of misery moving toward Virginia at 4:00 P.M. on July 4. The caravan stretched for seventeen miles on the northwest road toward Cashtown, Pennsylvania. Imboden estimated that fewer than one in a hundred of the wounded had received any medical treatment before being loaded onto the hard wooden beds of the springless wagons. The entire trip was accompanied by the sounds of wailing, screaming, cursing, and moaning men, many pathetically begging to be killed or set down by the roadside and left. The goal was to make it to Williamsport, Maryland, along the Potomac River and cross safely into Virginia. Imboden remembered the forty-mile trip: "On! On! We *must* move on. The storm continued, and the darkness was appalling. There was no time even to fill a canteen with water for a dying man; for, except the drivers and the guards, all were wounded and utterly helpless in that vast procession of misery. During this one night I realized more of the horrors of war than I had in all the two preceding years."[42]

The rest of Lee's battered army took a more direct route south than did the wagon train. The army withdrew under the cover of dark and storm on the night of July 4. General Meade ordered troops from the Sixth Corps forward at 3:00 A.M. on July 5 to reconnoiter the Confederate position. Word came back that the entire rebel army had evacuated. Federal cavalry units already were out along Lee's anticipated escape route, destroying a pontoon bridge at Falling Waters, Virginia, and attacking and harassing wagon trains.

Much has been made, and was made at the time, of Meade's perceived slowness in pursuing Lee's army. The rebels were low on ammunition, badly bloodied, exhausted, and in enemy territory. But morale was rarely a problem in the Army of Northern Virginia under Robert E. Lee. The Confederate army had ammunition enough to make a defense and would surely fight with the ferocity of a wounded bear if cornered.

While it was on its own turf, the Army of the Potomac had lost a quarter of its strength in casualties. The hard march to Gettysburg, and the hard fight there, had reduced uniforms to rags. Many of the filthy, exhausted troops were barefoot from the tough march up from Virginia; wet weather and bad roads had caused ankle boots to disintegrate altogether.

Private Marshall Sherman of the First Minnesota's Company C spoke of having been barefoot during the battle. In a case of the shoe literally being on the other foot, Sherman was hoping to find a dead Confederate soldier with a decent pair that he could "requisition." Ordinarily it was the rebel soldiers who were forever supplying themselves with footwear and other needed equipment from the bodies of Yankees. Sherman was lucky enough the night of July 3 to find a dead rebel who had obviously been part of a raiding party that captured a cache of new shoes at Gettysburg just before the battle.[43]

Meade was exhorted by telegraph from Washington to pursue Lee expeditiously. But he was also instructed, as was the case for every commander of the Army of the Potomac, to stay between Lee's army and Washington and Baltimore to the east. Despite the government's knowledge of Lee's defeat, the extent of his casualties, and the suspected status of his ammunition supply, there was the ever-present fear that the rebels might decide to make a dash for the federal capital.

Meade decided to have his cavalry continue to nip at the heels and flanks of Lee's columns but have the bulk of the army make an end run and cut Lee off before he reached the Potomac. Consideration was again given to available roads, essential for moving an army, and the necessity of getting over the South Mountain range through the passes. The continuous rain caused all the roads to become thick mud wallows, hampering the movement of men, artillery, and supply wagons.

The reconnaissance of the Sixth Corps turned into the beginnings of pursuit as the corps pushed farther toward Fairfield Gap and Monterey Pass in the South Mountain range, about eighteen miles southwest of Gettysburg. The mountain passes were found to be heavily fortified, and it would have cost much in time and casualties to dislodge the tenacious rebels covering the retreat.[44]

By the evening of July 5, the Army of the Potomac had about all the time it was going to get for recovering from the battle. The federal dead had been buried, as had some rebel dead, but Meade wired to Washington at 8:30 A.M. on July 5: "I cannot delay to pick up the debris of the battle-field, and request that all those arrangements may be made by the departments. After burying my own, I am compelled to employ citizens to bury the enemy's dead."[45]

It became a common practice to "sentence" civilians to twenty-four hours of burying corpses, or horse carcasses, if they were caught looting bodies or pilfering government property. The men of the First Minnesota and the rest of the Second Corps spent July 5 helping to bury the dead.[46] In the late afternoon they joined in the southward march in pursuit of Lee and his retreating army. The rest of the army followed on July 6.

On July 8 supply trains reached the new base of operations at Frederick, Maryland, where new ankle boots and other supplies were issued to the Army of the Potomac, now concentrated at Middletown, Maryland.[47] Reinforcements had been sent as well. One of these regiments was the elite Seventh New York Militia, a unit that had never left the state of New York but now was called down into Maryland because of the scare caused by the rebel invasion. This unit was closer to one of the "social club" militia units prevalent before the war, manned and officered by the wealthy upper class of New York City. As the First Minnesota passed the New York regiment resting by the road, William Lochren recalled that the New Yorkers, "had to bear, with meekness, all manner of jibes and jeers from the lines of dusty veterans."[48]

The flooded Potomac was almost the undoing of the Army of Northern Virginia. The pontoon bridge at Falling Waters had been destroyed by federal cavalry, and Lee was forced to entrench and defend a nine-mile-arcing line covering Falling Waters and Williamsport. The immense train of wounded led by General John Imboden had, miraculously, begun arriving in Williamsport on the afternoon of July 5. The rest arrived the next day, and the town immediately was turned into an enormous hospital, with the sympathetic townspeople volunteering to cook and care for the rebels.

Imboden organized a successful defense of the town when federal cavalry attacked on the afternoon of July 6. Positioning his artillery on high ground around the town and forming up wagoneers, dismounted cavalry, and even wounded officers into companies, he managed to drive off the federals and save what were, essentially, all of the transportation vehicles of the Army of Northern Virginia. He was relieved by the timely arrival of Confederate cavalry along roads to the flank and rear of the attacking Yankees, compelling the bluecoats to withdraw.[49]

By July 11 the Union army was in position facing the Confederate army, whose back was to the flooded Potomac River. Lee had been re-supplied with ammunition ferried across from the Virginia side of the Potomac on July 9.[50] He set about having the destroyed pontoon bridge salvaged at Falling Waters. Warehouses and other buildings were dismantled for wood and beams, and new pontoons were built and floated to Falling Waters to rebuild the bridge.[51]

As an engineer in the United States Army earlier in his long career, Lee was a master at judging terrain and configuring fortifications. His position was on high ground, partially masked from view in places by the bluffs.[52] The approaches to his flanks were protected by the river and by wide and open expanses of fields. No reconnaissance or assault force could approach without being subjected to intense and prolonged cross fire while moving toward the Confederate works.[53]

As daunting as the entrenched position appeared, Meade decided to make a determined probe of Lee's position around Falling Waters and Middletown and develop it into a full assault if conditions proved favorable. The advance was set for the morning of July 13. That evening Meade held a council in his headquarters tent. As one general in attendance recalled, "I do not think I ever saw the principal corps commanders so unanimous in favor of not fighting as on that occasion."[54]

Meade rethought the situation, acknowledging his own lack of specific information about Lee's position and the terrain. He ordered reconnaissance for July 13 instead of an advance, but fog, rain, and general foul weather limited its effectiveness. Resolving to lose no more time, he ordered the advance for the morning of July 14.

Lee would not wait. The reconstructed pontoon bridge was now finished at Falling Waters, and despite the previous day's rain the Potomac had dropped enough to risk fording troops. Beginning at dark on the night of July 13, Lee began moving his infantry back into the safety of Virginia.

When the Union advance began the next morning, all but two divisions of A. P. Hill's Third Corps had made it across the river. A sharp fight ensued between the rebel rearguard and the federal cavalry. Confederate Brigadier General J. Johnston Pettigrew, one of the division commanders in Pickett's Charge, was wounded mortally and about one thousand rebels were killed, wounded, or captured.[55] The last rebels across cut the pontoon bridge loose and let it float down the river, which already was beginning to rise again from the heavy rains the day before.

The Gettysburg Campaign was over. Meade would receive sharp criticism for allowing Lee's army to escape without at least engaging it in another major fight, if not outright annihilation. Although no one was anxious for more blood-letting, the morale of the Army of the Potomac was very high, especially after the victory at Gettysburg. Most of the soldiers were anxious to end it, and destroying Lee's army quickly would have brought that about.

After the discovery of Lee's escape, two soldiers were overheard talking, and one said, "Well, there goes for two more years!"[56] He was off by only three months. The next twenty-one months would witness the collapse and death of the Confederacy, bled out in a war of attrition. No matter that Lee continued to exercise his engineering expertise, the now defensive war, fought from entrenched positions and causing tens of thousands of casualties, inevitably led to Appomattox.

EPILOGUE

Ready to do it, whatever it might cost

BOTH ARMIES MOVED to the same war-torn land of the previous year—the area around the Rapidan River, the Rappahannock River, Chancellorsville, and the wilderness southwest of the burned-out crossroads. The Army of Northern Virginia took up a position south of the Rapidan, strung out from the Orange County Court House to Chancellorsville, a little over twenty miles northeast. Meade was directed from Washington to maintain an aggressive posture but to hold his line north of the Rappahannock.[1] By July 31, 1863, the First Minnesota and the rest of the Second Corps were on the north fork of the Rappahannock, about twenty miles northeast of Fredericksburg.

In mid-July the federal government implemented the new conscription law, and violent riots broke out in New York City in protest against the initial round of the draft. General Meade received orders to send four regiments to New York to suppress the rioters and maintain order. The orders specified that no Pennsylvania or New York regiments should be sent because it was felt they might be sympathetic to the rioters. This outbreak of violence was part of the reason that Meade had been ordered to hold his position and not pursue Lee. There were no reinforcements to send, but regiments were still going to be taken away. Meade would also eventually lose the Eleventh and Twelfth Corps in mid-September, when they were sent to the western theater of the war after the Union defeat at Chickamauga in northern Georgia.

On August 12 newly made Captain Charles Edward Davis of Company E wrote his father of the exhaustion, intense heat, and "very severe" guard and picket duty the men were enduring. The twenty-seven-year-old surveyor from St. Paul went on:

> Our wounded officers are getting along very slowly. Most of them though will never return for active duty in the field, but will join the Invalid Corps. Many of our wounded have died. Three of my old Company "A" have died in the hospital at Gettysburg—and it is rumored here that they did not receive much attention and that the greater part of the amputations were miserably performed, most of them resulting in death. Our colonel is still in the hospital at Gettysburg. I was told yesterday by General Harrow (commanding our division) that Col. Colville was to be made Brigadier General on account of the bravery of the regt. at Gettysburg—it's said his authority was General Hancock, who is next to General Meade in command of the Army of the Potomac. Colville is no military man, but he is as brave as a lion, and a commission to him as Brigadier would be a worthy tribute to the gallantry and courage of the "First."[2]

On August 15 a new request for still more regiments to control the situation in New York was telegraphed to Meade, and the Eighth Ohio, Seventh Michigan, and First Minnesota were ordered north. The regiments traveled by railcar to Alexandria and then were loaded on the steam transport *Atlantic* for a rough forty-eight hours of sea travel. Prior to departing from the dock, a tragic accident occurred when Lieutenant August Kreuger, a thirty-one-year-old Prussian immigrant in Company A, fell overboard in the night and drowned.[3] The crowded decks and stifling below-deck areas offered little in the way of comfort, and many of the seasick infantrymen vied for a spot to hang over the rail.

Arriving in New York harbor on August 23, the First Minnesota was initially posted on Governor's Island. Company D, under newly promoted Captain Christopher Heffelfinger, and Company C, now commanded by Lieutenant William Harmon,

Captain Charles Edward Davis, Company E, First Minnesota

reported to the provost marshal of Brooklyn. The sixty-five to seventy men comprising the two companies were posted in the borough's city hall in anticipation of the next round of the draft lottery. Heffelfinger was questioned by the provost marshal, who thought that at least two more companies needed to be on duty there. Heffelfinger assured him that his men could handle any contingency and that no more men could fit into city hall anyway. He recalled that the provost marshal asked him, "What would you do in case we were attacked by a mob of a thousand men or more?" We can only imagine the delivery of the cool, confident, battle-hardened Minnesota veteran as he replied, "We would do just the same as if there were one hundred, a thousand, or five thousand—we would drive them back."[4]

Fortunately the rioting spirit seemed to have burned itself out in the initial spasms of July. There was no trouble in the two weeks the regiment was in the city, and it became a much-needed and well-deserved holiday for the weary soldiers. Early in their stay on Governor's Island Company F had unexpected visitors. Harry Hoffman, the former sheriff of Goodhue County, Minnesota, and Abe Thomas, a merchant from Red Wing, were in New York and heard the regiment was in town and found where it was posted. Orderly Sergeant James Wright wrote of the reunion, "They looked natural and familiar to us who had know them well; while they declared we were all greatly changed and they expressed surprise at our bronzed and weather-beaten appearance, and the very few men there were left for duty. Until seeing the little skeletons of companies they had not realized how greatly they were diminished. It was the first time they, or any one else directly from our home town, had visited the regiment since it had left the state in June 1861. Their coming had turned our thoughts homeward and not much else was talked of for the rest of the day."[5]

On August 28 the regiment was ferried across to Brooklyn and set up camp in Washington Park in what had been Fort Greene in the colonial period. They came to the Brooklyn camp with newly issued uniforms and large wall tents, which Sergeant Wright noted, "were nice, large tents, in which we could stand up; something we had not had since we started for the Peninsula in the spring of 1862."[6] The men of Company D and C had even better accommodations, living within four solid walls and under a ceiling for the first time in more than two years. Corporal Edward A. Walker of Company D, a twenty-four-year-old machinist from Clearwater, Minnesota, wrote to a friend, "We are now right in the midst of the city and have our quarters under the [Provost] Marshal's Office. Have all the improvements, water (hot and cold), gas, cooking range, etc., etc."[7]

From the time the regiment stepped off the ferry onto Brooklyn soil they were constantly surrounded by admiring and inquisitive crowds. Not only had the New York papers run profile stories about the regiment and its bloody and honorable history, but the terrifying ordeal of the riots made people genuinely grateful to have the battle-hardened veterans in the city. The initial response of the regiment was irritation, but James Wright noted, "the expressions of interest and sympathy soon dissipated all our wishes to be left to ourselves and warmed our hearts towards the 'mixed multitude' about us until we were appreciative and grateful."[8]

Several men of the regiment admitted to being unaccustomed to being treated well by the general population, having spent more than two years in hostile Virginia. The outpouring of goodwill from the people of New York was reciprocated, and the men of the regiment would remember their stay fondly for the rest of their lives. There were still things to get used to, though, as Wright discovered the first evening they camped in Washington Park: "As the day drew to a close fires were started and coffee made and slices of pork were broiled or fried as we did in the field—each soldier his own cook. Some of the boys retired to their tents to eat but the most of us sat on the grass at the edge of the walk and masticated our pork and crackers and drank our black coffee, surrounded by a company that observed us with, apparently, the same interest that youngsters watch the animals feeding when the circus comes."[9]

Throngs of visitors, many bearing gifts of fruit and other food, continued to move freely in and out of the camp. The strict discipline of normal army life was relaxed, and the men were given a lot of time for sightseeing and visiting the homes of newly acquired friends among the many visitors. A Sunday service attended by several of the men blossomed into an invitation for the entire regiment to attend a dinner in their honor at the Carleton Avenue Methodist Church. An entry in

Daniel Bond's diary expressed what most of the men must have felt: "We were conducted to a beautiful repast spread under a spacious canopy erected for the purpose, where the ladies kind and beautiful as faeries were there to welcome us and make us at home. I must confess that I felt proud to be reconned among the number who were worthy of such honor. When we arose to depart they bestowed on each of us a bouquet of lilly flowers. Oh! It thrills ones heart with joy to endure such attentions. All the soldiers are happy."[10]

The entire New York episode must have seemed like a delightful dream to the men of regiment, and, like all dreams, it ended as abruptly as it started. At 8:00 P.M. on Saturday, September 5, the order was given to strike tents and pack knapsacks. By 10:00 A.M. the next morning the regiment was marching toward a steam transport ship to the cheers, good-byes, and fluttering handkerchiefs of the crowd that had gathered around them. James Wright noted, "It is not quite so bad as leaving home but something like it. Our stay here has been only long enough to make us realize that we are human beings, with social feelings still alive within us, and the many kindnesses shown us here has stirred them to lively activity. The brief stay of our regiment in Brooklyn was a rich, green oasis in the social desert of our soldier lives. It was perfumed with a generous kindness that touched our hearts then and it still exhales pleasant perfumes, when stirred by the touch of remembrance."[11]

By September 16 they were back on the battleground along the Rappahannock River in Virginia. The situation had changed very little since their departure. It was still an ongoing campaign of maneuvering by the armies, each looking for opportunities to strike the other. The Minnesotans discovered that Major General Gouverneur K. Warren had been given command of the Second Corps while Hancock recovered from his Gettysburg wound. Warren had been on Meade's staff. He was the chief engineer officer of the Army of the Potomac but had proved himself a brave and capable battle commander and had the confidence of the men. Warren was the one who had seen disaster awaiting on the abandoned Little Round Top at Gettysburg and rushed troops to its rocky summit just as the Confederate assault started. On October 4, Major Mark Downie returned to the First Minnesota and assumed command from Captain Henry Coates.

Constant marching, periodic skirmishes and leap-frogging back and forth across rivers was wearing on everyone. Corporal Edward A. Walker confided in a letter to a friend, "The campaigning in Virginia don't seem to amount to much. We have big battles, big advances, and big retreats but we don't take *Richmond*. I *blame* nothing, *know* nothing, but *do* object to so much useless marching especially when we carry 8 days rations."[12]

An opportunity presented itself to the rebel General A. P. Hill on October 14, 1863. Finding a gap in the federal line of march, Hill sent his men on an attack into the Union Fifth Corps. Unfortunately for him, he was not aware just how close the Second Corps was or where exactly it was positioned. To the sound of artillery fire, the Second Corps came onto the field running down the railroad track into Bristoe Station, the Minnesotans in advance of the rest of the corps.

The regiment deployed as skirmishers and moved toward the flank of the rebel line advancing on the Fifth Corps. The skirmish line, firing from the top of a hill, stopped the advance of a line of rebel skirmishers. Behind the heavy rebel skirmish line, the Minnesotans could see two fully deployed battle lines and a third column moving off the road preparing to deploy facing the First Minnesota.[13] It must have felt like Gettysburg all over again to the handful of Minnesotans.[14]

The regiment held its position until the last minute, firing from the cover of the top of the hill and from behind piles of rubbish and debris dumped there from surrounding army camps. Major Downie ordered the regiment back as the rebel skirmishers crested the hill and began to move around its ends. With artillery rounds exploding and shrieking overhead, the regiment took to its heels. The objective was an eight-foot-high railroad embankment, roughly three hundred yards away across open ground. James Wright remembered:

> When once I started I felt my life depended on the length of the steps down the gentle slope of the hill—and the rapidity with which I took them. It does not need to be said that I "struck by best gait" without ceremony. We had not covered half of the distance before our pursuers were at the top of the hill behind us, yelling and shooting. It was an intensely exciting moment which quickened all of the senses and brought every nerve and muscle into action. Their bullets fairly sizzled

as they passed over us and some of them struck the ground beside us, making the dirt fly and glancing away with a peculiar whining sound I never heard on any other occasion.[15]

Not seeing a single gun, flag, hat, or head above it, the men did not know for sure that any federal troops were on the other side of the railroad embankment, only that it was the nearest place of protection. They tumbled into the excavation ditch at the base of the embankment, then scrambled up and rolled behind it. They were relieved to discover they were sliding down into the line of the Nineteenth Maine. The men joined in the ferocious firefight along with the Maine regiment. Private Edward Bassett of Company G noted in his diary, "When we got behind the bank, we gave them [the rebels] some of our best rations of Uncle Sams cold load."[16]

Captain Ball ordered Company F to the left of the Nineteenth Maine to extend the line, and, by the time they were in place, the second rebel assault line was moving across the fields in front of the railroad embankment. Ball was concerned that, if the second wave piled into the ditch at the base of the embankment along with the first rebel line, one determined rush could bring them all over the embankment. He jumped to the top of the embankment and called for the rest of the men to follow, some of whom did. The captain fired his revolver into the mass of rebels at the bottom of the ditch, and, as a group of them charged up the embankment with fixed bayonets, Ball threw the empty weapon at them.[17]

At that moment Ball was hit in the groin by a bullet, which destroyed a testicle and lodged in his thigh. He tumbled backward off the embankment. Twenty-four-year-old Norwegian Private Hans Peterson was struck by two minié balls and was killed instantly, and two other men of Company F were wounded.[18] The rebel second line began to fall back, and most of those in the ditch surrendered. The Minnesotans went out again as skirmishers, aiding the rebel wounded as they were able and directing prisoners to the rear. They collected 322 prisoners and captured an abandoned artillery battery, bringing two of its guns back to the federal line.[19] The regiment sustained casualties of one killed and sixteen wounded.

The pattern of marching, countermarching, and river and stream crossings continued. On November 7, the Federal Sixth Corps defeated and drove away the rebel troops defending the railroad bridge at Rappahannock Station, which allowed the First Minnesota to move easily across Kelly's Ford downstream and take possession of well-constructed winter cabins abandoned by the rebels. The regiment was able to stay here resting and doing picket duty along the Rapidan River until November 26.[20]

On that date a general, coordinated advance was put into motion to strike Lee's right flank. A counterattack by Confederate forces stalled the advance long enough for the rebel army to fall back to defensive works on the hilltops west of Mine Run, a small stream about fifteen miles southwest of Chancellorsville. In the below-freezing night of November 29, 1863, the First Minnesota moved into position to take part in a morning assault on the Confederate entrenchments.

The regiment was to be deployed as skirmishers, and in the frigid dark they marched far to the Union left before moving forward into position, all the time expecting to receive a volley of musketry out of the blackness from the rebel pickets west of Mine Run. Finally they halted, faced west, and advanced, crossing the frozen twenty-foot-wide stream and falling through the ice. With legs wet up to their knees, the men moved forward to the first small rise they encountered and lay down to observe. The federal assault lines were forming several hundred yards behind them. Through the fog and darkness they could see fires in the rebel camps on the hilltops and hear men digging and chopping trees for trenches and breastworks. As they watched and listened, their trouser legs began freezing to their skin.[21]

Artillery fire was to begin the morning, five shots—one for each of the five corps of the army—as the signal for the advance. The assault was set for 8:00 A.M. The First Minnesota was to advance, shoot, and bayonet the rebels in the forward rifle pits, then join the general assault as it caught up to them. James Wright sent a letter to his mother describing that night of waiting:

> We prepared for the bloody work we expected. After writing our names on slips of paper and pinning them on our overcoats and blouses, that it might be known who we were in case we were not able to tell it ourselves, we exchanged last messages to be sent home, in case the receiver was in a condition to send them and the sender not. Then we

piled our knapsacks, examined our rifles and cartridges and, with silent prayer for safety and success, crept up to the crest of a little rise within pistol shot of their skirmishers and laid down to await the dawn. It was intensely cold; we suffered greatly and had to rub our hands and thump our feet against the frozen ground to save them from freezing. Their skirmishers were out of their pits, doing the same thing for the same reason and, though they must have known of our presence as well as we did theirs, neither offered to molest the other.[22]

Orders had been given for the men to leave behind their knapsacks and blanket rolls so as not to be encumbered during the charge. Captain Christopher Heffelfinger countermanded this order for his Company D, reasoning that, "if a man was wounded in the charge and left on the field, he would almost perish from the cold before relief could reach him."[23] Captain Charles E. Davis of Company E wrote to his sister later, "Captain [Thomas] Sinclair of our regt., who was wounded at Gettysburg and Bristoe, saw a pamphlet lying on the ground and picked it up. It proved to be a tract headed: 'Prepare to Meet Thy God.' Tom looked across the level plain in our front, over which we must charge full half a mile under a tremendous storm of artillery and musketry before we could reach their works, and laconically remarked, 'Yes, I think it's about time.' Many a brave soldier looked, as he supposed that morning, on the sun for the last time."[24]

General Francis A. Walker, the assistant adjutant general of the Second Corps, wrote, "While on the picket line, reconnoitering, my uniform concealed by a soldier's overcoat, I asked an old veteran of the noble First Minnesota, on picket, what he thought of the prospect. Not recognizing me as an officer, he expressed himself very freely, declaring it 'a damned sight worse than Fredericksburg,' and adding, 'I am going as far as I can travel, but we can't get more than two-thirds of the way up the hill."[25]

Fortunately the Army of the Potomac was no longer being led by Ambrose Burnside or anyone like him. The long night of anxious waiting would not end in another Fredericksburg-style slaughter. At first light General Warren could clearly see how formidable the rebel works were, noting with the precision of an engineer, "a run for eight minutes was the least time our line could have to close the space between us, during which we would be exposed to every species of fire. I at once decided not to attack, and so informed General Meade."[26]

Meade came to observe at 10:00 A.M. and concurred with Warren's decision. The Army of the Potomac fell back and established winter quarters. The Minnesotans took on the regular army camp routine of picket and fatigue duty, which mainly involved building corduroy roads. These roadways became essential, as much of the time the men lived in freezing rain and deep mud. Corduroying the road, the process of felling trees and laying them across a roadbed to prevent artillery and supply wagons from sinking, was necessary to keep supplies moving. On December 31, 1863, Private Edward Bassett wrote in his diary, "Just came in from picket. We were out three days, and altho it rained until the mud was eighteen inches deep, I enjoyed myself as well as I would in camp. . . . Mud, mud, mud everywhere, enough to lose an army in, if it attempts to move. We ended this year in mud."[27]

The regiment's three-year enlistment period was due to end in late April 1864, as would those of many of the other veteran regiments that spring and summer. The government was anxious for reenlistments. The veteran regiments were the cream, the original volunteers, and the quality of the conscripts and substitutes (men paid by wealthy draftees to serve in their place) made the reenlistment issue all the more important. The federal government offered a substantial inducement: any veteran with less than a year to serve as of September 23, 1863, could reenlist and receive a thirty-day furlough and $402.00 in cash and have his new three-year enlistment date from the day he reenlisted (not from the end of his original enlistment).[28]

Lieutenant Colonel Charles Powell Adams returned to the regiment on December 7, 1863, and took command. One of his first actions was to retire Colonel William Colvill from the army at half-pay. A general order from the War Department was in effect that all officers disabled by battle wounds were to be mustered out and put on half-pay. Because of Colvill's high standing with the men and most of the officers of the regiment and the short time until the regiment's enlistment was up, no one had even considered enforcing this general order in his case.

Some of the line officers, including Christopher Heffelfinger, became aware of Adams's action when the order retiring Colvill came to division headquarters. They had the head clerk of the division, Sam Coflin of the First Minnesota, hold up the order while they contacted the Minnesota congressional delegation and Colonel Colvill, who was still recovering from his wounds at his family home in New York state. Within forty-eight hours Colvill had been reinstated as colonel of the regiment at full pay. An indignant Adams threatened to resign over it, but as Christopher Heffelfinger noted, "he did not resign and I don't think he intended to."[29]

On January 21, 1864, Daniel Bond jotted in his diary, "Rumors are afloat that we are to be sent home."[30] The decision had been made that since active campaigning would not start until spring, after the First Minnesota's enlistment was up, the best thing to do was send the regiment back to the state to recruit actively. It was everyone's wish, particularly General Winfield Scott Hancock's, to fill out this veteran regiment so as to maintain the name and the organization. One sticking point was that the men did not want the offered thirty-day furlough but rather a sixty- to ninety-day furlough before they would reenlist. Only the thirty days were given, to date from the time they arrived in St. Paul.[31]

It had been a long and grueling three years, and even with the inducement of huge bounties to reenlist, it was not surprising that many men felt as did Corporal Edward A. Walker: "Will I pocket my $700.00 and reenlist? Not for a few days at least. If I am fortunate enough to get out of this I can look back over three years of my life, and say 'had a hard time' but I have learned lots about war, almost enough to pay me—but not quite."[32]

The final confirmation of the regiment's return home to Minnesota came on Thursday, February 4, 1864. James Wright noted in his diary:

> After these years of absence it is a most welcome order and the boys are wild with excitement at the thought of going home so soon, as they were when first ordered to Washington. Their different dispositions and temperments caused them to show, or try not to show, their feelings in a variety of ways; but every one was thrilling with a flood of emotions they could not hide. One of the least emotional of the company came into our tent and asked, almost in a whisper: "Is it true, sergeant, we are to go home?" Being told that it was, he caught my hand and almost crushed it in his and left without another word; but as he turned I saw the tears running down his bronzed cheeks and felt drawn

to him as I never have been before. We are to leave at 6 tomorrow morning.[33]

The regiment formed up and marched to division headquarters early the next morning and, in the cold darkness, were surprised to be greeted by a burst of music from the brass band of the Eighty-second New York Regiment. They found the entire brigade at attention in formation. Saluting them with the customary present arms, the brigade broke into cheers as the regiment marched to the tent of General Alexander Webb, commander of the division. Webb lauded the men and their excellent service record and said he genuinely regretted losing them from his division. As the First Minnesota marched out of camp, they were followed by the brass band playing "Auld Lang Syne." The Minnesotans began singing the song as they marched for the railcars at Brandy Station.[34]

The regiment arrived in Washington, D.C., that evening and stayed in the city an extra day to allow all men on detached duty, and all the sick or wounded who were able to travel, time to get to Washington and rejoin the regiment for the trip home. There were a little more than two hundred men actively serving with the regiment, and those coming in would bring the number up to about three hundred. The state congressional delegation, and other Minnesotans then in the capital, put together an enormous banquet for the regiment the next evening at the National Hotel. About fifty distinguished guests attended; among them were Vice President Hannibal Hamlin, Secretary of War Edwin Stanton, and other members of President Lincoln's cabinet.[35]

The biggest and most pleasant surprise for the men was when Colonel William Colvill was carried in. Still unable to walk or stand because of his severe wounds, Colvill was brought into the room on a stretcher by Captain Thomas Sinclair of Company B and Sergeant John Merritt of Company K. James Wright remembered the moment with, "His entrance into the banquet room was unexpected and when he was brought in there was a spontaneous outburst of shouting and cheering, which showed the feelings of the men toward him."[36]

The next morning, Sunday, February 7, 1863, the regiment boarded the train for Minnesota. On Friday, February 12, they arrived in LaCrosse, Wisconsin, which was the end of the railroad line. The Northwestern Transportation Company had made arrangements to have enough stage sleighs available to convey all the men of the regiment up the frozen Mississippi to St. Paul. Wrapped in buffalo robes and blankets, the men snuggled down as the sleighs slid over the three-foot-thick river ice, carrying them to family and friends they had not seen in nearly three years. The sleighs made stops in each of the river towns that had raised companies of the First Minnesota. Embraces, kisses, and tears flowed in Winona, Wabasha, Red Wing, and Hastings, each town giving the regiment a grand welcome and, at Winona and Red Wing, banquets. Wright recalled the scene at Red Wing, home of Company F:

> As soon as in the hall the boys were surrounded by the anxious waiting ones and there was a scene which no words of mine can even faintly reproduce on paper, and is best left to the imagination. It is sufficient to say that the boys were unceremoniously hugged and kissed with an earnestness and abandon that was, seemingly, intended to make up for all previous enforced omissions. Words—expression of feeling, questions and comments—were fired at them in volleys. It was a glad, joyous moment, and hearts thrilled with the intensity of human emotions, and tears were not lacking. Tears of gladness for those they were greeting and tears of sadness for those they never should greet again, and these were observable alike on fair faces and bronzed cheeks.[37]

The regiment arrived in St. Paul in the late afternoon of Monday, February 15. Daniel Bond wrote in his journal of the arrival, "All the city seemed insane. We were welcomed by the citizens with the most unbounded enthusiasm. Just as we came around the land of the river below the city, all the butchers [members of the city's Butchers Association] came riding on horseback to escort us in. The cannon pealed out the signal to the citizens that the regiment was in sight. All the bells opened their bronzen throats, so that by the time we landed over three thousand people were on the ice. It was with the greatest difficulty that we could form our ranks, every soldier's hand was grasped by a dozen acquaintences."[38]

The crowd included former members of the regiment who were back home after being discharged for disabilities. These men proudly wore white cloth trefoils on their coats to indicate their association with the returning warriors of the First Minnesota. The regiment paraded downtown to the Athenaeum, where they were again banqueted, toasted, and lauded in speeches by city and state dignitaries, and then all the men began their thirty-day furloughs.

Reenlistments had been slow in coming, and enlisting new recruits would not prove any easier. Captain Christopher Heffelfinger set up a recruiting office in the Nicollet House in Minneapolis but found most new recruits wanted to serve in one of the western theater armies, not with the Army of the Potomac back east. It seemed the same bloody history that had earned the First such praise and honor was working against it in getting more men to join and fight the war to an end. The reputation of the Army of the Potomac, with its string of inept commanding generals so often causing slaughter and defeat, was no help either. From March 10 to April 15, Heffelfinger was able to recruit only nineteen new men for the First Minnesota, and none of the other recruiting officers was any more successful.[39]

Considering the three hard years of service they had endured, it was expecting a lot of the veterans to reenlist for more of the same. They must all have felt they were living on borrowed time since the charge at Gettysburg and the endless, freezing night of waiting for the morning assault at Mine Run. Perhaps the biggest barrier for the veterans was the knowledge that they would be commanded by Lieutenant Colonel Adams. After the regiment reassembled at Fort Snelling in mid-March, Corporal Edward A. Walker wrote to a friend, "Not many have reenlisted as yet, and but few of the old members will, having seen about service enough. Our Lieut. Colonel is very anxious to have us go in again, he being ambitious and deserving a star [brigadier general's commission], but the men don't like him, and 'can't see it.'"[40]

Adams had further earned the men's resentment by working to have each man mustered out from the date of his own enlistment rather than from the date that the regiment mustered in on April 29, 1861, as they had been told at the time. The First Minnesota had originally been mustered into service on that date as a "three-month regiment," but orders immediately came to muster out each man and remuster them for "three years or the war," which had become the new standard for enlistments. Many of the original three-month men did reenlist for three years, and by May 24, 1861, the regiment was filled by recruits to take the place of the others who did not.[41]

Corporal Walker had enlisted on May 21, 1861, and he gave this analysis of Adams's motives: "The Lieutenant Colonel's object is this, to hold the May men and get what few recruits he can and have *us all* ordered to the front once more where recruits will be sent on as fast as our time expires thus keeping the regiment in the field as a stepping stone for a Brigadier's Commission. All this may help crush the rebellion—but men, however patriotic, don't love to be fooled."[42]

Charles Powell Adams finally got his star, in the form of a brevet commission to brigadier general. Colonel Colvill also earned his brevet brigadier general commission for the action at Gettysburg.[43]

Ultimately, nothing could hold the old First Minnesota together as a unit. Fifty-nine men joined the regiment as recruits at various times during its three-year term, and these men were retained to finish their

Veterans of Company A posed in 1897 among the boulders where they made their stand in Plum Run's ravine. The photograph's handwritten caption reads: "Lying on the ground—and on the very spot where they were wounded in that immortal charge at Gettysburg, July 2/63." From left to right are William Nixon, Charles F. Hausdorf, William H. Dooley, Stephen Lyons, John G. Sonderman, Rascellas S. Mowry, Edward Z. Needham (of Company G), Henry C. Coates, Melvin Fuller, and Daniel Farquhar.

own three-year enlistments. Thirty-six of the original members of the First Minnesota reenlisted, and 140 hard-won recruits were mustered in. But this group of 235 officers and men was not enough to bring the First Minnesota Volunteer Infantry up to the required minimum to maintain the organization.[44]

Veterans of the regiment during the 1897 dedication of the First Minnesota monument at Gettysburg. The bronze infantryman is at charge bayonet position and moving at double-quick march.

A grand, final review was held at Fort Snelling on April 28, 1864, and the men of the regiment officially mustered out on May 3, 4, and 5. The 235 officers and men were formed into two companies designated Companies A and B of the First Battalion, Minnesota Volunteer Infantry, a separate organization from the original First Minnesota Volunteer Infantry. They would go on to fight the final, hellish year of the war in the trenches around Petersburg, Virginia, and be there for the surrender at Appomattox Court House.

Through various evolutions of decommissioning, re-forming, and recommissioning through the nineteenth and twentieth centuries, the unit returned to the status of state militia and eventually became the state's National Guard. Now spanning three centuries of service as the twenty-first century begins, today's Second Battalion (Mechanized) 135th Infantry of the Minnesota National Guard sees itself as the direct descendant of the First Minnesota Volunteer Infantry of 1861.[45]

Perhaps for the First Minnesota Volunteer Infantry, the simplest and most meaningful memorial can be found in the words of Orderly Sergeant Wright, Company F, relating the harrowing night of waiting before the expected charge at Mine Run. It exemplifies the best of these Minnesotans in their sense of duty and purpose to the cause of preserving the Union:

> I do know this: that every man of the company who had left the camp with us was there, in his place, and ready to do his whole duty—if it cost him his life. Through a merciful providence, manifesting itself through the discreation of General G. K. Warren, none of them were required to give that "last, full measure of devotion." Yet, it was a severe, long-continued test of the very finest qualities of soldiership—fortitude and endurance—and they bore themselves through it all with commendable readiness and steadiness. I recall no six hours in the history of the company, or the regiment, when held inactive, where it bore itself more creditably. There was no display of heroics; none of us wanted our names in the casualty list; we all wanted to go home with a full complement of legs and arms; but we were there to meet the requirements of the occasion, and were ready to do it, whatever it might cost.[46]

APPENDIX 1

A question of time

THE HISTORY OF WARFARE in the twentieth century tells us the precise time of Zero-Hour for the beginning of D-Day, with all of the commanders' watches synchronized. But warfare of the mid-nineteenth century gives us conflicting times for both major and minor events. Orders were not for assaults to begin at 0700 hours but more often "as early as practicable" or "at first light." Frequently various components of an assault would not enter the battle until they saw those around them starting across the field. The sweep second hand was not the signal, but rather it was a volley of musketry or the booming of an artillery battery.

In the agrarian society of the mid-nineteenth century, folks awoke when the rooster crowed, ate breakfast as the sun was rising, and started work when they could see. When the sun was directly overhead, they stopped and had a midday meal and then went back to work and continued until the darkness of twilight. Even the battles of the Civil War were usually fought in this "while there's light enough to see" manner, and, except on very rare occasions, the fighting ended as the daylight faded.

Most of the fighting on the second day of the battle of Gettysburg took place in the late afternoon and early evening. It is puzzling to read of a charge taking place at 6:30 or 7:00 P.M. on an early day in July and then see the phrase: "the sun was nearly setting." Even allowing for the extra hour of our modern daylight-saving time, the sun should have been up until 8:00 P.M. or later.

The discrepancy, of course, is in whose "time" is being used. Today's international time zones, set according to the Greenwich, England, meridian did not exist in 1863. At the moment of the Battle of Gettysburg, there was something of a jumble of different time zones and different ways of considering and "clocking" time.

In the context of measured, "by-the-clock" time, the average person of the mid-nineteenth century functioned on "local time"—"noon" being the time the sun was at its highest point in the sky overhead.[1] Traveling north or south along the same meridian did not alter one's sense of time significantly. A pocket watch set to local time in Fredericksburg, Virginia, would not have to be reset as one journeyed roughly due north to Gettysburg, Pennsylvania. Traveling even a short distance east or west would make the watch inaccurate by a few more minutes the farther one went.

During the upsurge of progress in industry, finance, and railroad building during the 1840s and 1850s, standard time of some kind became increasingly important. There had to be some common time "currency" for distant financial transactions, for travelers making train connections, and for safety, as many railroads shared the use of large sections of track. By 1851 all railroads in New England were receiving daily telegraphic time signals from Boston and synchronizing station clocks and conductors' and engineers' watches to it. This was the first instance of an established time zone in the United States.[2] While other local and regional time zones appeared, nationwide time zones were not established until railroads in the United States and Canada adopted them in 1883. An international conference in Washington, D.C., led to the implementation of a worldwide standard—our current twenty-four time zones based on the prime, or zero, meridian at the Royal Observatory in Greenwich, England.[3]

In weighing the accuracy of any reference to time during the Battle of Gettysburg, many things must be considered. First, is it from a letter, journal entry, or battle report written shortly after the battle or years afterward in a reminiscence? Did the individual carry a watch, or was he relying on someone else's estimate or watch? In the heat of battle, what was the likelihood that the individual even had the time to consult his watch? If he had a watch, was it set to Gettysburg local time, to his home town's time, to the area's railroad time, or to the local time of the last place he camped?

Considering the passage of nearly 140 years since the battle, the imprecise nature of timekeeping at that point in history, and the general chaos of the battle itself, we can deal only in approximations of times during the battle. It is not surprising that individuals, sometimes in the same unit, gave differing times for a particular event. Some of these demonstrate several hours discrepancy. The text and notes cite the specific sources used by the author to explain his theory, or lack thereof, for the time of any given event or order of events.

APPENDIX 2

The tools of death

THE CIVIL WAR occurred during a period of transition in weaponry, and the war accelerated the process. Unfortunately for the soldier, tactical planning and the strategy of battle evolved at a slower pace. The fearfully high casualties during Civil War battles were the result of combining conventional methods of engaging the enemy with advanced weapons technology. Tactics evolved as the war progressed, but massed formations of men charging a defended enemy position, as in Pickett's Charge, remained common throughout the Civil War. The effect and outcome of these massed charges were much different with the more accurate weapons of the 1860s.[1]

The utilization of massed formations of fighting men dates back to the armies of Philip of Macedonia. The sheer weight of masses of men sent against an enemy position forces the other army from the field; they cannot kill or disable enough of the solidly deployed ranks to halt the advance and so must give way. The invention of firearms intensified the action without changing the tactics significantly. The early smoothbore weapons were loaded down the muzzle and fired a single round shot. While the smoothbore weapon was not much more accurate than hurling a brick at the enemy, its range was greater.

The military manuals had formulas for how much ground a body of troops could cover at a given rate of march, or charge, and how many times the enemy could load and fire in that time. Theoretically, the commanders of either side could almost figure out the winner of an engagement before the charge started. The first and sometimes second rank of troops might seriously be depleted by the time they arrived at the enemy position, but the supporting waves behind might make it almost intact. Hand-to-hand combat with fixed bayonets should in theory decide the winner.

A widely used weapon in the Mexican War of 1846–48 was the smoothbore flintlock. More modern weapons were available and coming into use at the time, but the flintlock was still routine issue in the armies of both the U.S. and Mexico. The firing system for this weapon was cumbersome and faulty. A hinged L-shaped piece of metal, called the frizzen, had to be pushed forward, exposing the flashpan. Gunpowder was poured into the flashpan and the frizzen pulled back down to cover it. The hammer of the flintlock was a small vise holding a piece of flint. When the hammer was cocked and the trigger pulled, the flint struck the upright face of the frizzen, flipped the frizzen forward and open, and threw a shower of sparks into the gunpowder in the flashpan. If everything worked as expected, the powder in the flashpan would flare up and jet down the touchhole of the barrel, which set off the powder charge in the barrel that actually propelled the lead musket ball.

By the early 1850s, the U.S. Army standard issue was a weapon with the modern and far more reliable percussion lock. In place of the flint, steel frizzen, and flashpan, the percussion rifle had a small metal nipple that was vented into the barrel where the powder charge was loaded. A small copper percussion cap, which looked somewhat like a miniature top hat with explosive matter inside, was placed over this nipple. The hammer had a small indention that smashed down and covered the nipple when it was cocked back and the trigger was pulled.

More important additions to this new weapon were rifling, a series of spiraling grooves cut into the bore of the barrel, and the introduction of the conical bullet in place of a round ball. When the weapon was fired, the projectile immediately expanded into the rifling and left the muzzle spinning, not unlike the way a football player puts a spin on the football he throws. The spinning conical-shaped bullet had greater distance because wind resistance was reduced by the shape and had much greater accuracy because the spinning kept it on its trajectory.

An experienced Civil War soldier could load and fire his weapon three times in a minute. Instead of being lucky to hit anything beyond a few hundred feet away, like his flintlock-armed Mexican War counterpart, he could bring down a man with a well-aimed shot at 250 to 300 yards. The bullet could still wound or kill a man at 600 to 800 yards. A sniper with a steady aim and a telescopic sight could drop a man at 1,000 yards.

In the rush to arm so many men so quickly, both the Union army and the Confederate army had to make do with an incredible hodgepodge of weaponry, particularly at the beginning of the war. Some Confederate soldiers fought with flintlocks in early months, and, in both armies, many flintlocks were converted to percussion locks and their barrels were rebored with rifling. In some instances, rifled tubes were inserted in the smoothbores, rather than reboring the weapon.

Usually some effort was made to provide weapons of the same caliber for any given regiment. Caliber is a measurement of the diameter of the bore of a weapon, measured in 1/100 of an inch. Uniformity made it easier to supply the units with ammunition.

The standard issue rifle-musket for the Union forces was the U.S. Rifle-Musket, Model 1861. It was known universally as the Springfield, named for the Springfield Arsenal where it originated, although nearly seven hundred thousand were also manufactured during the war by private contractors both domestically and in Europe. The Springfield was .58 caliber and fired the conical bullet developed by the French Colonel Claude Minié—known universally by Civil War soldiers as the minié ball. The .58 caliber minié ball weighed just over an ounce. As a result of the spin of this heavy bullet and the relatively low muzzle velocity, a buzzy kind of hum was created when one passed by a man's ear. They came to be nicknamed "bumblebees" by the soldiers.

There were also other models of muzzle loaders that were .69 caliber, which means the ball or bullet was nearly three-quarters of an inch in diameter. The .69 caliber minié ball is about the size of the top joint of an average-size male thumb.

The First Minnesota faced a wide variety of weaponry in the hands of the Confederates. Because of the lack of weapon and munitions factories in the South, the Confederacy scrambled to arm itself at the beginning of the war. As many weapons as possible were confiscated from U.S. arsenals, and the machinery for producing rifles was removed from the U.S. Arsenal at Harpers Ferry, Virginia. The machinery was sent to Richmond, Virginia, the Confederate capital, where it produced hundreds of thousands of rifle-muskets during the war.

As the Union blockade of southern ports grew tighter, the South depended more and more on weapons captured from the Union army. Some shipments from blockade runners occasionally made it through with loads of British Enfield rifles. These were very similar to the American Springfield, and though they were a slightly smaller caliber, .577, they could use the .58 caliber minié ball.

For the smoothbore weapon, the ammunition was often the "buck-and-ball" load, which was three round buckshot nested on top of a lead ball the same caliber as the weapon, usually the larger .69 caliber muskets. While it was not accurate at long range, the load gave the soldier four times the chance of hitting something with every shot.

The innovations in the machines of death in the period just before and during the Civil War were staggering. The hand-cranked Gatling gun, the first machine gun, was introduced in 1862. The Henry rifle, the forerunner of the famous Winchester repeating rifle of Old West fame, was invented in 1860. It held sixteen rounds of brass cartridges, similar to today's ammunition, in an inner chamber or magazine. Working the lever underneath the rifle would eject the spent cartridge, load the next one, and cock the hammer all in one down-and-up movement. The Spencer rifle held seven brass cartridges in a magazine inside the stock and was referred to by the rebels as "that damn Yankee gun you load on Sunday and fire all week." The Sharps rifle was single shot but used waxed linen or paper cartridges and loaded at the breech.

None of these weapons was in widespread use, especially among the infantry regiments. The Sharps and Spencer, and to a lesser extent the Henry, became common among the Union cavalry late in the war, most of them using the shorter carbine model, which was easier to handle on horseback.

Lincoln's War Department—unlike today's Defense Department—was reluctant to accept the new and innovative weapons. It was felt that the soldiers "wasted" enough ammunition as it was, and giving them easy to load repeating weapons would just allow them to waste more. Waste was a valid concern, however, since resupply of an army in the field always was dependent on the condition of dirt roads and was implemented with wagons and draft animals.

The artillery of the time was similar in design to the shoulder weapons: some innovative pieces, a few that loaded at the breech, but for the most part muzzle loaders. Most Union artillery batteries consisted of six cannon, and Confederate batteries had four cannon. The Union batteries were usually all the same type of cannon; the Confederate batteries were often a mixture of odds and ends.

Artillery was classified in four broad categories: mortars, rifles, howitzers, and guns. Mortars were short, squat tubes that lobbed solid cannonballs and exploding shells up and over the walls of forts or earthworks on an arching trajectory. Rifles had rifling like the shoulder weapons of the infantry, putting a spin on their conical projectiles that gave them long range and tremendous accuracy. One of the prized rifles of the time was the British Whitworth. Some Whitworths loaded at the breech like modern field artillery and fired an elongated solid iron projectile called a bolt, in addition to firing exploding shells. The rebel army had two breech-loading Whitworths at Gettysburg.

Howitzers were basically like smoothbore cannon except they often had a smaller chamber just behind the main chamber of the bore, which held the powder charge. Their trajectory arched more than the flat trajectory of a regular cannon, although not as elevated as that of the mortars. Artillery size designation usually depended on whether the piece was a smoothbore gun or a rifle.

Rifles generally were measured by the diameter of the bore, hence the designation as a three-inch rifle or an eight-inch rifle. Smoothbores commonly were designated by the weight of a round solid-shot projectile sized to fit the bore, as in the twelve-pound mountain howitzer. The gun could also be identified more generally as a twelve-pounder.

The real workhorse of the field artillery for both Union and Confederate armies was the twelve-pounder Napoleon, named after Emperor Napoleon III of France, where it was developed. Officially the gun was known as the Light Twelve-Pounder Gun-Howitzer, light indicating that it was designed to travel and fight with the infantry. This reliable and adaptable cannon was a standard smoothbore muzzle-loader with a bronze tube—as cannon barrels were called—that was always kept brightly polished. It fired a variety of projectiles and was accurate for use in general battle conditions, even at fairly long ranges.

The Napoleon fired four kinds of projectiles, the first three of which are representative of what other artillery fired. First was the standard solid-shot—the classic round black iron cannonball. These mainly were employed for pounding fortifications but were also extremely effective for counterbattery fire and for breaking up oncoming troop formations. Not surprisingly, they caused severe distress among men subjected to their bouncing and ricocheting within their ranks. They had a relatively low muzzle velocity that often allowed a man to see a solid-shot flying through the air at him, but he could not always react in time to get out of its path. If the solid-shot was airborne, it had the ability to cut through a column of ten men before it stopped.

Another projectile was the common shell. This was a cannonball that was cast with a cavity inside filled with gun powder and a fuse inserted into it. One type of fuse was paper inserted in a hole in the ball. The paper fuses were marked with lines that told the gunner how long to cut it to allow for a specific number of seconds before the shell would explode. In theory, the powder charge inside the cannon would ignite the paper fuse as it was blown out of the tube. A more common fuse used by the federal artillery was the Borman fuse, a more reliable device that the gunner screwed into the shell and then set for a specific detonation time. The gunner used a special tool to punch a hole in the soft lead top of the fuse, exposing a powder trail at a preselected number that designated the seconds until the shell exploded.

The fuses of the period were not entirely reliable, and it was not uncommon for the shell to explode inside the tube or just as it left the muzzle, particularly with the poor quality Confederate ammunition. This explains the shells exploding in the air in all of the Civil War battle lithographs and paintings. When they exploded as planned, the casing of the ball ruptured, and the fragments would shower down and forward on the enemy troops.

A third projectile was spherical case shot, also called shrapnel, after the British artillery officer, Captain Henry Shrapnel. Spherical case was like a shell but was more effective at killing and maiming because the cavity was packed with lead or iron balls in addition to the powder charge. The balls as well as the fragments of the shell casing would rip through the enemy troops.

The fourth projectile was devastatingly deadly at close range. There were two variations of it, one called grapeshot and the other canister shot. Grapeshot was a pile of small iron balls held between two or more metal plates, the plates joined by a rod through the center, referred to as a stand of grape. Grapeshot had been around as military ordnance for a good many years. It was mainly used by the navy but saw some field artillery use, especially during the first years of the war. Many soldiers referred to grapeshot flying around the battlefield in their letters and journals even long after it ceased actually being used by the land armies.

Canister shot was a lightweight tin can packed with cast iron or lead balls. The size and number of balls depended on which artillery piece was firing it. The Napoleon's canister round had twenty-seven balls one and a half inches in diameter. The can would tear apart as it left the muzzle and spray the balls among the oncoming troops, turning the cannon into a giant shotgun. It was not unusual during a particularly ferocious enemy charge, for the cannoneers to load double canister— two of the cans in one shot. A battery firing canister could chop down entire ranks of charging troops at between two and three hundred yards.

Unlike the smokeless powder of today, which is light gray in color, the weapons of the Civil War used black powder. This propellant produced a tremendous amount of thick, white smoke when ignited. Under the best of conditions, a battle, in the eyes of the combatants, is an exercise in terror and utter chaos. The element of being literally blinded by huge clouds and curtains of dense smoke, which quickly enshrouded the battlefields, was a major part of the combat experience of the Civil War soldier. The smoke left a pungent, acrid smell of burned sulfur in the air, clothing, and hair. The noise was deafening, and more often than not the men could not hear shouted orders from their officers. Drums and bugles were used to relay commands on the battlefield, various orders having a different drum beat or roll or bugle call, but even these could usually not be heard or distinguished from more than a few feet away. The men were often left to advance, hold on, or retreat depending on their nerve and what the men on either side of them were doing.

The men loaded their muskets by tearing off the end of the paper cartridges with their teeth, pouring the powder down the barrel, and then ramming home the minié ball with the ramrod. The weapon was then primed by half-cocking the hammer, removing the remnants of the used percussion cap, and placing a new percussion cap on the nipple. The hammer was then pulled back into full-cocked position, and the rifle-musket was brought to the shoulder to be aimed and discharged with a pull of the trigger.

The process of tearing paper cartridges open with the teeth caused each soldier quickly to have a distinctive black smear down the right corner of his mouth. The powder smoke would leave an oily, black film over exposed, sweaty skin. Appropriate to the work they were doing and the rank smell of burning sulfur, the men quickly took on a hellish appearance.

History has shown that any entity as large, well-established, and steeped in tradition as the military is slow to change. But the scope of the American Civil War brought change, out of necessity, to arms, tactics, and the logistics of warfare. Innovation in the tools of death was coming along in any case; the war merely accelerated the pace. If the Civil War had come five or ten years later, the universal use of rapidly loading and firing weapons would have made the casualty totals even more horrendous. Tactics eventually changed with increase in firepower and accuracy. Massed assaults, with their enormous loss of life, were still occasionally and foolishly employed but eventually gave way to both armies settling in to siege and trench warfare. It was a foreshadowing of the brutal, protracted misery of stalemate and attrition in World War I, forty-nine years later.

APPENDIX 3

The mythology of the First Minnesota

MYTHOLOGY IS ENDEMIC to the human condition. There is, of course, the classic mythology of Greece and Rome, but every culture has its mythologies and a very real need to have and maintain them. A culture's mythology can explain the unexplainable or embellish the remarkable. It can pass along the values and expectations of a society, generation to generation. It can also give meaning and order to bewildering events, loss, and chaos, making the unbearable bearable. Dr. Bruce Lincoln, a former professor of humanities and religious studies at the University of Minnesota, wrote:

> The authority of myth is somewhat akin to that of charters, models, templates, and blueprints, but one can go beyond this formulation and recognize that it is also (and perhaps more important) akin to that of revolutionary slogans and ancestral invocations, in that through the recitation of myth one may effectively mobilize a social grouping. Thus, myth is not just a coding device in which important information is conveyed, on the basis of which actors can then construct society. It is also a discursive act through which actors evoke the sentiments out of which society is actively constructed.[1]

As Professor Lincoln pointed out, mythmaking, and the passing on of a culture's myths, are emotional acts — they "evoke the sentiments" that construct and maintain a society's values. Second, perhaps, only to a culture's creation mythology is its war/hero mythology. It establishes the ethos of sacrifice for the greater good; it helps to establish and maintain the ideology of the group. It sets the standard for courage that enables the individual—or individual within the group—to withstand the trial, to endure, and to die if needed for the greater good of the society and its values.

As psychiatrist Dr. R. William Betcher and psychologist Dr. William R. Pollack expressed it: "Even the defeated warrior can achieve greatness, for if he fought without cowardice he, no less than his conqueror, has placed honor above death. Indeed, the fallen hero may be especially honored—he has defied his fate at the hands of a superior foe, and also basks in the reflected glory of his conqueror."[2]

Throughout history most cultures have embraced the entire process of war, death, and destruction as both repugnant and somehow necessary and unavoidable. If it is not outright conquest—to maintain and expand one's own society or defeat and "tame" some "savage" society—it is fighting to defend one's own country, society, and culture. This was the mindset of both sides in the American Civil War.

The North was trying to maintain the Union and its vision of what the Founding Fathers established and intended, and they had to defeat the rebellious, arrogant, slave-holding southern aristocracy to do it. The South saw itself as parting from a freely entered confederation, since their vision of the Founding Fathers had been appropriated and perverted by the dominant, industrial North. They wanted to go their own way and only fought because the federal government of the United States invaded their new Confederate States of America.

But any war, especially a civil war, requires that a society draw heavily on its shared mythologies to maintain its cause and to enable it to endure. As sociologist Dr. James A. Aho noted: "The intentional destruction of human beings always contains the potentiality to devastate mankind's fragile cultural creations and thrust him into total darkness. And yet, killing and dying, particularly when done 'well,' when done courageously in the name of an ethical principle, are among man's most convincing witnesses to the facticity and solidity of social order. In the sacrifice of the warrior, the reality of society is symbolically cleansed of any taint of chaos and its members are persuaded of its immortality."[3]

The line between fact, embellished fact, and mythology is probably a product of time as much as anything else. In the case of the First Minnesota, the immensity of what they faced and their loss at Gettysburg is not in question, but the circumstances and scope of it grew and became part of the mythology of the regiment. The diminished number involved in the charge and the inflated casualties were established by William Fox in 1889, based on miscalculation on his part. These figures readily were picked up by William Lochren, Fox's book having been published while Lochren was gathering information for his regimental history of the First Minnesota.

This was a godsend to Lochren. His letters to other veterans of the regiment, and their responses, indicate they were all scouring their memories, personal records, and diaries to try and calculate the number of men in the charge and the number wounded or killed in it. The actual casualty lists were quite difficult to access at that time because the government was in the process of compiling the massive 127-volume Official Records of the War of the Rebellion series. All records were horded in Washington, D.C., until the series was written.

Lochren's job was made easier, and the numbers given legitimacy, by the fact that Fox was a prominent historian and Civil War veteran himself (who had fought at Gettysburg). It was the word of a respected individual with no direct investment in fabricating numbers for the First Minnesota or in saying, "The greatest regimental loss in any battle, in proportion to the number engaged, occurred in the ranks of the First Minnesota, at Gettysburg," unless he felt it was true. Prior to the publication of Lochren's regimental history in 1890, the number participating in the charge was consistently estimated, or said to be, greater than 262 men. After that historians and others consistently cited the Fox–Lochren figures; they became codified and a keystone of the regimental mythology.

The First Minnesota was ripe for glorification and mythologizing. It was one of the few regiments from a western state in an army predominantly made up of regiments from the East and New England. While the Minnesotans were all natives of other states, or immigrants, they comprised the only Minnesota regiment in the Army of the Potomac and represented the state farthest west of any in the army. They were not only known to be hard fighters and excellent soldiers but also carried the ethos of hardy, adventuresome, pioneer stock with them.

Their reputation was established with the earliest major battle of the war—Bull Run—when the First held its position in an open field under withering fire. Despite a 20 percent casualty rate for the regiment of new soldiers, they did not withdraw until ordered, and the Minnesotans received special commendation in the reports of both their brigade and division commanders.[4] At Antietam, fourteen months later, they likewise held and made an orderly withdrawal while much of their division was routed by a massive flank attack by Stonewall Jackson's rebels.

At Fredericksburg, in December 1862, they occupied hastily dug rifle pits on the open fields in front of the Confederate position. Enfilading rebel artillery fire drove other units out of the pits, but the First Minnesota held on. Observing this, division commander General Oliver O. Howard commented to the regiment's brigade commander (and former regimental colonel) General Alfred Sully, "Sully, your First Minnesota doesn't run," to which General Sully replied, "General, the First Minnesota never runs."[5]

The Confederates even displayed a grudging respect for the First Minnesota and its division after Gettysburg. The rebels fighting the Minnesotans at Bristoe Station in October 1863 were some of those who had participated in Pickett's Charge three months before. As rebel prisoners were gathered after the battle, they saw the white trefoil division insignia on the hats and uniform blouses of the federal soldiers and exclaimed, "Here's those damned white clubs again."[6]

It is not unusual to read contemporary statements about the regiment similar to Lieutenant Frank Haskell's, written several weeks after the Battle of Gettysburg. Telling of his directing Harrow's brigade to the right to staunch the rebel penetration at the Angle during Pickett's Charge, Haskell wrote, "The 19th Maine, the 15th Massachusetts, the 32nd New York [*sic;* 82nd N.Y.], and the shattered old thunderbolt, the 1st Minnesota—poor Farrell was dying then upon the ground where he had fallen,—all men that I could find I took over at the double quick."[7] Likewise, in a letter to Governor Henry Swift of Minnesota, Lieutenant Colonel William G. LeDuc, chief quartermaster of the Eleventh Corps, wrote glowingly of the regiment. Trying to convince Governor Swift not to allow the Minnesotans buried on the battlefield to be removed to other graves, LeDuc wrote:

> There where the 1st Regiment not only of Minnesota but of the world was ground to powder—but the enemy was turned to flight—There when the "glorious first" (so long the exemplar and boast of the whole Army of the Potomac) went down and was extinguished, but as ever, triumphant. There on the western slope of Gettysburg should be their resting place. Altho I have not the coveted honor of a place on their muster rolls yet I have served with them, always in the same army, for a long time in the same division, and through all the vicesitudes of the army of the Potomac; they were my countrymen, my comrades and many of them my friends. I beg of you use your influence to prevent any illconsidered or unwise action. We should not think of this as of momentary gratification, but of its appropriateness for all time.[8]

This reputation, coupled with the suicide charge at Gettysburg, is the stuff of legend and mythology even by today's standards. During the war and throughout the nineteenth and early twentieth centuries, the men and the regiment as a unit were held up as paradigms of heroic sacrifice for the "holy" cause of preserving the Union. One of the earliest profile pieces on the regiment after Gettysburg was written on July 7 and appeared in the *New York Tribune* on July 10, 1863. Correspondent Charles Anderson Page felt "induced" to give the reader a "brief sketch" of the regiment because of the Lieutenant Edgar Sproat letter (see Chapter 9) of July 4, which was published for the first time in Anderson's story.

The article gave a capsule biography of the regiment, indicating the regiment's losses at the First Battle of Bull Run "exceeded that of any other regiment" and declaring that their former corps commander, Edwin V. Sumner, "was in the habit of coupling it with the 8th Illinois Cavalry and pronouncing them the best infantry and cavalry regiments, respectively, in the service." After mentioning an inflated number in the original muster, as well as an inflated addition of recruits up to that time, Page stated the regiment "has been in twenty-one battles, (and) has literally fought itself down to less than 100 men."[9] While that number, armed and equipped and in the ranks, might have been briefly true, it reads like hyperbole and budding mythology: an inflated number of original members, and recruits, and the implication that all but a hundred have been killed in battle since the beginning of the war. Detailed computations made by a committee of veterans of the First Minnesota in 1898 showed 1,242 men—original members and recruits—served with the regiment. The mortality rate was calculated at 18.13 percent: 14.15 percent killed in battle and 3.9 percent dying by disease or by accidents.[10]

The *Stillwater Messenger* of July 14, 1863, published a July 9 letter from the former lieutenant colonel of the regiment, and future Minnesota governor, Stephen Miller. Miller's love of and devotion to the regiment is understandable, but he spoke for most Minnesotans when he wrote, "In addition to resolutions commemorating the honored dead, and condoling with the many surviving sufferers, would it not be well to inaugurate an association for the erection of a suitable monument in St. Paul or vicinity upon which to inscribe the names of the fallen heroes, of the now immortal Minnesota First?"[11] Miller's use of "heroes," "fallen heroes," and "immortal" is the earliest use of the terminology that was forever after tied to the First Minnesota Volunteer Infantry.

The "scrappy" nature of the Minnesotans received an early airing in a July 6, 1863, *New York Times* piece by correspondent Samuel Wilkeson. The long story, headlined "Details from Our Special Correspondent" and datelined "Headquarters Army of the Potomac, Saturday Night, July 4," gave his eyewitness description of the battle and human-interest incidents during and after. He also include a casualty list of officers of various units, which incorporated the information that all the field officers of the First Minnesota were wounded and that Lieutenant Colonel Charles Powell Adams was mortally wounded (which proved not to be true). The wounding and subsequent death of Captain Wilson Farrell was also mentioned.

Of particular interest was a short passage about Corporal Anson R. Hayden of Company I. Hayden either sought out the reporter, or the story was circulating and Wilkeson checked into it and inserted the somewhat dubious bit of heroism: "Corp. Hayden of the First Minnesota, was captured—escaped, seized a musket and seized a rare opportunity, and actually made ten Rebels surrender. While marching them to Gen. Gibbon's quarters, a rebel behind a tree on the way drew a bead on him with his rifle. Hayden saw him in time to bring his piece to a level, and cry out, 'Surrender.' The fellow actually threw his gun and joined the cavalcade, and Hayden came in with eleven captives."[12]

There were no Minnesotans taken prisoner at Gettysburg. The only real opportunity for this story to have happened, however unlikely, would have been at dusk on July 2 as the Confederates were withdrawing and the federal troops were falling back to Cemetery Ridge and collecting rebel prisoners. Perhaps a clutch of rebel soldiers isolated Hayden along Plum Run and started to march him back as a prisoner. However, the rebels would have all been armed and it seems unlikely, even had Hayden slipped away from his captors and picked up a rifle, that ten armed rebel soldiers would simply drop their weapons and surrender to him, let alone an eleventh—behind a tree, no less—drop his rifle and surrender.

Hayden's Company I was the second company from the left in the regiment during the charge and the stand on Plum Run. The other accounts of the fighting on the left of the regiment indicate that this portion of the First Minnesota probably never came within direct, hand-to-hand combat distance of the rebels. It seems unlikely Hayden could have been isolated, captured, and marched back as a prisoner of the rebels.

If this episode did happen, perhaps Hayden took part in rounding up the isolated three to four hundred rebels who had been cut off from retreat on the regiment's right, and he was embellishing. These Confederates, bunched up between the First Minnesota and the Nineteenth Maine, were gathered by the Minnesotans, Mainers, and rallied members of the Third Corps. They were fought out and knew they were cut off from retreat, so it is not totally beyond belief that eleven of them dropped their muskets when covered by a federal soldier with a single-shot musket. This area was also lightly timbered, so there was a tree or two for a rebel soldier to have stood behind to "draw a bead" on the Minnesotan. Hayden might have had only one shot, but one can imagine that each of the exhausted rebels did not want to be the one to receive it, and there were plenty of other armed federal soldiers nearby gathering prisoners.

It is hard today to sit in judgment over the line between reality and hyperbole in early missives from the regiment. To the men, having participated in the Battle of Gettysburg and seeing the aftermath, it probably did not seem an exaggeration to write, as Lieutenant Edgar Sproat did, "The 1st Minnesota is gone."[13] His next sentence belies this with, "But 87, officers and men, [are] left out of 220 that went into the fight." The devastation was very real, but Sproat's figures do not account for the many on detached service, nor the fact that some were not badly wounded and rejoined the ranks in the coming weeks. The regiment was hardly "gone."

Likewise, regimental quartermaster Francis Baasen's letter, dated July 3, 1863, indulged in heroic imagery: "Every man without exception, had his clothing riddled—some of them all to rags."[14] As quartermaster, Baasen was the one requisitioning and keeping records for uniforms and equipment, so he would know the men's needs and condition of their uniforms. However, the hard march to the Gettysburg battlefield had taken a toll not only on the men's physical condition, but on shoe leather and uniforms as well. Undoubtedly, given the amount of close-range lead being hurled at the eight companies fighting along Plum Run, there was bound to be a great deal of damage done to hats, forage caps, loose-hanging sleeves, and trouser legs. But who today can say what was wear-and-tear of hard use and what was "bullet-riddled." Baasen did, however, give a more accurate picture of those still on their feet, stating, "about one-hundred fifty men are left for duty."

Independent praise of the regiment continued in the days following Gettysburg. A September 1, 1863, letter was published in the September 9 issue of the *Saint Paul Daily Press*. The writer, identified only as "a lady" who wrote the letter to a relative in St. Paul, was in Brooklyn and visited and observed the First Minnesota in their Washington Park, then called Fort Greene, camp. She wrote, in part:

> Do you know that the remnant of the glorious old Minnesota First is now encamped here at Fort Greene in Brooklyn? . . . A great deal of enthusiasm is manifested and great respect paid to the war-worn veterans.
>
> Yesterday I went over with Mr. H. and paid the Minnesotians a visit. I happened to reach the ground just as the bugle call was sounding for the evening parade. Captain Coates was in command. No company numbered more than twenty men, and one mustered only five. The regiment counts up 230, but some of them are on duty in Washington, where the draft is now going on.

As I saw this little fragment of the once splendid Minnesota First march by me, carrying their stained and tattered flag, scarcely a shred of which is left, except the design close by the staff, and take their places in line of battle just as they stood on that bright morning more than two years ago at Fort Snelling, when so many of us were there and heard General Gorman's last directions and Mr. Neil's prayer—previous to their breaking camp and embarking for the war, and their glorious destiny, I absolutely shivered with emotion. There the brave fellows stood, a grand shadow of the regiment which Fort Snelling knew. Their bronzed faces looked so composed and serious. There was a history written on every one of them. I never felt so much like falling down and doing reverence to any living men. The music of the band, as the men went steadily through the changes of the drill was very sweet, but it seemed to me all the while like a dirge for the fallen.[15]

The New York City and Brooklyn newspapers had many New York heroes of their own to write about, but they took several column inches to single out the First Minnesota during its brief stay in Brooklyn. The Sunday, September 3, 1863, *New York Herald* ran a profile piece on the regiment, giving a battle history and a list of officers and past colonels and mentioning that the recent battle at Gettysburg claimed "224 men out of 315, with which they entered the fight."[16] With more than a bit of jingoistic pride, the *Brooklyn Daily Eagle* noted that the regiments stationed in the New York area were "all veterans—men who have passed through many battles and have borne the old flag proudly, through reverses which would have made an army of any other nation dissolve into its original elements." In a nod of respect to another region of the Union, the story went on to say, "The regiments are mainly from the West, and Western soldiers have always given good account of themselves. They have very few defeats to regret, but many victories to be justly proud of."[17] In a story mentioning the troops stationed through-out Brooklyn's various wards, the First Minnesota was highlighted with, "The headquarters are guarded efficiently by two companies, C and D, of the First Minnesota Volunteers under charge of Captain Heffelfinger, whose services in Virginia with one of Minnesota's most gallant regiments we have before now chronicled in these columns."[18]

Whatever accolades the regiment was garnering on a national scale, the true pride, love, and devotion were at home in Minnesota. Being the premier regiment of the young state, the regiment was raised, praised, and glorified with a level of enthusiasm the other Minnesota regiments were never accorded. The severe test at Gettysburg, and the regiment's performance there, solidified their place in the hearts and history of their state.

Upon the regiment's arrival back in St. Paul in the winter of 1864, the men were lavishly feted and toasted. The mayor's speech, even allowing for the florid, mid-nineteenth-century prose and hyperbole, is a good indication of what these hard-used veterans meant to the people of Minnesota.

> Soldiers of the Minnesota First—the regiment offered to the country in its hour of need, consecrated with the blood of more than twenty battles and the loss of more men than composed its original number—it is with the most heartfelt pleasure that I welcome you to the hospitalities of St. Paul.
>
> By your bravery, your sufferings and your patriotic sacrifices in the cause of our common country, you have won yourselves an imperishable renown. You have reflected glory upon your State, and have earned the gratitude of its citizens as a permanent legacy for your wives and children.

The mayor then plunged into territory more appropriate for returning warriors of ancient Greece or Rome: a near offering of the grateful country's "daughters" to the loins of the heroes.

> And those of you who have neither wives nor children to love and pray for you while fighting for the unity and immortality of your country, I can assure you that should you survive the perils of the war, and witness again the starry banner of freedom floating in all its beauty on every part of our beloved land, 'not a stripe erased, not a star obscured,' the fairest and loveliest daughters of America will take your hands with pride and give you their hearts with joy. It matters not how battered you may be, though you may have lost an arm, or a leg, or an eye. Your very disfigurements will but increase their admiration, and your scars will be looked upon as badges of nobility!

Then he returned to a reverent supplication of the citizenry to the warriors and the cause:

> We rejoice to see you among us! We bow our heads in reverence, as we behold your stalwart forms and call to mind the terrible scenes through which you have passed.

You have come forth from the fiery furnace, pure gold, tried and purified. But still you have determined, with a nobleness of purpose that has never been surpassed, to devote yourselves again, of your own free will, to the rescue of our own imperiled country. It is this fact, so grand, so disinterested, so patriotic, that fills our hearts with a kind of awe, and opens them to you as we would open them to a returning brother or cherished friend. And I look upon you with this thought in my mind, it seems to me as if each one of you had a crown upon his brow and a scepter in his hand.

You are the true kings! The people's kings, and when this war shall have ended, as end it will, the control of civil affairs will be committed to your hands. You will be the saviours of the country.[19]

This mayoral prediction proved true, both in Minnesota and the country as a whole. State legislatures, the Congress, state and the federal executive branches, as well as the judiciary were filled with Civil War veterans throughout the nineteenth and early twentieth centuries. This was not a surprising outcome, given the enormous number of men who served in uniform in the Civil War and the level of respect and deference given to them. Some went into uniform from successful political careers, but the war itself made successes of many others, not least of whom was Ulysses S. Grant—a failure at everything in civilian life until he found his niche as a winning Union general. It would lead to two terms for him as president of the United States.

The glory of the First Minnesota was always kept well polished during the remainder of the nineteenth and into the twentieth century. In 1903 a monument was placed in St. Paul's Summit Park to all Minnesotans who served in the federal armies and navies during the Civil War. The granite pillar monument is surmounted by a bronze statue of Josias Redgate King, embraced as the first man to volunteer for the First Minnesota Volunteer Infantry. In 1905, when the colors of all the Minnesota Civil War regiments were moved from the old Capitol to the new one, the First Minnesota and its veterans had the place of honor at the front of the parade. To this day, one of the regiment's colors and the spliced flagstaff from Gettysburg are the only items to have their own glass display case in the Capitol rotunda.

One of the best examples of the state's response to the First Minnesota was the honor and near reverence bestowed on Colonel (and

Brevet Brigadier General) William Colvill after Gettysburg, throughout his lifetime and after his death. Colvill was the fifth and last in a line of brave and able colonels to command the regiment. Having come into command two months before Gettysburg and not able to take active field command after the battle before the regiment was mustered out of service, he remained in everyone's hearts and minds as the colonel of the regiment.

As Gettysburg codified a place in history for the regiment, so it did for Colvill. In 1928—twenty-three years after his death—his gravesite in Cannon Falls, Minnesota, was memorialized. An all-day dedication program was highlighted by a speech by President Calvin Coolidge, with the unveiling of an appropriately larger-than-life bronze statue of Colvill atop a stone pedestal. It is a companion bronze to the Colvill statue dedicated in 1909 on the upper level of the Capitol rotunda in St. Paul. The feelings for Colvill and the First Minnesota, as late as 1928, can be summed up in this passage from the Cannon Falls dedication program: "The heroic charge of the already decimated regiment is credited with saving the Union Army from defeat and thus making possible a Union victory on the following day. In the final analysis, Col. Colvill, perhaps, saved not only the Union Army and the day at Gettysburg, but turned back 'the high tide of the Confederacy' and saved the Union."[20]

Periodically the regiment's place in history was bolstered and the mythology enhanced in state newspapers when there was a major reunion of the regiment. The biggest events, though, were the dedication of the regiment's Gettysburg monument in July 1897 and the fiftieth anniversary of the Battle of Gettysburg in July of 1913.

In keeping with the scope of the regiment's sacrifice at Gettysburg, comparisons constantly were made to other famous, and some not-so-famous, charges and stands against a greater enemy force throughout history. The earliest, and certainly the most popular comparison throughout the nineteenth and early twentieth centuries, was the charge of the British Light Brigade in the Crimean War. The annihilation of the Three Hundred Spartans at the Thermopylae Pass was also a favorite.

But many famous, and some arcane, battles from all over the world and throughout history were culled for dramatic comparison in newspaper articles and speeches. The "unknown sergeant" who wrote the long, detailed, and quite literate letter to the *Saint Paul Pioneer,* published on August 9, 1863, calls up the Light Brigade, a snippet of poetry to the "veterans of Fontenoy," the "Old Guard at Waterloo," and says of the First Minnesota's charge, "It reads like the legend of 'Chevy Chase.'"[21] In time, the First Minnesota acquired a good number of "heroic" poems penned to honor its exploits at Gettysburg.

For the most part, the interviews with officers and men of the First Minnesota stuck to the facts of the regiment having charged into a Confederate brigade. There was some confusion about whether it was Barksdale's or Wilcox's brigade. Barksdale's brigade seems to have been mentioned because William Barksdale was a prominent Mississippi politician at the time, and there was a need to support the contention that a member of the First shot him from the saddle. It was not until others began speaking and writing about the charge that the Confederate force grew exponentially.

The greatest, and doubtless the most influential, exception to this was William Lochren's capsule history of the regiment written for the book series *Minnesota in the Civil and Indian Wars,* published in 1890. This work codified the figures of 262 men making the charge, 215 being killed or wounded in the charge, and (so that the math would work) only 17 casualties for July 3 during the repulse of Pickett's Charge. Lochren's text ran forty-eight pages, and the article was an entire regimental history, so of necessity it lacked the detail of later, fuller regimental histories. Only one-and-a-half pages are devoted to the charge at Gettysburg.

Lochren was selective in what he left out, whether for space considerations or to embellish the heroism of the regiment. He did mention that the regiment was supporting Evan Thomas's Battery C, Fourth U.S. Artillery, which was on the regiment's right. But he failed to point out that the Nineteenth Maine was a short distance on the other side of the battery. Even more relevant was there being no mention of Colonel George Willard's brigade coming in on the Minnesotans' left and attacking Barksdale's brigade of Mississippians.

While it is true that, "No other troops were then near us," as Lochren stated, the "then" is crucial: he was speaking of the time when the regiment was first posted beside the battery. He omitted any mention of the incident two hours later when Willard's men came into position and charged Barksdale shortly before the Minnesotans charged Wilcox. Likewise, Lochren noted "the large brigades of Wilcox and Barksdale" breaking the Union Third Corps line and pursuing it toward the First Minnesota's position. With no reference to Willard's troops stopping Barksdale and no mention of "the Plum Run Line" of federal artillery pounding the rebels, one is left to surmise that the First Minnesota faced down and charged into Barksdale's and Wilcox's brigades with no support of any kind.[22]

In the coverage of the monument dedication in 1897, the *Saint Paul Pioneer Press* ran a story under the headline "No Feat of Arms Like It," with a subhead describing the story as an "Appreciative Sketch of the Immortal Sacrifice of the First Minnesota Regiment."[23] The story was a recounting of the First Minnesota story by an unnamed New York colonel who was a veteran of the battle and was visiting the field at Gettysburg. The colonel stated, "There were no other Federal troops in sight" around the small band of Minnesotans—thus giving no recognition to the hard fighting of Willard's brigade of New Yorkers to the First Minnesota's left nor the Nineteenth Maine to their right. To make his version of the story even more heroic, the colonel provided the then-accepted number of Minnesotans in the charge—262—and went on to say, "the Confederates were a whole division, led by Wilcox's brigade."[24] This story was reproduced at least once more, in a 1901 issue of the *Minneapolis Journal*.[25] Said to be a clipping from the *New York Sun* "of some years back," it was submitted to the newspaper by Stephen Lyons, formerly of Company A, First Minnesota.

Likewise, a *Minneapolis Journal* story in 1897 asserted that the Minnesotans, "kept up a continuous fire that forced back and held the two brigades which acted much as a man does when he is suddenly and unexpectedly hit by a heavy club."[26] In this story, the three to four regiments of Wilcox's brigade that the First Minnesota actually engaged became the two full brigades of Wilcox and Barksdale. The 1897 *Saint Paul Pioneer Press* issue, mentioned above, also contained a non-bylined staff-written story of the charge. This story stated, "No other troops were near on either flank" of the Minnesotans, and the regiment, "like a great granite boulder of their state, went rolling down the hill directly upon the center of the advancing Confederate host—262 men against 3,000, with thousands more on either flank."[27] The April 6, 1902, issue of the *Minneapolis Sunday Times* gave a recounting of the story, declaring the regiment faced down "a division of the enemy."[28]

Any disclaimers that the veterans of the regiment might have made to such inflated Confederate opposition never seem to have made it into print. At the time of the battle, it must have felt as though they were fighting against a division. They had all earned the right to bask in the hyperbole. As the old veterans of the First Minnesota passed on, the obituaries uniformly read like Stephen Lyons's in 1908: "War Hero Is Dead: Stephen Lyons, at Gettysburg with the Famous First, Passes Away: Stephen Lyons, who survived the deluge of lead during the memorable charge of the famous First Minnesota regiment at the battle of Gettysburg and had lived for many years an honored resident of Minnesota, passed away in the Northwestern hospital in Minneapolis. He was severely wounded in the historic charge of his regiment and it was from injures there received that his death resulted."[29]

An unexpected disruption in the established story of the regiment came in 1903, in the pages of the *Minneapolis Journal*. The son of the then deceased Charles Powell Adams, former lieutenant colonel of the First Minnesota, submitted a letter under the headline, "Commander at Gettysburg—Some Prevalent Misconceptions Cleared Up by Official Records."[30] The things mentioned in the letter read like a passing on of family lore (and rancor) from one generation to the next—things that Charles Powell Adams undoubtedly told his family and perhaps close friends but never spoke of publicly or committed to publication. W. H. Adams maintained, as a result of Colonel Colvill being under arrest, that General Hancock gave the order to charge to his father, Lieutenant Colonel Charles Powell Adams, and that he led the charge.

Since Colvill was known to have been in the charge and there still were many living veterans of the regiment in 1903 (including Colvill), Adams had his father leading the charge on horseback (no officers were, in fact, mounted) and Colvill, having just been released from arrest, riding to him and taking command. They both then led the charge until Colvill, almost immediately, was shot from his horse. Adams was said to have been shot six times (he was shot three times), and "falling well to the front," he "was left there for dead for five days and six nights." He actually was evacuated from the field that night, and as badly wounded as he was, it seems unlikely he would have lived, unattended, for five days. It is also puzzling that he would have been left on a field that had been checked carefully for wounded, from which the dead already had been gathered and buried in the daylight and from which the Confederates had withdrawn completely two days before Adams supposedly was found.

W. H. Adams also claimed to have a copy of an official record written by General Hancock that proclaimed Lieutenant Colonel Adams was the officer to whom he gave the charge order. If such a record ever existed, it never made it into the Official Records of the War of the Rebellion. There was also the apocryphal story of Hancock seeing Adams after both had healed and returned to the army after Gettysburg. Hancock was said to have placed his hands on Adams's shoulders while saying, "This is the officer to whom I gave the command for the First Minnesota regiment to charge at the battle of Gettysburg." In truth, there seems to be no published record, letter, or anything else by Hancock—during the war or after—that mentioned Charles Powell Adams.

Minnesota historian William Watts Folwell conducted an interview with W. H. Adams, in Adams's Minneapolis office, on November 28, 1903. Folwell's typed notes of the interview make no mention of Adams showing, or offering to show, the historian any of the documentation mentioned in his letter to the *Minneapolis Journal*. An indication of the family venom toward Colvill, which fortunately never made it into print, was the outright defamatory statement by W. H. Adams that Colvill "was much of the time in arrest for drunkenness" during the war.[31] There are no documents, statements, or even rumors in letters or journals that this author has found to substantiate this claim. It seems unlikely that Colvill would have risen from captain to colonel to brevetted brigadier general if he were "much of the time in arrest" for being drunk. He more likely would have been cashiered from the army.

Fortunately W. H. Adams's outlandish statements did not go unanswered for long. Christopher Heffelfinger wrote "To the Editor of the Journal," and countered Adams's assertions, point-for-point. He ended with: "There can be no mistake as to who commanded the regiment during the charge at Gettysburg. It was Colonel William Colvill and not the lieutenant colonel. The facts, as recorded in Judge Lochren's history of the Gettysburg campaign (see "Minnesota in the Civil War," pp. 32–38) were well known to and not disputed by Lieutenant Colonel Adams during his lifetime—facts which can be readily verified by the survivors in our midst. There was glory enough for all; let not the living be denied their proper share."[32]

The embellishments of history surrounding the charge of the First Minnesota at Gettysburg fit a fairly standard pattern for heroic battlefield exploits throughout history. The dividing line of fact, hyperbole, and pure invention can sometimes be hard to discern. Whatever we can piece together from the historical record, informed conjecture, and 20/20 hindsight does not, in any way, lessen or detract from what the men of the First Minnesota did along the dry ditch of Plum Run on that hot July day in 1863.

Cultural anthropologist Dr. Jarich G. Oosten wrote: "Myths themselves exist in the context of history, they may alter or disappear, and new myths may come into being, as historical circumstances change. New myths must, however, fit into existing mythical patterns if they are to be significant to the participants. Consequently, the structure of a mythology changes much more slowly than individual myths."[33] The mythology, and factual circumstances, of a small group of soldiers making a stand and fighting—potentially to utter annihilation—a larger force of the enemy is itself a "structure of mythology" that is unchanged for millennia. Fact, and the myth, seem to join in history and communal consciousness in events like the First Minnesota sacrificing itself across three hundred yards of Pennsylvania soil to help preserve the Union.

In this merging of fact, myth, history, and heroism, the inscription to the three hundred Spartans on the monument in Greece's Thermopylae Pass can truly be applied to the First Minnesota Volunteer Infantry:

> *Go, stranger, and to Lacedaemon tell*
> *That here, obeying her behests, we fell.*

APPENDIX 4

Casualties

THERE IS QUITE A BIT OF DOCUMENTATION on the number of men in the First Minnesota Regiment at the time of the Battle of Gettysburg. From it we can extrapolate how many should have been in the eight companies that made the charge and how many were engaged in the battle overall. But there is no consistency between what should have been and what many of the combatants claim there to have been.

First, there was inconsistency in which parts of the regiment were counted. Company L, the sharpshooters, were at various times considered "attached to" and "detached from" the regiment. They were considered "attached" during Gettysburg, having been formally attached the previous year at the Battle of Fair Oaks during the Peninsula Campaign in Virginia. At Gettysburg the sharpshooters immediately were sent as support for Woodruff's artillery battery in Ziegler's Grove and never fought with the regiment during the battle. Still, some listings of the regiment's strength and casualties included Company L. Likewise, Company C, part of the division's provost guard since January 1863, was sometimes counted and sometimes not.

In the case of the charge, we have to subtract the men of Company F when that company went out as skirmishers. We know from Colonel Colvill that twenty men had been sent on picket duty the night of July 1, and the regiment marched so early on the morning of July 2 that the picket detail was left behind. Lieutenant Jasper Searles was on detached duty commanding the division ambulance corps. He came up later in the morning and found the twenty men from the picket detail and took charge of them, but they did not reconnect with the regiment until after the charge, when Searles was supervising the removal of the First Minnesota's wounded after dark on July 2.[1] There were also two men wounded earlier in the day to subtract from the count of those in the charge.

The figures, which are still universally cited, are: 262 men went into the charge on the evening of July 2, 1863. Of those, 215 were killed or wounded and 47 were still standing when the regiment formed around its colors back on Cemetery Ridge. This is said to have produced a casualty rate of 82 percent, which is supposed to be "the greatest regimental loss in any battle, in proportion to the number engaged."[2] Since the late nineteenth century, these figures have, literally, been carved in stone and cast in bronze and repeated endlessly in books, articles, and newspaper stories about the regiment.

The figures are wrong.

These numbers were incorporated into the history and legend of the regiment for the first time in 1890 when former Second Lieutenant William Lochren's regimental history was published in the two-volume work *Minnesota in the Civil and Indian Wars.* Lochren mentioned these figures in several letters written in 1889 to fellow veterans of the First Minnesota.[3] He quoted them from the book *Regimental Losses in the American Civil War* by Union veteran William Fox, published that same year. There seems to be no version of these figures before Fox's.

Fox did not explain his methodology in his 1889 book but did in the introduction to a three-volume work, published in 1900, universally cited and referred to as *New York at Gettysburg.*[4] Undoubtedly, he already had developed and used the methodology in his 1889 book. This is a compelling theory when we examine the statistics after applying his computation formula to the First Minnesota.

Fox arrived at his tabulations in a statistically valid manner. For a number of units, ranging in size from regiments to full corps, he had exact figures of how many men went into battle at Gettysburg. He also had the June 30, 1863, payroll figures for the entire Army of the Potomac. Taking the difference in these two figures for each unit, he arrived at an average percentage of men "present and equipped" for battle at Gettysburg that he applied to the entire army.

The figure Fox used was 85.2 percent, which allowed for individual men absent due to sickness, straggling, detached service, and so on.[5] Fox apparently used the figure 385, instead of 399, when doing his calculations on the First Minnesota's June 30, 1863, pay muster roll total. This figure was also given in the regiment's 1916 regimental history, but it does not correspond to the 399 figure of the muster rolls. Perhaps Fox made his own initial deductions from the 399 figure, and the men of the regiment involved in writing the regimental history took his 385 figure as the most accurate. Fox was a respected veteran and historian of the time, and he had done wonderful things for the regiment's legacy by writing of 82 percent casualties for the charge and that being "The greatest regimental loss in any battle, in proportion to the number engaged," and "It is the largest percentage of loss recorded in the annals of modern warfare."[6]

Taking 385 and multiplying it by 85.2 percent, then dividing by ten—the number of companies in a regiment—gives an average number of men in each company. Multiplying that number by eight should give the correct number of men in the eight companies that made the charge on the evening of July 2, 1863. Using this formula, that number is 262.416, rounded down to 262.

The problem with this, aside from the fact that the 385 figure is fourteen men short, is that the 399 (or the 385 figure, for that matter) represents nine companies, not the full ten companies of the regiment. Company C is listed as detached, and those men are not part of the 399. Using Fox's formula, and his 385 figure, but dividing by nine instead of ten gives a figure of 291.57, which rounds up to 292 men in the eight companies that made the charge. Using the 399 figure with Fox's formula gives 302 in the eight companies.

Leaving William Fox's and William Lochren's statistics aside, the extant record varies according to the source: Consolidated Morning Reports for the regiment compiled on June 28, 1863—four days before the regiment's engagement at Gettysburg—show 396 officers and men present for duty, not including Companies C and L; regimental payrolls made out on June 30, 1863—two days before the regiment's fight—

indicate 399 officers and men present for duty; various firsthand accounts soon after the battle, and in the following few years, indicate that anywhere from 300 to 384 men were engaged at Gettysburg, and 269 to 300 made the charge on the evening of July 2, 1863.[7]

Significant reasons for the absence of men from the regiment at this time were heat stroke and detached service. With the intermittently hot and humid weather, the whole army suffered heat stroke casualties during the march to Gettysburg. While no men of the First Minnesota died, there is no way of telling how many—if any—may have been in a field hospital recovering.

It is likely, given the attitudes of the time, that it was considered to reflect poorly on one's "manhood" to drop from sunstroke. It is mentioned, in a general way, that it happened to men in the regiment and in the rest of the Second Corps, but no numbers are given and there is no indication anyone from the First Minnesota missed the battle because of it. There are no letters, diaries, or reminiscences where an individual admits to having missed the battle because of sunstroke. Typical of any mention of the event is this Monday, June 15, 1863, diary entry by Private Isaac L. Taylor of Company E: "It has been very warm & many cases of 'sun-stroke' occur. I don't recolect of ever seeing so many 'sun-struck' and 'fagged-out' on a march. I stand the march 'first rate.' Among those 'fagged-out' are many officers."[8]

In addition to normal detachment of men for use as clerks, aides, hospital stewards, and couriers, the artillery went around the regiments while the army was still camped at Falmouth, Virginia, and several men from the First Minnesota volunteered, or were assigned, to help fill the artillery gun crews. This service made the man technically "detached," while he was still a member of the regiment.[9]

Similarly, there is no way of knowing if any other officers had the same luck as Lieutenant Christopher Heffelfinger and persuaded some of the retreating Third Corps troops to join the First Minnesota in the charge. Daniel Bond also mentioned that when Company F was falling back from the advanced skirmish line, his brother Hezekiah and Ole Johnson were both separated from the company and ended up back with the regiment. Bond claimed both went on to fight in the charge, and Hezekiah was wounded in the eye by a bursting shell after he had made it back from Plum Run. Bond said that the explosion not only "seriously injured" one eye but knocked the rifle out of his brother's hands and broke a photograph he carried of his family.[10] There are no records that indicate that Hezekiah Bond was wounded at Gettysburg.

In the well-researched and documented 1994 book, *Regimental Strengths and Losses at Gettysburg,* John W. Busey and David G. Martin use a tabulation technique similar to Fox's. They made it more accurate by tabulating a percentage of "those engaged" for each corps, as opposed to the entire army. Their calculations indicate that only about 83.5 percent of the Second Corps actually participated in the battle.[11]

If we use that percentage with the First Minnesota's June 30, 1863, pay muster rolls, we get 296 men in the eight companies that made the charge. This is thirty-four more than the Lochren/Fox claim and is within the range of numbers given in several other accounts by officers and men of the regiment. All of these accounts are from before 1890, because after the publication of Lochren's regimental history nearly everyone who wrote about the regiment quoted the Lochren/Fox statistics.

The Morning Reports and the payroll records were a detailed accounting of the men in the regiment. With accurate records as recent as two days before the fight, it is hard to justify taking those figures and decreasing them to 83.5 percent in order to arrive at what should have been the actual number in the battle. If men dropped out from heat stroke or were on detached service, it showed in both the Morning Reports and payroll muster reports, unless it happened July 1 or 2.

The Morning Reports became somewhat sporadic after the army marched from the Rappahannock River. The "comments" section of the June 18, 1863, Morning Report gave a grab bag of reasons why men were absent: one discharged; two detached to Division Headquarters, probably as clerks or couriers; six sent to the general hospital; one arrested; and one absent without leave. Still, this date shows a total of officers and men present, including "present-sick," as 394.

Having an exact count of the number of men present for duty on June 30, 1863, from the payroll muster record affords us the opportunity to do the math, subtracting the approximate number we know were missing just before the charge. The payroll figure is 399 officers and men present. The subtractions from the battle line are: 10 musicians—these men were assigned (as was usual) to be stretcher-bearers for the division's ambulance corps once the fighting started; 20 men on picket detail on the night of July 1; 6 teamsters with the regimental baggage and supply wagons;[12] 33 of Company F out as skirmishers; 2 casualties before the charge; 3 to 4 orderlies holding the field and staff officers' horses during the charge. Subtracting 75 men from 399 gives a total of 324.

According to this method, about 324 men were in the charge. But this is not the whole story. Thirty-seven men appear on the muster rolls as having "extra or daily duty." Extra duty was work for the quartermaster department, to which the soldier was assigned for more than ten days. Daily duty was work that could pull the man out of the day's regular duty rotations of his company. This might include clerking, being assigned as a cook for the regimental hospital, or being delegated as a teamster.[13]

The specific assignments would not necessarily mean that all these men were away from the regiment during the charge, but it is likely that many were. The thirty-seven men included one from Company C and two from Company F. Company C was not part of the calculations anyway, and the two from Company F were included in the already subtracted thirty-three from that company, so removing them from the thirty-seven makes the figure thirty-five men on extra or daily duty. Subtracting these thirty-five men from the 324 figure gives a total of 289 men in the eight companies that made the charge. It is the author's opinion that this figure is closer to the actual number of Minnesotans in the charge on July 2, 1863, than the Lochren/Fox figure of 262.

This total does not factor in straggling within the regiment. But given the fact that the regiment was posted within three miles of their final position on the battlefield the night of July 1, was in a stationary position in reserve for most of the day of July 2, and was in its battle-line position for about two hours prior to the charge, it seems most stragglers would have had an opportunity to catch up and join the regiment. And, as indicated, a certain number of stragglers would be counterbalanced by the fact that not every man assigned to extra or daily duty necessarily would be away from the regiment at the time of the charge.

But, even given this analysis and these calculations, there is still an argument to be made for somewhat fewer men having made the charge on July 2. Former Orderly Sergeant James Wright left the following observation in his memoir, "The Story of Company 'F,' 1st Regiment," finished in 1911. As orderly sergeant for his company, Wright was well versed in calling roll, tabulating numbers, accounting for men, and the uncertain nature of what rolls might show compared to the actual number of men "present and equipped" at any given moment.

It will be remembered that at the close of December, 1862, as computed, the total enrollment of the company was 60: 3 officers and 57 men. Of this number there was one officer (Lt. Spencer) and 5 men on detached duty, and one officer (Captain McCallum) and at least ten men absent sick or wounded. During the succeeding five months there had been a number of changes. We note them as follows: Capt. McCallum had been transferred to the Invalid Corps, Lieut. Ball had been made captain and Sergt. Bruce had been promoted to second lieutenancy. C. E. Adams had died, Corps. J. Barrows, W. D. Bennett and J. Williams, and Privates J. Clausen, G. D. Leighton, C. W. Mills, R. Mott, O. Oscar, D. Seamans and Wm. Shadinger had been discharged.

These were mostly wounded men who had "got it" on the Peninsula or in later fights. Barrows had been wounded at Bull Run. This made a total permanent loss of 13 (1 officer and 12 enlisted men) or a total remaining enrollment of 47 officers and men. The promotion of Sergt. Bruce made the number of officers 3 again and the enrolled number of enlisted men 44, but these were not all present.

Twenty-five percent or more were not present in the ranks. We make the best calculations that we can: Two, C. E. Hudson and W. C. Riddle, were absent without leave as already stated. Five were detached—Lt. Spencer and G. L. Lewis were with the signal corps; C. A. Brooks was with the surgical department; John Brown was wagon master, and Corp. T. A. Wood was in the commissary department. H. T. Bevans was absent on a furlough, and was later discharged, and I find a notice that indicates that Geo. F. Daucher and Thos. Peterson were in hospital about this time. There was also one non-combatant present—M. L. Bevans, acting musician. This makes one officer and ten men absent or on duty other than in line of battle, and leaves a possibility of two officers and thirty-four men for duty.

While this is possible it was not probable. It was a rare case indeed if there were but two men absent sick or wounded. Just about this time demands were made for men to fill the quotas of the artillery, sufficiently to man their guns properly, and, as usual, details were made from the infantry for this purpose. This took two more men, Henry Burgtorf and A. L. M. Decker, from the company.

It is not possible that Company "F" started on the Gettysburg campaign with more than two officers and 32 men, and it is not probable that there were more than thirty officers and men, as it is very unlikely that there were but two men absent sick at this time. From this statement it will be seen that the fighting strength of Company "F" could not have exceeded thirty-two rifles and two swords, and was probably four or five rifles less than that number. Company "F" was only a fair sample of the other companies of the regiment, and of the other, older, regiments in the corps and army.[14]

The *Official Records of the War of the Rebellion* lists 224 casualties for the First Minnesota at Gettysburg: 3 officers and 47 enlisted men killed, 14 officers and 159 enlisted men wounded, and 1 enlisted man missing. The one missing was the result of an early battlefield count. The missing man was Private Mike Devlin of Company A, severely wounded during the repulse of Pickett's Charge and inadvertently taken to another division's hospital. At the time of the battle Second Lieutenant Lochren—as acting adjutant for the regiment after the battle—wrote two official reports that were sent in over the signature of Captain Henry Coates, then commanding the regiment. The first, dated July 5, 1863, was submitted to Minnesota's new senator and very recently resigned governor, Alexander Ramsey.

The version of this report usually cited is the published version, printed in *Minnesota in the Civil and Indian Wars*. It indicated a total casualty count of 232, "out of less than 330 men and officers engaged." The second report was submitted to the regiment's division headquarters and was dated August 3, 1863, and shows the total casualty count at 227.

These conflicting reports have perplexed historians for years. But by comparing the original handwritten July 5 report in the state adjutant general's archives with the published one reveals errors in the latter. The former states that 222 were killed and wounded, not 232. In fact there was even a slight discrepancy between the formal battle report submitted on July 5 and the list of names that accompanied it. The handwritten report showed 5 officers killed and 12 wounded, 45 enlisted men killed, 160 wounded, and 1 missing—a total of 223. It is likely that the report somehow counted the one missing man twice by also incorporating him into the wounded column, since he was found to be wounded and not in fact missing.

The handwritten list of names that accompanied the report shows 5 officers killed and 12 wounded, 45 enlisted men killed, 159 wounded, and 1 missing, totaling 222. Inexplicably, the tabulations in the published version of the battle report in *Minnesota in the Civil and Indian Wars* showed 4 officers killed and 13 wounded, 47 enlisted men killed, 162 wounded, and 6 missing. Complicating things further is yet another list of names, which accompanied the August 31, 1863, Consolidated Morning Report for payroll. This list was noted in the 1916 regimental history, which stated that the list totals were: 7 officers killed and 9 wounded, 88 enlisted men killed, 141 wounded, and none missing—a total of 245.

Clearly there was some moving of men between the "wounded" and "killed" columns, depending on the date the specific report was written. Just as clearly, there are discrepancies among cumulative casualty totals of 222, 223, 227, 232, and 245.

Men died for weeks after the battle, and no one can say what effect the wounds had on shortening lives in the years after the war. For instance, Private Moritz Ehrhardt of Company B would be reminded of the charge every day of his life. He had been shot in the ankle, and the wound became a running sore that never healed properly. In the winter of 1908 he finally had to have the leg removed just below the knee in surgery at the Minnesota Soldiers Home in Minneapolis. The stump would not heal properly either, and in due course another amputation was done above the knee. At 9:00 A.M. on December 17, 1908—forty-five years after the battle—the Confederate minié ball that dropped Moritz Ehrhardt at Gettysburg finally took his life.

Between the two extant casualty lists we can be fairly certain that all the major wounds, and most of the minor, were enumerated. But there were surely some instances of a man bleeding who did not end up on the lists. One was the case of Sergeant Wright, who was peppered with lead and wood fragments in the chest and face when a bullet struck a gun stock near him. But Wright was the one taking the names of the wounded and killed in his company to report to acting Adjutant Lochren, and Wright purposely said not to put his name on the casualty list. His motive is not known, but it is likely that he did not want the newspapers in Minnesota to get it wrong and list him as dead. Even the simple label "wounded" in a newspaper could cause anguish to friends and loved ones, with no way of dispelling the misinformation until, or if, a letter made it home from the soldier. Lochren himself was a victim of this through a fellow officer who wrote to a Minnesota senator with mistaken information.

In the chaotic aftermath of the battle, it was inevitable that mistakes would be made. Differences in the two lists mainly were wounded men appearing in the dead section of the second one, understandable after the passage of a month. In the case of Private Charles Ely of Company K, there was a resurrection between the lists of July 5 and August 3. Other information confirmed that he was not killed but was seriously wounded and survived.

Six men from the July 5 list inexplicably were left off of the August 3 list: Private John Farquhar of Company A, Private John Anderson of Company B, Private William Bassett of Company E, Private Edmund Parker of Company F, Private William Riddle of Company F, and Private A. S. Wood of Company H. Other records indicated that some of these men were wounded. Farquhar may have been overlooked on the second list because his brother Daniel was also wounded in the leg and was in the same company. At some point someone may have thought they were the same person and deleted John from the final list.

Bassett did not appear in the diary list of First Sergeant Henry Taylor of Company E. This is puzzling because every other name on the lists from Company E did. As first sergeant for the company, Taylor was the one who compiled and submitted his company's list. However, he included in his diary list a name that does not appear on either of the regimental casualty lists: Private William Cundy, whom Taylor indicated was wounded in the charge on July 2. It could not have been too serious a wound since he was one of the two men Taylor mentioned helped bury his brother Isaac on the morning of July 3.[15] Perhaps the six men were so slightly wounded that they were completely recovered by the time the August 3 list was compiled, and they simply were not included on the second list. It is also possible that none was wounded at all, and that was known by the time the August 3 list was made out.

Eleven men are on the August 3 list who do not appear on the July 5 list. They are: Sergeant George Oliver and Privates George Arnold and Albert Sebers of Company B; Private Maurice Leonard of Company C; Private Daniel Waite of Company E; Privates James Bachelor, Artemus Decker, and Charles Hubbs of Company F; Privates Adam Areman and William Brown of Company G; and Private Byron Welch of Company I. All the men of Company F, except Bachelor, were wounded while serving Cushing's artillery battery during the repulse of Pickett's Charge on July 3. Being wounded while on detached service probably had something to do with their being omitted from the earlier casualty list.

Inexplicably, the August 3 list contained separate sections for officers killed, enlisted men killed, and enlisted men wounded but had no listing of officers wounded. Correcting that omission adds twelve more names to the actual total of the August 3 list. There was one duplication on this list: Private Edwin Paul of Company I appeared in both the dead and the wounded sections of enlisted men; he died on July 14, 1863. Subtracting one and adding twelve makes the total 227. When the six names that appeared only on the July 5 list are added, the total reaches 233.

Inclusion on the list that follows required being on either or both of the July 5 and August 3, 1863, casualty lists. Details on the nature of the wounds are compiled from a variety of sources, including published lists from newspapers, diaries, letters, reminiscences, and regimental records of varying kinds. A short list of names follows the main list. There is evidence that these men were also wounded, but they do not appear on either of the two regimental casualty lists.

First Minnesota: Killed and Wounded at Gettysburg

♣ Man is confirmed killed or wounded in July 2 charge.

† Man is in marked grave at Gettysburg National Cemetery.

* Date enclosed in brackets indicates that this name was found only on casualty list submitted on that date, [July 5] or [August 3].

FIELD AND STAFF OFFICERS

♣ Colvill, William, Col.   Shot through right ankle/foot and right shoulder

♣ Adams, Charles Powell, Lt. Col.   Shot in the chest, groin, and leg

♣ Downie, Mark W., Maj.   Shot once in foot and twice in right arm

♣ Pellar, John Lt., (Adj.)   Left arm broken

COMPANY A

♣ Adams, Lucius A., Pvt.   Shot in hand

† Brandt, Clark, Pvt.   Right leg amputated above knee; died July 21, 1863

† Crawley, Timothy, Cpl.   Shot through left leg, above knee; died July 20, 1863

Dehn, John, Cpl. of Color Guard   Shot through the hand July 3, 1863

Devlin, Mike, Pvt.   Wounded July 3, 1863 [reported as missing on July 5 list]*

Dooley, William H. H., Sgt.   Wounded in wrist July 3, 1863

Drake, Charles S., Pvt.   Wounded in arm July 3, 1863

♣ Edler, Julius, Cpl.   Killed in action

♣ Farquhar, Daniel W., Pvt.   Shot through left thigh, above knee, and left ankle

Farquhar, John, Pvt.   Wounded in thigh on July 3 [July 5]*

♣ Geiser, Frederick, Pvt.   Wounded in the side

♣†Glave, Frederick, Pvt.   Shot through left knee; died of wound August 3, 1863

♣ Hausdorf, Charles F., Sgt.   Shot in the leg (served under the pseudonym "Frank Houston")

♣ Hauser, John, Pvt.   Killed in action

♣ Keyes, James N., Cpl.   Killed in action

♣ Lyons, Stephen, Cpl.   Wounded in thigh

† Marks, Peter, Cpl.   Wounded in right ankle; right foot amputated; died July 23, 1863

♣ Miller, William F., Pvt.   Killed in action [July 5: "W. F.," August 3: "John F."]*

♣ Mowry, Rascellas S., Pvt.   Shot in the side

♣ Muller, Charles, Pvt.   Shot in the right thigh

♣†Nickell, Henry, Pvt.   Shot through left thigh, fractured femur; died of wound on August 10, 1863

♣ Sanders, Benjamin, Pvt.   Wounded

♣ Schmucker, Joseph, Cpl.   Killed in action

♣†Simonson, Hans M., Pvt.   Shot through left calf and knee; died of wounds August 3, 1863

♣ Steen, Charles, Sgt.   Shot through left thigh; leg amputated

♣ Theim, Joseph, Pvt.   Wounded in arm

Wagner, Warren, Pvt.   Died of wounds July 6, 1863

♣ Wilson, John G., Pvt.   Killed in action

Wright, Henry C., Sgt.   Wounded in head; died of wound July 6, 1863

COMPANY B

♣ Sinclair, Thomas, Lt.   Minié ball flattened itself against his sternum
May, William M., Lt.   Shot in upper left forearm and in right leg on July 3
Anderson, John, Pvt.   Wounded [July 5]*
♣ Arnold, George, Pvt.   Shot through right shoulder and left calf [August 3]*
♣ Aucker, William H., Pvt.   Shot through both hips
♣ Bates, William F., Pvt.   Killed in action
Blanchard, Rufus G., Cpl.   Wounded in side July 3, 1863
♣ Caplazi, Albert, Pvt.   Wounded in thigh
♣ Carriegiet, Bartholomew, Pvt.   Shot in thigh
♣ Crome, Frederick, Sgt.   Wounded
♣ Densmore, John D., Sgt.   Wounded (five wounds)
♣ Ehrhardt, Moritz (Morris) W., Pvt.   Shot in left ankle
♣ Everson, Peter, Pvt.   Shot in neck
♣†Gove, Charles H., Pvt.   Shot in shoulder and spine; died of wounds
♣ Hamann, Charles, Pvt.   Wounded in face and head (hand?)
♣ Henry, Martin J., Pvt.   Wounded
♣ Johnson, David, Pvt.   Wounded
♣ Koenig, Augustus, Pvt.   Killed in action
♣ Lord, David, Sgt.   Wounded in shoulder
♣ Marty, Adam, Pvt.   Shot in the right thigh
♣ Marty, Fridolin, Pvt.   Shot in the hand
♣ Nickerson, Samuel B., Sgt.   Killed in action
♣ Nytsedt, Erick, Pvt.   Wounded
♣ Oliver, George A., Sgt.   Slight wound in chest [August 3]*
♣ Quist, Andrew P., Pvt.   Wounded [July 5: "killed," August 3: "wounded"]
♣ Schoebeck, John P., Pvt.   Wounded
♣ Sebers, Albert, Pvt.   Wounded in head and leg [August 3]*
♣ Stevens, John B., Cpl. of Color Guard   Shot in chest
Tanner, Joseph A., Pvt.   Wounded in leg and head July 3, 1863
♣ Thompson, Ole, Pvt.   Shot in leg; died of wound
♣ Wells, Edwin, Cpl.   Wounded in leg

COMPANY C

(All wounded or killed on July 3, 1863, repelling Pickett's Charge)
Farrell, Wilson B., Capt.   Wounded in head; died late July 3, 1863
Harmon, Willam, 1st Lt.   Slightly wounded; shot in the waist belt
Mason, Charles H., 2nd Lt.   Wounded in hand; died of wound
August 18, 1863
Atherton, Minor, Pvt.   Wounded in thigh

Clancy, Daniel, Pvt.   Wounded in right shoulder

† Ellsworth, John, Pvt.   Wounded; leg amputated above knee; died July 20, 1863

Gilman, James B., Pvt.   Wounded

Greenwald, Aaron, Quarter Master Sgt.   Shot through head, ball entered shoulder; died of wound July 7, 1863

Hayford, Faxon, Pvt.   Wounded

Howard, Henry H., 1st Sgt.   Wounded in arm; died of wound

Krueger, Andrew F., Sgt.   Wounded

Leonard, Maurice F., Pvt.   Wounded [August 3]*

† Lufkin, Wade, Sgt.   Killed in action

Squires, Gideon L., Cpl.   Shot in arm

COMPANY D

♣ Heffelfinger, Christopher B., Lt.   Hit in chest; bullet stopped by memo book in pocket

Allen, William Russel, Pvt.   Shot through bowel; died July 8, 1863

♣†Baker, Charles E., Pvt.   Killed in action

♣ Bartlett, George W., Pvt.   Wounded in thigh

♣ Bryant, James, Cpl.   Wounded in thigh

♣ Geer, Charles W., Cpl.   Wounded in shoulder and arm

♣ Geer, Lewis B., Pvt.   Shot through right lung, side, and hand

♣ Goeppinger, August A., Pvt.   Wounded in hand and foot

† Grady, George, Pvt.   Shot in chest; died of wound

† Hayden, Alonzo C., Pvt.   Killed in action July 3, 1863 (possibly hit in July 2 charge; died July 3)

♣ Howe, Archibald E., Pvt.   Wounded in hip

♣ Kouts, Jacob W., Cpl.   Shot in arm

♣†Lawrence, Irvin, Pvt.   Wounded; died July 7

♣ Nason, Thomas B., Cpl.   Shot in wrist (breast?)

♣ Noel, Benjamin F., Pvt.   Wounded in leg

♣ Past, Marcus A., Pvt.   Shot through chest; died July 6, 1863

♣ Perkins, Ellet P., Color Sgt.   Shot in thigh

♣ Prime, Joseph H., Pvt.   Killed in action

♣ Rines, Charles H., Pvt.   Five wounds in side

♣ Robinson, Calvin D., Sgt.   Wounded

♣ Rollins, Franklin, Pvt.   Died of wounds

♣ Smith, William C., Pvt.   Shot in shoulder

♣ Smithyman, Joseph, Cpl.   Wounded

♣ Sullivan, Daniel, Pvt.   Shot through the heel

♣ Walsh, James W., Pvt.   Gunshot wound

COMPANY E

⚜ Muller, Louis, Capt.   Killed in action; shot through the head

⚜ Demerest, David B., 1st Lt.   Shot in the hip; died of wounds July 30, 1863

⚜ Adams, George M., Pvt.   Wounded in shoulder

⚜ Bassett, William H., Pvt.   Wounded in arm and thigh (not in P. H. Taylor's diary list) [July 5]*

⚜ Berry, Amos O., Pvt.   Wounded in leg

⚜ Berry, Charles A., Pvt.   Wounded in leg

⚜ Bradley, Henry C., Cpl.   Shot in ankle

⚜ Curry, John, Pvt.   Shot in left shoulder

⚜ Davis, John W., Pvt.   Killed in action

⚜ Drake, Hiram, Pvt.   Wounded in foot

⚜ Fisher, Henry I., Pvt.   Wounded in foot

⚜ Fowler, Norman, Pvt.   Killed in action

⚜ Hill, Jonas R., Pvt.   Wounded in both legs

⚜ Holden, William W., Pvt.   Wounded in side and leg

⚜ Jackins, Israel, Pvt.   Killed in action

⚜ Jefferson, Ernest, Pvt.   Wounded in leg and foot; leg amputated

⚜ Losse, William H., Pvt.   Wounded in chest

⚜†McKenzie, John, Pvt.   Shot through both thighs; died of wounds

⚜ Middlestadt, Vincent, Pvt.   Wounded in foot

O'Brien, Henry D., Cpl.   Shot through hand and in head July 3, 1863; Medal of Honor

Stites, Adam C., Pvt.   Wounded in head July 3, 1863

⚜ Stites, Samuel B., Sgt.   Shot in arm

⚜ Staples, Benjamin F., Cpl.   Wounded

⚜ Taylor, Isaac Lyman, Pvt.   Killed in action by artillery fragments

⚜ Taylor, Mathew F., Cpl.   Shot through left lung

⚜ Trevor, Joseph G., 1st Sgt.   Killed in action

⚜ Waite, Daniel H., Pvt.   Wounded in leg [August 3]*

⚜ Weaver, Elijah, Pvt.   Shot in neck (shoulder?)

⚜†Welin, Peter, Pvt.   Left leg amputated above ankle; died of wounds

COMPANY F

Abbott, Marion, Cpl.   Wounded in right arm (bone shattered) on July 2, 1863

Bachelor, James F., Pvt.   Wounded in foot on July 2, 1863 [August 3]*

Barber, Horatio N., Cpl.   Wounded July 3, 1863

Bondurant, Cyrus, Pvt.   Wounded in hand July 3, 1863

Burgetorpf, Henry, Pvt.   Wounded July 3, 1863 (working Cushing's battery) [August 3]*

Decker, Artemus L. M., Pvt.   Wounded; knee July 3, 1863 (working Cushing's battery) [August 3]*

† Hamlin, Philip, Sgt.   Killed in action; shot in left leg, thigh, neck, and heart July 3, 1863

Hubbs, Charles L., Pvt.   Wounded; wrist, leg July 3, 1863 (working Cushing's battery) [August 3]*

Jacobs, Romulus E., Pvt.   Wounded in shoulder by sharpshooter early on July 3, 1863

King, Levi, Pvt.   Shot in the face; jaw broken July 2, 1863

Parker, Edmund F., Pvt.   Wounded (not on James Wright's list) [July 5]*

Riddle, William C., Pvt.   Wounded in leg (not on James Wright's list) [July 5]*

† Squires, Leonard J., Cpl.   Killed in action July 3, 1863

COMPANY G

† Messick, Nathan S., Capt.   Killed in action; shot through the head July 3, 1863

♣ DeGray, James, Lt.   Wounded; skull had a four inch "rip" from bullet grazing

♣ Areman, Adam, Pvt.   Wounded in shoulder [August 3]*

♣ Barton, Dana S., Pvt.   Wounded in chest and wrist

♣ Brown, William W., Pvt.   Wounded in leg [August 3]*

♣ Carney, James H., Pvt.   Wounded in hip

♣ Coen, William G., Pvt.   Wounded in leg

♣†Dunham, Phineas L., Pvt.   Shot in left thigh and testicles; died July 14, 1863

Ernst, Anthony B., Pvt.   Wounded in shoulder July 3; died of wounds

♣ Farnsworth, Jerome, Pvt.   Wounded in thigh; died of wound

♣ Gatzke, John, Pvt.   Wounded in thigh

♣ Goodrich, Jonathan, Pvt.   Wounded in left leg

♣ Hopkins, George J., Pvt.   Wounded in right wrist

Jones, Anthony, Cpl.   Wounded in head July 3, 1863

♣ Lilly, Samuel, Pvt.   Wounded in the back

♣ Magee, George, Pvt.   Shot in the chest

♣ Mosher, Ludwell L., Pvt.   Wounded in thigh and wrist

♣ Reed, Walter S., Pvt.   Wounded in shoulder

♣ Rhorer, John M., Pvt.   Shot in hand

♣ Sawyer, George P., Cpl.   Killed in action

♣†Sisler, Joseph, Pvt.   Killed in action

♣ Strothman, John M., Cpl.   Killed in action

COMPANY H

✿ Akers, James, 1st Sgt.   Killed in action

Bradbury, George W., Pvt.   Wounded in shoulder July 3, 1863

✿ Clauser, John, Pvt.   Shot in chest; killed in action

Cronkhite, Samuel S., Pvt.   Wounded July 3, 1863 ("contusion")

† Diehr, Frederick, Sgt.   Shot through the lung July 3, 1863; died July 21, 1863

Docken, John H., Pvt.   Shot in arm July 3, 1863

✿ Drondt, Kellian, Pvt.   Shot in head; died of wound

✿ Essencey, John H., Cpl.   Killed in action

Galvin, Thomas, Pvt.   Wounded in arm July 3, 1863

✿ Hess, Reinhald, Pvt.   Shot in the face; died of wound

Smith, Benjamin, Pvt.   Wounded July 3, 1863

✿ Wicoff, William H., Sgt.   Killed in action

Wood, A. S., Pvt. (Roster says "Edward L. Wood")   Wounded [July 5]*

COMPANY I

✿ Boyd, George Jr., 1st Lt.   Wounded in left leg, slightly

✿†Farrar, Waldo, 2nd Lt.   Shot through head; killed in action

✿ Abbott, Henry, Pvt.   Wounded in leg

✿ Donovan, Jeremiah, Pvt.   Shot in wrist

✿ Ellis, Philander C., Pvt.   Killed in action

✿ Freeze, Jacob F., Pvt.   Shot in hand, foot; died of wounds

✿ Frey, Joseph, Pvt.   Killed in action

✿†Hale, Edward P., Pvt.   Wounded in hip, shot through right knee; died of wounds

✿ Howell, William D., Pvt.   Shot in hand

✿ Hutchins, Daniel, Pvt.   Wounded

✿ Jackson, Benjamin, Pvt.   Wounded in leg

Knight, Oliver M., 1st Sgt.   Wounded in arm by artillery round (before charge) July 2, 1863

Lawson, Herman, Cpl.   Shot in hand July 3, 1863

✿ Mason, Charles F., Pvt.   Wounded in leg

✿ Miller, Ernst L. F., Cpl.   Wounded in leg

✿ Milliken, George A., Cpl.   Wounded in foot; foot amputated

† Paul, Edwin, Pvt.   Wounded in left leg; amputated below knee; died July 14, 1863

† Peck, William N., Cpl.   Wounded in left leg; amputated below knee; died July 21, 1863

✿ Philbrook, William B., Pvt.   Wounded in thigh

♣ Rabaca, Herman, Pvt.   Wounded
  Richards, William K., Sgt.   Wounded in leg July 3, 1863
  Roe, William J., Sgt.   Wounded July 3, 1863; died [lists say "Oliver Roe"
    and "O. Roe"]
♣ Weaver, Daniel S., Pvt.   Wounded in leg
♣†Welch, Byron, Pvt.   Killed in action [August 3]*
♣†Wellman, William F., Cpl.   Wounded in leg; died of wound
♣ Widger, Henry, Pvt.   Wounded in hip
  † Woodard, Oscar, Sgt.   Killed in action by artillery round (before charge)
    July 2, 1863

COMPANY K

♣†Periam, Joseph, Capt.   Shot in nose; bullet exited behind left ear; died
    July 7, 1863
♣ Behr, Charles, Pvt.   Wounded in chest and head
♣ Carpenter, Alfred P., Sgt.   Wounded in foot
  Durfee, Chester H., Pvt.   Wounded July 3, 1863
  † Durr, Israel, Pvt.   Shot through lung July 3; died of wound July 4, 1863
♣ Eaton, Joseph S., Pvt.   Shot in left thigh
♣ Einfeldt, John, Cpl.   Wounded in shoulder
♣ Ely, Charles E., Pvt.   Shot through right breast
♣ Geisreiter, Jacob, Pvt.   Killed in action
♣ Goddard, Charles E., Cpl.   Shot in thigh and shoulder
♣ Gore, Leslie P., Cpl.   Killed in action
♣ Hanson, Lewis, Pvt.   Wounded in calf
♣ Keiley, Timothy, Cpl.   Wounded in thigh and calf
♣ Kinyon, William H., Pvt.   Wounded
♣ Marvin, Mathew, Sgt.   Shot through foot
♣ North, Charles, Cpl.   Wounded
♣ Smith, Augustus H., Pvt.   Killed in action
♣ Taylor, David, Pvt.   Killed in action
♣ Tenney, Samuel S., Pvt.   Wounded in leg
♣ Towner, James, Pvt.   Wounded
  Vosz, Peter, Pvt.   Shot through the bowel July 3; died July 3, 1863
♣ Winters, Henry C., Pvt.   Killed in action
  Wright, Randolph, Cpl.   Killed in action July 3, 1863

COMPANY L
SECOND MINNESOTA SHARPSHOOTERS

Baker, Ozias B., Pvt.   Wounded in thigh July 2, 1863
Brown, Sylvester, Pvt.   Killed in action July 3, 1863
Coleman, William M., Pvt.   Wounded in right side of head July 3, 1863;
1″ x 2″ piece of skull carried away by minié ball

Possibly Wounded, Not on Casualty Lists

These are men not on either the July 5 or August 8 casualty lists but for whom there is otherwise some indication of having been wounded at Gettysburg. Names appear on this list if no conclusive information is found to dispute "wounded" information, such as the individual having been killed in an earlier battle or discharged before the Battle of Gettysburg. The source of "wounded" information is in parentheses.

COMPANY A

Guntzer, Nicholas, Pvt.   Wounded (roster)
Lyons, Harrison, Pvt.   Wounded in charge (roster)

COMPANY B

Graf, Emil, Pvt.   Wounded by accident while on detail, July 2, 1863 (roster; letter from former Sergeant Myron Shepard of Co. B to William Lochren, dated March 10, 1890)
Pooler, Albert, Pvt.   Wounded (roster; letter from former Sergeant Myron Shepard of Co. B to William Lochren, dated March 10, 1890)

COMPANY E

Austin, Edward A., Corp.   Wounded (roster)
Brower, James S., Corp.   Wounded (roster)
Cundy, William, Pvt.   Wounded in charge (Sgt. P. H. Taylor diary list)
Fenton, Benjamin, Pvt.   Wounded in charge on July 2 (roster)

COMPANY F

Davis, Almeron, Pvt.   Wounded (wartime "descriptive book" of regt., which says wounded on July 2, 1863; 1st Sgt. James A. Wright's personal reminiscence says July 3, 1863)
Wright, James A., 1st Sgt.   Wounded by fragments of shattered gunstock and lead minié ball on July 3, 1863 (his personal reminiscence; roster)

COMPANY G

Coombs, Charles A., Pvt.   Wounded (roster)
Hall, Edward Philo, Sgt.   Wounded (roster)

COMPANY H

Raymond, Frederick W., Pvt.   Wounded July 3 (roster; *Saint Paul Pioneer* for Wednesday, July 29, 1863, says he was in the South Street Hospital in Philadelphia. The final "descriptive book" for the regiment, compiled at the end of its service, indicates Raymond was "Dropped from roles as a deserter, July 30, 1863." Roster indicates that he died October 10, 1863. Service record in National Archives indicates he committed suicide on that date.)

COMPANY I

O'Neil, James, Sgt.   Wounded (roster)
Price, Edward B., Sgt.   Wounded (roster)
Seymour, Samuel O. K., Pvt.   Wounded (roster)
Sutliff, Omar H., Pvt.   Wounded (roster)
Worthington, William H., Sgt.   Wounded (roster)

COMPANY K

Boardman, Charles B., Pvt.   Wounded (roster)
Chandler, Joseph C., Pvt.   Wounded (roster)

BIBLIOGRAPHY

Given the focus of this work—a single Minnesota regiment in a single campaign and battle—it is not surprising that the bulk of the useful material was found in the collections of the Minnesota Historical Society. As indicated in the preface, many other archives and individuals were consulted. Two of the more prominent, aside from the Minnesota Historical Society, are the Gettysburg National Military Park archives and the U.S. Army Military History Institute, Carlisle Barracks, in Carlisle, Pennsylvania. Having a complete catalog listing of the Minnesota-related holdings of these two institutions, the author discovered that the majority of their material on the First Minnesota is, in fact, copies of material from the Minnesota Historical Society. There is also some original material that the author used and is cited below.

In one instance, a copy in the Gettysburg Archives led to original material in the Wisconsin State Archives.

The staffs of both archives were tremendously helpful, through phone calls, letters and e-mail. Much information was acquired this way, especially from the Gettysburg staff, pertaining to other units and specifics of the field itself at the time of the battle.

ARCHIVES AND INSTITUTIONS CONSULTED AND UTILIZED

Minnesota
Anoka County Historical Society
James J. Hill Group
Minneapolis Public Library
Minnesota Historical Society (MHS)
Morrison County Historical Society
St. Paul Public Library
Star Tribune News Research Library
University of Minnesota—Wilson Library
Winona County Historical Society

Other
Beverly Historical Society and Museum, Beverly, Massachusetts
Gettysburg National Military Park, Gettysburg, Pennsylvania
National Archives and Records Administration, Washington, D.C.
New York Historical Society, New York, New York
New York State Archives and Records Administration, Albany, New York
New York State Historical Association, Cooperstown, New York

U.S. Army Military Institute, Carlisle Barracks, Carlisle, Pennsylvania

PRIMARY SOURCES
Papers, diaries, letters

Adams, Charles Powell. Papers. MHS.

Adjutant General, Civil and Indian Wars. Papers. MHS.

Bassett, Edward H. and George S. Letters, 1861–1863. MHS.

Bloomer, Samuel. Papers. MHS.

Bond, Daniel. "Reminiscences." Unpublished manuscript, 1916(?), (microfilm). MHS.

Carpenter, Alfred P. Letter, typed transcription, dated "30 July, 1863." MHS.

Coleman, Leslie F. Letter and historical narrative of Wilber Coleman, 2nd Minnesota Sharpshooters, July 5, 1883. Gettysburg National Military Park.

Davis, Charles Edward. Letters (microfilm). MHS.

Durfee, Chester S. Letter and manuscript narrative of 50th Anniversary trip to Gettysburg. MHS.

Folwell, William Watts. Papers. MHS.

Goddard, Charles. Letters, 1861–1864. Orrin Fruit Smith and Family Papers. MHS.

Gorman, Willis A. and Family. Papers. MHS.

Hamlin, Philip Rice and Jacob Leslie. Letters. MHS.

Hospes, Adolphus Conrad. Letters (microfilm). Wisconsin Historical Society.

Lochren, William. Papers. MHS.

Marty, Adam. Papers. MHS.

Marvin, Matthew. Papers, 1861–1863. MHS.

McColley, Charles E. "Story of the 1st Minnesota." Unpublished manuscript. MHS.

Minnesota Infantry, 1st Regiment. Papers, 1861–1864. MHS.

Muller, Charles. "History of Company A, 1st Minnesota." Unpublished manuscript. MHS.

Muller, Louis. Family Papers. MHS.

National Archives and Records Administration, Army Service and Pension Records for: Duffy, Wilbur F.; Chase, John M.; Colvill, William; Smith, DeWitt C.

——. Old Military and Civil Records, Record Group 94.2.4.

Pressnell, Thomas H. "Incidents in the Civil War." Unpublished typescript. MHS.

Ramsey, Alexander. Family Papers. MHS.

Sullivan, Daniel. Letters (typed transcripts). Private collection.

Swift, Henry A. Papers, 1855–1868. MHS.

Taylor, Patrick Henry. Letters (copies). Morrison County (Minnesota) Historical Society.

——. Typescript of diary entries for June 30, 1863–July 5, 1863. MHS.

Wright, James A. "Story of Company F." Unpublished manuscript. MHS.

BOOKS

Adams, Silas. "The Nineteenth Maine at Gettysburg," in *War Papers, Read Before the Commandery of the State of Maine, Military Order of the Loyal Legion.* Portland: Lefavor-Tower Co., 1898–1919, 4:250–63.

Alexander, E. Porter. *Military Memoirs of a Confederate.* 1907; reprint with introduction and notes by T. Harry Williams, Civil War Centennial Series. Bloomington: Indiana University Press, 1962.

Alleman, Mrs. Tillie (Pierce). *At Gettysburg, or What a Girl Saw and Heard of the Battle: A True Narrative.* 1889; reprint with introduction by William A. Frassanito. Baltimore: Butternut and Blue, 1994.

The Annals of the Civil War. 1878; reprint with introduction by Gary W. Gallagher. New York: De Capo Press, 1994.

Bassett, M. H. *From Bull Run to Bristow Station.* St. Paul: North Central Publishing Co., 1962.

Battles and Leaders of the Civil War. Vol. 3. 1883. Reprint, Edison, N.J.: Castle Books, 1995.

Billings, John D. *Hardtack and Coffee: Or The Unwritten Story of Army Life.* 1887. Reprint, with introduction by

William L. Shea. Lincoln: University of Nebraska Press, Bison Books, 1993.

Casey, Silas. *Infantry Tactics, For the Instruction, Exercise and Manoeuvres of the Soldier, A Company, Line of Skirmishers, Battalion, Brigade or Corps d'Armee.* New York: D. Van Nostrand, 1862.

Coffin, Charles Carleton. *Eyewitness to Gettysburg.* 1889. Reprint, with introduction and notes by John W. Schildt. Shippensburg, Pa.: Burd Street Press, 1997.

Fox, William F. *Regimental Losses in the American Civil War: 1861–1865.* Albany: Albany Publishing Co., 1889.

Gallagher, Gary W., ed. *Fighting for the Confederacy: The Personal Recollections of General Edward Porter Alexander.* Chapel Hill: University of North Carolina Press, 1989.

Gibbon, John. *The Artillerist's Manual, Compiled from Various Sources and Adapted to the Service of the United States.* 2d ed. Rev. and enl., New York: D. Van Nostrand, 1863.

———. *Personal Recollections of the Civil War.* New York: G. P. Putnam's Sons, 1928.

Groat, J. W. *Civil War Memoirs of J. W. Groat.* Anoka, Minn.: Anoka County Historical Society, 1988.

Hardee, W. J. *Hardee's Rifle and Light Infantry Tactics, For the Instruction, Exercises, and Manoeuvres of Riflemen and Light Infantry. Including School of the Soldier and School of the Company.* New York: J. O. Kane Publisher, 1862.

Haskell, Frank Aretas. *The Battle of Gettysburg.* 1878(?). Reprint with introduction by Bruce Catton. Boston: Houghton Mifflin Co., 1969.

Heffelfinger, Lucia L. Peavey. *Memoirs of Christopher B. Heffelfinger.* Santa Barbara, Calif., 1915; Minneapolis, 1922.

Holcombe, Return I. *History of the First Regiment Minnesota Volunteer Infantry, 1861–1864.* Stillwater, Minn.: Easton and Masterman Printers, 1916.

Humphreys, Andrew A. *From Gettysburg to the Rapidan: The Army of the Potomac, July 1863 to April 1864.* 1883. Reprint. Baltimore: Butternut and Blue.

Jaquette, Henrietta Stratton, ed. *South after Gettysburg: Letters of Cornelia Hancock, 1863–1868.* 2d ed. New York: Thomas Y. Crowell Co., 1956.

Ladd, David L., and Audrey J. Ladd, eds. *The Bachelder Papers.* 3 vols. Dayton, Ohio: Morningside Press, 1994.

Livermore, Thomas L. *Numbers and Losses in the American Civil War.* 1900. Reprint, Civil War Centennial Series. Bloomington: Indiana University Press, 1957.

Lochren, William. "The First Minnesota at Gettysburg," in *Glimpses of the Nation's Struggle.* Vol. 3. St. Paul: D. D. Merrill Co., 1893, p. 42–56.

———. "Narrative of the First Regiment," in Minnesota Board of Commissioners on Publication of History of Minnesota in the Civil and Indian Wars, *Minnesota in the Civil and Indian Wars, 1861–1865.* Vol. 1. St. Paul, 1891, p. 1–66.

Maine Gettysburg Commission. *Maine at Gettysburg: Report of Maine Commissioners Prepared by the Executive Committee.* Portland: Lakeside Press, 1898.

Nelson, A. H. *The Battles of Chancellorsville and Gettysburg.* Minneapolis, 1899.

New York Monuments Commission for the Battlefields of Gettysburg and Chattanooga: Final Report of the Battlefield of Gettysburg. Vol. 1 and 2. Albany: J. B. Lyon Co., 1900.

Revised United States Army Regulations of 1861. With an Appendix, Containing the Changes and Laws Affecting Army Regulations and Articles of War to June 25, 1863. Washington, D.C.: Government Printing Office, 1863.

Rollins, Richard, ed. *Pickett's Charge: Eyewitness Accounts.* Redondo Beach, Calif.: Rank and File Publications, 1994.

Sauers, Richard A., ed. *Fighting Them Over: How The Veterans Remembered*

Gettysburg in the Pages of the National Tribune. Baltimore: Butternut and Blue, 1998.

Searles, Jasper Newton. "The First Minnesota Volunteer Infantry," in *Glimpses of the Nation's Struggle.* Vol. 2. St. Paul: St. Paul Book and Stationary Co., 1890, p. 80–113.

Simons, Ezra de Freest. *A Regimental History: The One Hundred and Twenty-Fifth New York State Volunteers.* New York: E. D. Simons, 1888.

Smith, John Day. *The History of the Nineteenth Regiment of Maine Volunteer Infantry, 1862–1865.* Minneapolis: Great Western Printing Co., 1909.

Walker, Francis A. *History of the Second Army Corps in the Army of the Potomac.* New York: Charles Scribner's Sons, 1891.

The War of the Rebellion: A Compilation of the Official Records of the Union and Confederate Armies. Series 1. Vol. 27. Part 2—Reports. U.S. War Department. Washington, D.C.: Government Printing Office, 1889. (Also *The Civil War CD-ROM* version, Carmel, Ind.: Guild Press of Indiana, 1997.)

Willson, Arabella M. *Disaster, Struggle, Triumph: The Adventures of 1000 "Boys in Blue," From August, 1862 to June, 1865.* Albany: Argus Co., 1870.

Young, Jesse Bowman. *The Battle of Gettysburg: A Comprehensive Narrative.* New York: Harper & Brothers Publishers, 1913.

PERIODICALS

Clark, George. "Wilcox's Alabama Brigade at Gettysburg." *Confederate Veteran* 17, no. 5 (May 1909): 229–30.

Early, Jubal A. "General Early's Reply to the Count of Paris." *Southern Historical Society Papers* 6 (1878): 12–36.

Long, A. L. "Letter from General A. L. Long, Military Secretary to General R. E. Lee." *Southern Historical Society Papers* 4 (1877): 118–23.

[Taylor, Isaac Lyman]. "Campaigning with the First Minnesota: A Civil War Diary."

Edited by Hazel C. Wolf. *Minnesota History* 25 (Mar., June, Sept., Dec., 1944): 11–39, 117–52, 224–57, 342–61.

Wilcox, Cadmus M. "Letter from General C. M. Wilcox." *Southern Historical Society Papers* 4 (1877): 111–17.

NEWSPAPERS

Adams, W. H. "Commander at Gettysburg: Some Prevalent Misconceptions Cleared Up by Official Records." *Minneapolis Journal*, Dec. 9, 1903, p. 9.

"Amid Flying Shot and Shell: Standards Borne by Minnesota Regiments." *Saint Paul Pioneer Press*, July 21, 1893.

Baasen, Francis. "Our Army Correspondence: Letter From Lieut. Baasen of the First Regiment, A Partial List of the Casualties." *St. Paul Pioneer*, July 16, 1863, p. 1.

Benedict, George G. "Wilcox's Brigade at Gettysburg." *National Tribune*, Aug. 19, 1886, p. 6.

"Birthday Celebrated by Conflict." *Minneapolis Tribune*, June 29, 1913, p. 10.

"A Charge of Peace! Survivors of the First Minnesota Meet Again on Memorable Ground." *Minneapolis Tribune*, July 3, 1897, p. 1.

Colvill, William. "The Old First Minnesota at Gettysburg." *Minneapolis Daily Tribune*, July 28, 1884, p. 2.

"Complete List of the Casualties in the First Minnesota, At Gettysburg." *Saint Paul Pioneer Press*, July 18, 1863, p. 2.

Conwell, F. A., and J. J. McCallum. "Letters from Adj. McCallum and Chaplain Conwell to Mrs. Messick, on the Death of her Husband." *Central Republican* (Faribault, Minn.), Aug. 5, 1863, p. 1.

Dey, Charles W. "Willard's Brigade." *National Tribune*, Sept. 24, 1908, p. 7.

Doane, E. "1st Minnesota at Gettysburg." *National Tribune*, Apr. 4, 1912, p. 11.

"The Draft in Brooklyn: The Drawing Commenced." *Brooklyn Daily Eagle*, Aug. 31, 1863, p. 2.

"The Dreadful Casualties of the First Minnesota." *Central Republican* (Faribault, Minn.), July 15, 1863, p. 2.

Eastman, P. M. "Cemetery Hill: How the 1st Minn. Gathered in the Prisoners." *National Tribune*, Nov. 16, 1905, p. 3.

"The First Minnesota," and "Terrible Slaughter in the First Minnesota." *Saint Paul Pioneer*, July 9, 1863, p. 1.

"The First Minnesota at Brooklyn, New York: The Boys Having a Grand Time." *New York Herald*, story reprinted in *Saint Paul Pioneer*, Sept. 5, 1863, p. 1.

"1st Minnesota at Gettysburg." *National Tribune*, Oct. 23, 1890, p. 4.

"The First Minnesota's Monument at Gettysburg." *Picket Guard*, July (?), 1897.

"The 1st Minnesota—The Recent Battles—But 87 out of 220 left—Sketch of the Organization." *State Atlas*, July 22, 1863.

"The First Regiment: The Return Home." *Saint Paul Pioneer*, Feb. 16, 1864, p. 1.

"From the First Minnesota." *Saint Paul Daily Press*, Sept. 9, 1863, p. 1.

Hagadorn, D. C. "On the Field of Gettysburg." *National Tribune*, Jan. 8, 1903, p. 3.

Hancock, Cornelia. "Young Girl Army Nurse at Gettysburg." *National Tribune*, Oct. 14, 1926, p. 5.

Harmon, William. "Co. C at Gettysburg." *Minneapolis Journal*, June 30, 1897.

Heffelfinger, C. B. "Says Colvill was in Command: Major C. B. Heffelfinger Writes to Correct Statement of W. H. Adams Concerning the Old First at Gettysburg." *Minneapolis Journal* (clipping from MHS scrapbook, "December 1903" given as date indicator).

"The History of a Regiment of Heroes." *Saint Paul Pioneer Press*, July 3, 1897, p. 2.

"In Honor of the Fallen Soldiers of the Minnesota First," and "From the First Minnesota." *Stillwater Messenger*, July 14, 1863, p. 2.

Hospes, Adolphus C. "From the First Minnesota." *Stillwater Messenger*, July 14, 1863, p. 2.

"The Killed and Wounded in the First Minnesota." *Central Republican* (Faribault, Minn.), July 29, 1863, p. 1.

Knox, Thomas W. "The Battle Field at Gettysburg." *Saint Paul Pioneer*, July 16, 1863, p. 4.

[Lochren, William]. "The First Minnesota: A Graphic Account of the Great Battle. Interesting Letter from an Officer" and "Wounded of the First Minnesota." *St. Paul Pioneer*, July 29, 1863, p. 1.

"Losses at Gettysburg Greatest in History." *Minneapolis Sunday Times*, Apr. 6, 1902, p. 13.

Maginnis, Martin. "The First Minnesota. The Most Gallant Charge of the War." Article from newspaper identified only as "Gouverneur, N.Y. newspaper, 1881[?]."

"The Military Force in the City." *Brooklyn Daily Eagle*, Aug. 29, 1863, p. 2.

Minneapolis Times, April 29, 1907 (multiple stories).

"Monuments at Gettysburg." *New York Times*, Oct. 4, 1888.

"No Feat of Arms Like It: Ride of the Six Hundred Out-done at Gettysburg." *Saint Paul Pioneer Press*, July 3, 1897, p. 2.

O'Brien, Henry D. "The 1st Minnesota at Gettysburg." *National Tribune*, Nov. 18, 1886, p. 3.

———. "The 1st Minnesota at Gettysburg." *National Tribune*, Dec. 7, 1893, p. 1.

———. "At Gettysburg. Troops at the Stone Wall, The High Water Mark of the Rebellion." *National Tribune*, Sept. 15, 1892, p. 4.

———. "Gettysburg." *National Tribune*, July 29, 1886, p. 3.

"One of the Grandest Charges in History: Graphic Account of the Work of the First Minnesota at the Battle of Gettysburg." *Minneapolis Journal*, Apr. 13, 1901, p. 5.

Page, Charles Anderson. "The 1st Minnesota—The Recent Battles—But 87 out of 220 Left—Sketch of the Organization." *New York Tribune*, July 10, 1863, p. 1.

Plummer, John W. "Correspondence: Letter from a Soldier of the First Minnesota." *State Atlas*, Aug. 26, 1863.

"A Prominent Citizen at Rest. Judge P. H. Taylor Died of Pneumonia at the Family Home Friday." *Cass County Democrat* (Mo.), Dec. 26, 1907.

"Roster of the Regiment—The Men Who Went into the Charge—The Survivors." *Minneapolis Journal,* June (?), 1897.

"Sergeant." "Battle of Gettysburg and the First Minnesota." *St. Paul Pioneer,* Aug. 9, 1863, p. 2.

"Story of the Regiment that Never Ran." *Minneapolis Journal,* June 26, 1897, p. 12.

Sonderman, J. G. "The 1st Minnesota's Daring." *National Tribune,* Jan. 17, 1901, p. 3.

"State's Heroes at Gettysburg: Artist Will Portray Charge of First Minnesota." *Saint Paul Pioneer Press,* Apr. 26, 1905.

Sweet, George M. "Willard's Brigade at Gettysburg." *National Tribune,* Aug. 12, 1915, p. 7.

"Vermont and Minnesota at Gettysburg." *National Tribune,* May 8, 1913, p. 3.

Walker, Francis A. "Hancock at Gettysburg." *National Tribune,* Oct. 28, 1886, p. 1.

"War Hero Is Dead." *Saint Paul Pioneer Press,* May 1, 1908.

Wheeler, Henry. "Willard's Brigade at Gettysburg." *National Tribune,* Sept. 24, 1908, p. 7.

"Where Many Fell: First Minnesota Veterans Arrive at Gettysburg." *Minneapolis Tribune,* July 2, 1897, p. 1.

Whitney, H. C. "Battle Field near Gettysburg, Pa.—July 5, 1863." *Central Republican* (Faribault, Minn.), July 29, 1863, p. 2.

"Who Wounded General Hancock?" *National Tribune,* Apr. 18, 1889, p. 5.

Wilkeson, Samuel. "Details from Our Special Correspondent." *New York Times,* July 6, 1863, p. 1.

Wright, J. A. "The 1st Minnesota. Its Part in the Battle of Gettysburg." *National Tribune,* Feb. 12, 1885, p. 3.

Youngs, Frank. "Willard's Brigade." *National Tribune,* Aug. 26, 1915, p. 7.

SECONDARY SOURCES
Books

Aho, James A. *Religious Mythology and the Art of War: Comparative Religious Symbolisms of Military Violence.* Westport, Conn.: Greenwood Press, 1981.

Bailey, Ronald H. *The Bloodiest Day: The Battle of Antietam.* Alexandria, Va.: Time-Life Books, 1984.

Betcher, William, and William Pollack. *In a Time of Fallen Heroes: The Re-Creation of Masculinity.* New York: Macmillan Publishing Co., 1993.

Buell, Thomas B. *The Warrior Generals: Combat Leadership in the Civil War.* New York: Three Rivers Press, 1997.

Busey, John W. *The Last Full Measure: Burials in the Soldiers' National Cemetery at Gettysburg.* Hightstown, N.J.: Longstreet House, 1988.

———. *These Honored Dead: The Union Casualties at Gettysburg.* Hightstown, N.J.: Longstreet House, 1988.

Busey, John W., and David G. Martin. *Regimental Strengths and Losses at Gettysburg.* Hightstown, N.J.: Longstreet House, 1994.

Campbell, Joseph. *The Hero with a Thousand Faces.* Bollingen Series 17, 3rd printing. Princeton: Princeton University Press, 1973.

———. *The Power of Myth.* With Bill Moyers, edited by Betty Sue Flowers. New York: Doubleday, 1988.

Carley, Kenneth. *Minnesota in the Civil War.* Minneapolis: Ross and Haines, 1961.

———. *Minnesota in the Civil War: An Illustrated History.* St. Paul: Minnesota Historical Society Press, 2000.

Catton, Bruce. *Glory Road.* New York: Doubleday, 1952.

———. *Mr. Lincoln's Army.* New York: Doubleday, 1951.

———. *Never Call Retreat.* Garden City, N.Y.: Doubleday, 1965.

Clark, Champ. *Gettysburg: The Confederate High Tide.* Alexandria, Va.: Time-Life Books, 1985.

Coco, Gregory A. *A Concise Guide to the Artillery at Gettysburg.* Gettysburg: Thomas Publications, 1998.

———. *A Strange and Blighted Land: Gettysburg—The Aftermath of a Battle.* Gettysburg: Thomas Publications, 1995.

———. *The Civil War Infantryman: In camp, on the march, and in battle.* Gettysburg: Thomas Publications, 1996.

Coddington, Edwin B. *The Gettysburg Campaign: A Study in Command.* New York: Charles Scribner's Sons, 1968.

Coggins, Jack. *Arms and Equipment of the Civil War.* 1962. Reprint, Wilmington, N.C.: Broadfoot Publishing Co., 1990.

Curtiss-Wedge, Franklyn, ed. *History of Goodhue County.* Chicago: H. C. Cooper, Jr., 1909.

Davis, William C., and Bell I. Wiley, eds. *Photographic History of the Civil War.* Compilation in 2 volumes by arrangement with Cowles Magazines. New York: Black Dog and Leventhal Publishers, 1994.

Dyer, Gwynne. *War.* New York: Crown Publishers, 1985.

Folwell, William Watts. *A History of Minnesota.* Vol. 3. Rev. ed. St. Paul: Minnesota Historical Society, 1956.

Foote, Shelby. *The Civil War: A Narrative. Fredericksburg to Meridian.* New York: Random House, 1963. Reprint, New York: Vintage Books, 1986.

Frassanito, William A. *Antietam: The Photographic Legacy of America's Bloodiest Day.* New York: Charles Scribner's Sons, 1978.

———. *Early Photography at Gettysburg.* Gettysburg: Thomas Publications, 1995.

———. *Gettysburg: A Journey in Time.* New York: Charles Scribner's Sons, 1975.

Furgurson, Ernest B. *Chancellorsville 1863: The Souls of the Brave.* New York: Alfred A. Knopf, 1992.

Gallagher, Gary W., ed. *The Second Day at Gettysburg: Essays on Confederate and Union Leadership.* Kent, Ohio: Kent State University Press, 1993.

———. *The Third Day at Gettysburg & Beyond.* Chapel Hill: University of North Carolina Press, 1994.

Gambone, A. M. *Hancock at Gettysburg... and beyond.* Army of the Potomac Series. Vol. 18. Baltimore: Butternut and Blue, 1997.

Gram, Kent. *The Chances of War: Lee, Longstreet, Sickles, and the First Minnesota Volunteers.* In *The Gettysburg Nobody Knows,* Gabor S. Boritt, ed. New York: Oxford University Press, 1997.

Griffith, Paddy. *Battle Tactics of the Civil War.* New Haven: Yale University Press, 1989.

Hess, Earl J. *The Union Soldier in Battle: Enduring the Ordeal of Battle.* Lawrence: University of Kansas Press, 1997.

Imholte, John Quinn. *The First Volunteers: History of the First Minnesota Volunteer Regiment, 1861–1865.* Minneapolis: Ross & Haines, 1963.

Jordan, David M. *Winfield Scott Hancock: A Soldier's Life.* Bloomington: Indiana University Press, 1988.

Lincoln, Bruce. *Discourse and the Construction of Society: Comparative Studies of Myth, Ritual, and Classification.* New York: Oxford University Press, 1989.

Lord, Francis A. *Civil War Collector's Encyclopedia.* New York: Castle Books, 1963.

———. *They Fought for the Union.* New York: Bonanza Books, 1960.

Luvaas, Jay, and Harold W. Nelson. *The U.S. Army War College Guide to the Battle of Gettysburg.* Carlisle, Pa.: South Mountain Press, 1986.

Lyman, Darryl. *Civil War Wordbook.* Conshohocken, Pa.: Combined Books, 1994.

McPherson, James M. *Battle Cry of Freedom: The Civil War Era.* New York: Oxford University Press, 1988.

McRandle, James H. *The Antique Drums of War.* Military History Series 33. College Station: Texas A&M University Press, 1994.

Moe, Richard. *The Last Full Measure: The Life and Death of the First Minnesota*

Volunteers. New York: Henry Holt and Co., 1993; reprint, St. Paul: Minnesota Historical Society Press, 2001.

Murry, R. L. *The Redemption of the "Harper's Ferry Cowards": The Story of the 111th and 126th New York State Volunteer Regiments at Gettysburg*. The author, 1994.

O'Malley, Michael. *Keeping Watch: A History of American Time*. Washington: Smithsonian Institution Press, 1990.

Oosten, Jarich G. *The War of the Gods: The Social Code in Indo-European Mythology*. London: Routledge & Kegan Paul, 1985.

Pfanz, Harry W. *Gettysburg: Culp's Hill & Cemetery Hill*. Chapel Hill: University of North Carolina Press, 1993.

——. *Gettysburg: The Second Day*. Chapel Hill: University of North Carolina Press, 1987.

Priest, John Michael. *Antietam: The Soldiers' Battle*. New York: Oxford University Press, 1989.

——. *Into the Fight: Pickett's Charge at Gettysburg*. Shippensburg, Pa.: White Mane Books, 1998.

Rollins, Richard. *"The Damned Red Flags of the Rebellion": The Confederate Battle Flag at Gettysburg*. Redondo Beach, Calif.: Rank and File Publications, 1997.

Ross, Steven. *From Flintlock to Rifle: Infantry Tactics, 1740–1866*. London: Associated University Presses, 1979.

Sears, Stephen W. *Controversies & Commanders: Dispatches from the Army of the Potomac*. Boston: Houghton Mifflin Co., 1999.

——. *Landscape Turned Red: The Battle of Antietam*. New York: Warner Books, 1983.

Stackpole, Edward J. *They Met at Gettysburg*. 3d ed. Harrisburg, Pa.: Stackpole Books, 1986.

Stevenson, Paul. *Wargaming in History: The American Civil War*. New York: Sterling Publishing Co., 1990.

Stewart, George R. *Pickett's Charge: A Microhistory of the Final Attack at Gettys-*

burg, July 3, 1863. Boston: Houghton Mifflin Co., 1959.

Svehla, Joe. *A Monumental Story of Gettysburg: A Complete Tour Guide to the Monuments at Gettysburg*. The author, 1993.

Tucker, Glenn. *Hancock the Superb*. Indianapolis: Bobbs-Merrill Co., 1960.

——. *High Tide at Gettysburg*. 1958. Reprint, New York: Konecky & Konecky, 1993.

United States of America's Congressional Medal of Honor Recipients and Their Official Citations. Columbia Heights, Minn.: Highland House II, 1994.

Warner, Ezra J. *Generals in Blue: Lives of the Union Commanders*. Baton Rouge: Louisiana State University Press, 1964.

Wheeler, Richard. *Witness to Gettysburg*. New York: Harper and Row, 1987.

Wiley, Bell Irvin. *The Life of Billy Yank: The Common Soldier of the Union*. Baton Rouge: Louisiana State University Press, 1952.

PERIODICALS

Austerman, Wayne R. "Case Shot and Canister: Field Artillery in the Civil War." *Civil War Times Illustrated* 26, no. 5 (Sept. 1987): 16–29, 43–48.

Campbell, Eric. "'Remember Harper's Ferry': The Degradation, Humiliation, and Redemption of Col. George L. Willard's Brigade." (Part 1 and 2) *Gettysburg Magazine*, no. 7 (July 1, 1992): 51–75, no. 8 (January 1993): 95–110.

Carmichael, Peter S. "Who's To Blame?" *Civil War Times Illustrated* 37, no. 4 (August 1998): 54–66.

Elmore, Thomas L. "A Meteorological and Astronomical Chronology of the Gettysburg Campaign." *Gettysburg Magazine*, no. 13 (July 1995): 7–21.

——. "The Florida Brigade at Gettysburg." *Gettysburg Magazine*, no. 15 (1996): 45–59.

Hadden, R. Lee. "The Granite Glory: The 19th Maine at Gettysburg." *Gettysburg Magazine*, no. 13 (July 1995): 50–63.

James, Garry. "The Union's Most Ready Rifle." *Civil War Times Illustrated* 28, no. 5 (Sept./Oct. 1989): 10–14.

Martin, Samuel J. "Did 'Baldy' Ewell Lose Gettysburg?" *America's Civil War* 10, no. 3 (July 1997): 34–40.

Maust, Roland R. "The Union Second Corps Hospital at Gettysburg, July 2 to August 8, 1863." *Gettysburg Magazine*, no. 10 (Jan. 1994): 53–101.

Meinhard, Robert W. "The First Minnesota at Gettysburg." *Gettysburg Magazine*, no. 5 (July 1991): 79–88.

Murphy, David J. "On the Line." *Civil War News* 25, no. 6 (July 1999).

Myers, J. Jay. "Who Will Follow Me?" *Civil War Times Illustrated* 32, no. 3 (July/Aug. 1993): 29–37, 73.

Narewood, Ermin D. "Attack and Counter Attack (Letters to the Editor column)." *Gettysburg Magazine*, no. 10 (Jan. 1994): 120–21.

Pfanz, Harry W. "The Gettysburg Campaign after Pickett's Charge." *Gettysburg Magazine*, no. 1 (July 1989): 118–24.

Rice, Gary R. "Devil Dan Sickles' Deadly Salients." *America's Civil War* 11, no. 5 (Nov. 1998): 38–45.

Samito, Christian G. "Lost Opportunity at Gettysburg." *America's Civil War* 13, no. 3 (July 1998): 46–53.

Selcer, Richard. "Pickett: Another Look." *Civil War Times Illustrated* 33, no. 3 (July/Aug. 1994): 44–49, 60–73.

Stefanon, Dyon. "Pickett's Charge by the Numbers." *Civil War Times Illustrated* 32, no. 3 (July/Aug. 1993): 34.

Welch, Richard F. "Gettysburg Finale." *America's Civil War* 6, no. 3 (July 1993): 50–57.

Wendel, Vickie. "First of the First." *Civil War Times Illustrated* 35, no. 4 (Aug. 1996): 42–47.

Wiggins, David. "The Civil War." *Roots* 12, no. 3 (spring 1984).

Winschel, Terrence J. "Their Supreme Moment: Barksdale's Brigade at Gettysburg." *Gettysburg Magazine*, no. 1 (July 1989): 71–77.

Zimmerman, Daniel. "J. E. B. Stuart: Gettysburg Scapegoat?" *America's Civil War* 11, no. 2 (May 1998): 50–57.

MAPS

The Battlefield at Gettysburg (map set)—Developed and Produced by Thomas A. Desjardin. A Project of the Friends of the National Parks at Gettysburg, 1998.

Illustrated Gettysburg Battlefield Map and Story. Gettysburg: TEM, 1984.

John B. Bachelder relief map set—Gettysburg Battlefield and troop positions, July 1, 2, 3, 1863. Morningside Press (reprint), 1995.

McElfresh Map Co.—two-map set: Watercolor historical (1863) base maps, Gettysburg Battlefield, 1994.

Topographic map of the Battle Field of Gettysburg, Showing the field as it was in 1863 and showing the field as it is in modern times, including the Cavalry Field—Kevin P. Twine, cartographer, 1988.

United States Geological Survey—digital satellite photos of Gettysburg National Military Park, www.terraserver.microsoft.com.

NOTES

NOTES TO THE PREFACE

1. Research Librarian Vickie Wendel of the Anoka County (Minnesota) Historical Society has done some fascinating research that indicates another man might deserve the honor of being first to volunteer. Documents, diaries, and newspaper stories led to Aaron Greenwald, a 28-year-old miller from Anoka. When Governor Ramsey telegraphed Adjutant General William Acker back in St. Paul, he also telegraphed Willis A. Gorman, an attorney and a former territorial governor of Minnesota, former congressman from Indiana, and a Mexican War veteran. Gorman was in district court in Anoka at the time. Since there was no telegraph connection between Anoka and St. Paul, a mounted courier rode to Anoka and delivered the telegraph message from Governor Ramsey.

Gorman asked to have the court session recessed, promptly delivered an impromptu speech to a group of assembled citizens, and began signing up volunteers. Greenwald was the first to sign an offer to enlist, shortly after 10:00 A.M. on Monday, April 15, 1861. Gorman went on to become the First Minnesota's first colonel and later a brigadier general, and Greenwald fell at Gettysburg, mortally wounded while fighting to repulse Pickett's Charge on July 3, 1863. He died on either July 5 or July 7, 1863.

2. See Appendix 4 for an assessment of the casualty rate and a list of dead and wounded.

NOTES TO CHAPTER 1

1. Diary, Sept. 20, 1862, Samuel Bloomer Papers, 1835–1917, Minnesota Historical Society (hereafter MHS).

2. Stephen W. Sears, *Landscape Turned Red: The Battle of Antietam* (New York: Warner Books, 1983), 130.

3. Sears, *Landscape Turned Red*, 359.

4. Bruce Catton, *Mr. Lincoln's Army* (New York: Doubleday, 1951), 327.

5. Ernest B. Ferguson, *Chancellorsville 1863: The Souls of the Brave* (New York: Alfred A. Knopf, 1992), 11.

6. Bruce Catton, *Glory Road* (New York: Doubleday, 1952), 34.

7. Shelby Foote, *The Civil War, A Narrative: Fredericksburg to Meridian* (New York: Vintage Books, 1986), 25.

8. John Quinn Imholte, *The First Volunteers: History of the First Minnesota Volunteer Regiment, 1861–1865* (Minneapolis: Ross and Haines, 1963), 110.

9. Thomas H. Pressnell, "Incidents in the Civil War," unpublished typescript, Twelfth Paper, p. 10, MHS.

10. Daniel Bond, Reminiscences, p. 72, unpublished manuscript (microfilm), MHS.

11. Catton, *Glory Road*, 93.

12. Charles Goddard letters, Orrin Fruit Smith Family Papers, 1829–1932, MHS.

13. Bond, Reminiscences, p. 74–75.

14. Bond, Reminiscences, p. 75.

15. Catton, *Glory Road*, 88.

16. [Isaac Lyman Taylor], "Campaigning with the First Minnesota: A Civil War Diary," ed. Hazel C. Wolf, *Minnesota History* 25 (Sept. 1944): 244.

17. Ferguson, *Chancellorsville 1863*, 18, 19.

18. Ferguson, *Chancellorsville 1863*, 25; see also Glenn Tucker, *Hancock the Superb* (Indianapolis: Bobbs-Merrill Co., 1960), 116, 117.

19. Darryl Lyman, *Civil War Wordbook* (Conshohocken, Pa.: Combined Books, 1994), 85.

20. Catton, *Glory Road*, 211.

21. Ferguson, *Chancellorsville 1863*, 158, 159.

22. Ferguson, *Chancellorsville 1863*, 339.

23. James M. McPherson, *Battle Cry of Freedom: The Civil War Era* (New York: Oxford University Press, 1988), 645. See also Bruce Catton, *Never Call Retreat* (Garden City, N.Y.: Doubleday, 1965), 160.

24. Sears, *Landscape Turned Red*, 74.

NOTES TO CHAPTER 2

1. James Wright, "The Story of Company F," p. 526, unpublished typescript, 1911, MHS. See also James A. Wright, *No More Gallant a Deed: A Civil War Memoir of the First Minnesota Volunteers*, ed. Steven J. Keillor (St. Paul: Minnesota Historical Society Press, 2001), which is an edited version of Wright's memoir.

2. Wright, "Company F," 538.

3. Wright, "Company F," 558.

4. Chester S. Durfee, journal of trip to 50th reunion of the Battle of Gettysburg, July 1913, MHS.

5. Return I. Holcombe, *History of the First Regiment, Minnesota Volunteer Infantry 1861–1864* (Stillwater, Minn.: Easton & Masterman, 1916), 313.

6. Hamlin Family Papers, 1861–1948, MHS.

7. Wright, "Company F," 542.

8. Wright, "Company F," 545, 546.

9. Wright, "Company F," 546.

10. [Taylor], "Campaigning," 358.

11. Daniel Zimmerman, "J. E. B. Stuart: Gettysburg Scapegoat?" *America's Civil War,* May 1998, p. 52, 53.

12. Zimmerman, "J. E. B. Stuart," 53.

13. The fact that the lost order, "Special Order No. 191," had been found by the Union army became publicly known in the spring of 1863. With that knowledge fresh in his mind as he was planning his Pennsylvania campaign, Lee was undoubtedly in an almost paranoid state about issuing written orders.

14. Edwin B. Coddington, *The Gettysburg Campaign: A Study in Command* (New York: Charles Scribner's Sons, 1968), 7, 8.

15. Thomas B. Buell, *The Warrior Generals: Combat Leadership in the Civil War* (New York: Three Rivers Press, 1997), 222–23.

16. Wright, "Company F," 552.

17. Charles Muller, "History of Company A," unpublished manuscript, MHS.

18. Harpers Ferry was, by the date of the battle, a part of the new state of West Virginia, which had been admitted to the Union on June 30, 1863, as a free state.

19. Holcombe, *History of the First Regiment,* 309, 310.

20. Bond, "Reminiscences," 84.

21. David L. Ladd and Audrey J. Ladd, eds., "Report of Lt. Col. Charles H. Morgan," in *The Bachelder Papers: Gettysburg in Their Own Words,* vol. 3 (Dayton, Ohio: Morningside Press, 1995), 1348. Morgan said that the marching orders for the day were delivered to corps headquarters and left on a table by a courier who did not, as was custom, deliver them to a staff member and obtain a receipt for the delivery. The orders were for the Second Corps to march at 4:00 A.M. on the morning of June 29; they were not found until 6:00 A.M., and the corps did not start marching until 8:00 A.M.

22. Holcombe, *History of the First Regiment,* 349.

23. William Lochren, "The First Minnesota at Gettysburg," in *Glimpses of the Nation's Struggle*, vol. 3 (St. Paul: D.D. Merrill Co., 1893), 45.

24. Wright, "Company F," 559.

25. James Wright noted that, overall, inspectors were not regarded very warmly by the men in the ranks. But Lieutenant Colonel Morgan seemed to have almost gone out of his way to irritate. With the Second Corps late start, Morgan made it his personal business to "flog" the troops along to make up the time. He would frequently ride up and down the line, ordering the various regimental colonels to hurry their troops along. Wright said, "More than once in his hurried rushes to the front he had ridden so close to the marching column as to spatter men with dirt or mud and giving the impression that he would about as soon ride over an ordinary man as not" (Wright, "Company F," 559).

By the time Morgan had placed Colonels Colvill and Ward under arrest, the men of the First Minnesota were nearly ready to take care of Morgan themselves. Wright said, "There were expressed desires to 'mar his visage' with a boot heel or the butt of a musket, and some even suggested the use of the other end of the gun in the usual way. However, strong as was our resentment, it was clearly understood that our colonel was in disgrace, wholly on our account, and any further demonstrations on our part would only 'make a bad matter worse,' and there was a prompt compliance with his wish to 'drop it for his sake'" (Wright, "Company F," 560).

26. M. H. Bassett, *From Bull Run to Bristow Station* (St. Paul: North Central Publishing Co., 1962), 27.

27. Wright, "Company F," 561. The emphasis on "*real* doughnuts" is Wright's. No doubt Wright was impressed, and pleased, with being served the real thing after eating so much of the ersatz version concocted from field rations. The innovative Civil War soldier, in his quest to add some variety (and taste) to his rations, came up with "skillygalee." Mainstay of the marching, or field, rations was hard bread, or hardtack as it commonly was known. Hardtack looked like a modern soda cracker, only the dimensions were roughly three inches square and half an inch thick. Nine or ten of these were issued per soldier as a day's bread ration. The ubiquitous nickname "sheet-iron cracker" gives an idea of how palatable they were.

Soldiers were also commonly issued fresh, pickled, or salt pork, which they would fry (and sometimes eat raw while marching or when too exhausted to cook). Skillygalee was born of left-over pork grease and crackers too tough to bite and chew. The soldier would soak a piece of hardtack in water until it was puffy and soft, then fry it in the grease. He would then rub it in sugar or salt. Depending on the seasoning, he would have the rough equivalent of a cake donut or a soft pretzel. Civil War reenactors have told the author that actually it is not too bad, for a bacon-flavored donut.

28. William Lochren, "Narrative of the First Regiment," in Minnesota Board of Commissioners on Publication of History of Minnesota in the Civil and Indian Wars, *Minnesota in the Civil and Indian Wars, 1861–1865*, vol. 1 (St. Paul, 1891), 34.

29. William Colvill mentioned that the people of Uniontown "gave a ball for the First at the principal hotel" on the evening of June 29 and that many of the officers and men who attended "did not come away till the small hours." It must be that Colvill was misremembering, given that this is mentioned in Folwell's interview in 1904; see typed and signed statement of Colvill, Dec. 22,1904, for William Watts Folwell, Folwell Papers, MHS. The author cannot discern any particular link that would induce the people of a small Maryland town to throw a ball, on very short notice, specifically for a regiment of Minnesotans. There is also no mention of the event by anyone else. In fact, after review-

ing Colvill's signed statement to Folwell, William Lochren told Folwell that he had no recollection of such a ball being given for the First Minnesota. While Lochren had been sent out on picket duty, as an officer he undoubtedly would have been invited to such an event and would surely have been told about it by anyone else attending.

It must also be remembered that Colvill was under arrest at this time, so it seems odd that he would be allowed out of camp to attend a party in town. The men of the regiment had also endured one of their longest and most grueling marches that day. Most accounts said, as the text indicates, that the men shuffled to the roadside and fell out to sleep. It is hard to imagine, however many die-hard, party-loving fellows were in the regiment, that any of these men were in the mood or condition to attend a ball. They had not been out of their clothes in nearly two weeks. Exhausted, ragged, filthy, stinking—it is inconceivable that any of them would attend a party, let alone stay "till the small hours" on the evening of June 29, 1863.

30. [Taylor], "Campaigning," 359.

31. Catton, *Glory Road*, 266.

32. Wright, "Company F," 573.

33. Wright, "Company F," 574.

NOTES TO CHAPTER 3

1. Wright, "Company F," 575; see also A[lanson] H. Nelson, *The Battles of Chancellorsville and Gettysburg* (Minneapolis, 1899), 78.

2. Diary, Mathew Marvin Papers, 1861–1895, MHS. Like many of his contemporaries, Marvin used a variety of spellings of his name, which appears in his letters and in the regimental history as Mat, Matt, Mathew, and Matthew; the author has chosen to use Mat as it was the spelling Marvin himself used most often.

3. Letter of John W. Plummer to his brother, published in *Minneapolis Atlas*, Aug. 26, 1863.

4. Wright, "Company F," 576.

5. Wright, "Company F," 575–56

6. Patrick Henry Taylor, unpublished typed transcript of Civil War diary, MHS.

7. Colvill statement to Folwell, p. 3, 10.

8. Wright, "Company F," 582.

9. The First Minnesota was shown as the last regiment in the reserve column in a map drawn by William Watts Folwell. The map was based on his interview with Colvill and accompanied the typed and signed statement Colvill made in 1904 for Folwell. John Bachelder's map indicated that the order of the brigade, front to back, was the Nineteenth Maine, Fifteenth Massachusetts, First Minnesota, and Eighty-Second New York. However, the battle report of Lieutenant Colonel George C. Joslin of the Fifteenth Massachusetts (commanding at the end of the battle) indicated not only that the brigade was in "close column by regiments" but that his regiment was behind the First Minnesota. See also *The War of the Rebellion: A Compilation of the Official Records of the Union and Confederate Armies*, ser. 1, vol. 27, part 1—Reports, U.S. War Department (Washington: Government Printing Office, 1889, hereafter cited as O.R.), 423.

10. Bond, "Reminiscences," 86.

11. *Minneapolis Morning Tribune*, June 29, 1913, p. 10.

12. Colvill, statement to Folwell, Dec. 22, 1904, p. 3, 4.

13. Colvill, statement to Folwell, Dec. 22, 1904, p. 4.

14. Muller, "History," 6.

15. Wright, "Company F," 247.

16. Wright, "Company F," 583.

17. Letter of William Lochren, March 3, 1893, *Bachelder Papers*, 1849. The battery that the sharpshooters supported was known as Kirby's battery, after former commander Edmund Kirby. Kirby had died from wounds received at the Battle of Chancellorsville. Minnesota actually had two companies of sharpshooters, and both were at Gettysburg. The First Company of Minnesota Sharpshooters had become Company A of the Second U.S.

Sharpshooters, commanded at Gettysburg by Major Homer R. Stoughton. On July 2 it was engaged near Little Round Top, and on July 3 it was near the center of the federal line during the repulse of Pickett's Charge.

The Second Company of Minnesota Sharpshooters became the eleventh company of Colonel Hiram Berdan's First U.S. Sharpshooters during the Peninsula Campaign in May 1862. This was somewhat unusual because the standard number of companies for any infantry regiment was ten. It was given the designation of Company L within Berdan's regiment. Less than a month later it was detached from Berdan's command and attached to the First Minnesota during the Battle of Fair Oaks. It remained with the First Minnesota until the regiment finished its three-year enlistment and returned to Minnesota. The company was still designated as Company L when it appeared on the rolls of the First Minnesota, but it was never officially consolidated with the regiment. It was always, officially, considered "detached" from Berdan and "attached" to the First Minnesota, although (as at Gettysburg) it was often detached from the regiment and sent where it was needed to do its "special kind of work."

18. Wright, "Company F," 584.

19. Muller, "History," 7.

20. Plummer letter, *Minneapolis Atlas*, Aug. 26, 1863.

21. This is a point of dispute among the various sources. John Plummer's letter indicated that the shell killed a sergeant named "Woodworth" and wounded three other men. He specifically stated that artillery did not start falling among them with any regularity until "about two o'clock"—therefore this incident happened after 2:00 P.M. but before the regiment shifted to the left and moved into the final position from which it charged later in the day. The roster for the First Minnesota calls the sergeant "Woodard."

Alfred Carpenter of Company K in a letter dated July 30, 1863, stated, "At about 10 o'clock the enemy commenced throwing shells at us, and owing to the peculiar shape of our line, they fell fast and close among us, massed as we were, behind a little eminence." Carpenter was referring to the fact that the brigade was just behind the crest of Cemetery Ridge and that they were massed within the brigade in column by regiment. This was a deadly formation with artillery falling because the massed block of men was such an easy target—one shell can have a devastating effect. Carpenter mentioned men "falling to rise no more" and others "being carried to the rear with more or less severe wounds." He went on to mention that before sunset they were ordered to the left. While he does not mention artillery casualties by name or specifically from the First Minnesota, his chronology and description indicated that the men were wounded while in the regiment's first, reserve, position.

Daniel Bond's history, probably written in 1916, did not specify the movement from the original reserve position to the final position of the regiment. It is hard to tell if he was indicating the artillery casualties happened at the first, reserve, position or at the final position. Bond also wrote that three men "in the next company to the right of us" were hit by the shell. One was killed, one's foot was blown off, and the third was "severly wounded."

James Wright in his memoir of 1911 stated that the artillery round fell into Company I after the shift to the left into the final position. He said that "Sergeant Oscar Woodward" was killed and "Sergeant O. M. Knight" was wounded. The way Wright phrased this does not necessarily indicate that no others were wounded but simply that these were the ones he was mentioning (perhaps because they were fellow sergeants and he knew them well).

Finally there is Charles Muller of Company A and his 1921 reminiscence. As the text indicates, Muller wrote that the artillery casualties occurred in the first, reserve, position behind Cemetery Ridge and only that "several of our men were badly wounded."

I tend to trust Plummer's and Carpenter's letters more than any other because they were both written within a few weeks of the battle. They also do not conflict with any other account except James Wright's, written several years after the battle. Wright is probably correct about the names, however.

22. Stephen W. Sears, *Controversies & Commanders: Dispatches from the Army of the Potomac* (Boston: Houghton Mifflin Co., 1999), 199.

23. Harry W. Pfanz, *Gettysburg: The Second Day* (Chapel Hill: University of North Carolina Press, 1987), 83, 93.

24. Pfanz, *Gettysburg*, 86–87, 91.

25. Pfanz, *Gettysburg*, p. 97–101; O.R., 515.

26. The exact time that this forward movement by Sickles commenced was another episode in the battle that was given a broad range. Various accounts mention everything from noon to 4:00 P.M., somewhere between 2:00 and 3:00 P.M. being the predominating approximation. The fact is, it was not one big push. Rather, Sickles moved his two divisions forward at different times, which accounts for at least some of the discrepancy. Birney's First Division went forward first, followed some time later by Humphreys's Second Division.

In his official report Birney stated that he sent out Berdan's reconnaissance party at noon, and when they returned with their information Sickles ordered Birney's division forward. This would have been after 2:00 P.M., since Berdan stated in his official report that this was the time he reported back to General Birney. Humphreys's official report stated that at noon he was ordered to form line of battle and to move forward to the base of Cemetery Ridge. His division maintained this position—probably just west of Plum Run, down in the swale—until 4:00 P.M., when the division moved forward to the

Emmitsburg Road. Any particular observer's notation of the time depended on what part of the Third Corps he saw moving forward and what sequence of the advance he saw.

27. McPherson, *Battle Cry of Freedom*, 657.

NOTES TO CHAPTER 4

1. Pfanz, *Gettysburg*, 107.

2. Pfanz, *Gettysburg*, 113; see also Coddington, *Gettysburg Campaign*, 377, 383, 384.

3. Jesse Bowman Young, *The Battle of Gettysburg: A Comprehensive Narrative* (New York: Harper & Brothers Publishers, 1913), 262, 263.

4. Pfanz, *Gettysburg*, 144.

5. O.R., 532.

6. O.R., 379; see also *Bachelder Papers*, 1194, 1195.

7. Pfanz, *Gettysburg*, 374.

8. Colvill statement to Folwell, Dec. 22, 1904, p. 5.

9. Wright, "Company F," 594.

10. John Day Smith, *The History of the Nineteenth Regiment of Maine Volunteer Infantry 1862–1865* (Minneapolis: Great Western Printing Co., 1909), 70.

11. It must have been either Turnbull's or Weir's battery, as there is no record of another being posted at this time or in this area that would have threatened nearly to run down the Nineteenth Maine.

12. Letter of Francis Heath to John Bachelder, Oct. 12, 1889; see also Pfanz, *Gettysburg*, 358, 375; O.R., 532.

13. Wright, "Company F," 594.

14. Wright, "Company F," 594–95. Wright said Colvill gave the order for Company F to go out as skirmishers, but he does not know if the order originated with Colvill or whether the colonel was himself acting on orders. Wright said, "We were only a single, little regiment—at most but 290, officers and men—posted alone on a hillside, and, apparently, forgotten in the surge of greater events around us." As indicated by Wright, given

the isolated position and circumstances of the First Minnesota, it is likely that Colvill acted on his own.

15. See Appendix 4 for a full discussion.

16. Pfanz, *Gettysburg*, 341.

17. Wright, "Company F," 595.

18. Bond, "Reminiscences," 89.

19. Wright, "Company F," 595.

20. Pfanz, *Gettysburg*, 333.

21. O.R., 483 (report of General Birney).

22. Pfanz, *Gettysburg*, 333.

23. Pfanz, *Gettysburg*, 334n134.

24. John W. Busey and David G. Martin, *Regimental Strengths and Losses at Gettysburg* (Hightstown, N.J.: Longstreet House, 1994), 137.

25. Pfanz, *Gettysburg*, 332.

26. Busey and Martin, *Regimental Strengths*, 185.

27. O.R., 618.

28. Herbert to John Bachelder, July 9, 1884.

29. Pfanz, *Gettysburg*, 374.

30. Pfanz, *Gettysburg*, 349; see also Wright, "Company F," 596.

31. Pfanz, *Gettysburg*, 156.

32. Pfanz, *Gettysburg*, 349 (both quotes).

33. Bond, "Reminiscences," 89.

34. Wright, "Company F," 595.

35. Paddy Griffith, *Battle Tactics of the Civil War* (New Haven: Yale University Press, 1989), 148–49; see also Garry James, "The Union's Most Ready Rifle," *Civil War Times Illustrated* 28, no. 5 (Sept./Oct. 1989): 14. As indicated in Appendix 2 on weapons and tactics, the rifle-musket had much greater range than the smoothbore weapons of earlier times (although smoothbores saw use through the end of the war). But there is a great difference between "effective range" of a weapon and the range where a man in the heat of battle may actually hit something. Needless to say, there were more than a few distractions to a man trying to fire a steady, well-aimed shot on a Civil War battlefield. The tendency to jerk the trigger, and thus pull the weapon upward as it fired, was the cause of countless mentions of officers

ordering the men to "fire low" and even to fire at the enemy's feet.

The standard rifle of the Union army, the Springfield .58 caliber rifle-musket, had an adjustable rear sight that could be calibrated for 100, 300, and 500 yards. The documented effective range was about 1,000 yards. While a bullet fired from one might travel that far, and even potentially hit and kill someone, the range at which most soldiers fired and could hit a man-size target was, at most, 250 yards and usually closer to 100. Many firefights occurred at even closer ranges.

36. Wright, "Company F," 595.

37. Silas Adams, "The Nineteenth Maine at Gettysburg," in *War Papers, Read Before the Commandery of the State of Maine, Military Order of the Loyal Legion* (Portland: Lefavor-Tower Co., 1898–1919), 251.

38. Lochren, "Narrative of the First Regiment," 1:35.

39. The only reference to "fixing bayonets" that the author has found is from Henry O'Brien in an 1893 article he wrote for the *National Tribune*. O'Brien was prone to hyperbole and some exaggeration in his postwar reminiscences, and this article is no exception: "Without hesitation the order was given: 'Forward—fix bayonets—charge!'" This is an unlikely sequence of orders. The order to fix bayonets would have been given before the men were ordered forward, but it indicates that the order could have been given just before the men advanced. Henry D. O'Brien, "The 1st Minnesota at Gettysburg," *National Tribune*, Dec. 1893, p. 1.

NOTES TO CHAPTER 5

1. O.R., 370; see also Pfanz, *Gettysburg*, 376.

2. Eric Campbell, "'Remember Harper's Ferry': The Degradation, Humiliation, and Redemption of Col. George L. Willard's Brigade" (Part 1), *Gettysburg Magazine*, July 1, 1992, p. 64.

3. R. L. Murry, *The Redemption of the "Harper's Ferry Cowards": The Story of the*

111th and 126th New York State Volunteer Regiments at Gettysburg (The author, 1994), 38; see also Sears, *Landscape Turned Red*, 170.

4. Like most accounts of events at Gettysburg, Willard's movement south was given a broad range of start times. Times of 4:00 and 5:00 P.M. were given in regimental commander's Official Reports; 5:30 P.M. by one participant in an 1868 letter; 7:00 P.M. in a 1900 report of the New York Monument Commission. This is probably closer to the correct time, in relation to the times of other events. Willard's brigade probably moved south from its place in the Second Corps line sometime between 6:30 and 7:00 P.M.

5. O.R., 370.

6. Former Sergeant George M. Sweet of Company I, 125th New York Regiment, wrote that Hancock met Willard's brigade "where the 1st Minn. monument now stands," or, in other words, right behind the First Minnesota as the regiment was lying on the slope of Cemetery Ridge; George M. Sweet, "Willard's Brigade at Gettysburg," *National Tribune*, Aug. 12, 1915, p. 7.

7. Wright, "Company F," 596.

8. Bond, "Reminiscences," 90.

9. Pfanz, *Gettysburg*, 346. See also Coddington, *Gettysburg Campaign*, 416; Gregory A. Coco, *A Concise Guide to the Artillery at Gettysburg* (Gettysburg: Thomas Publications, 1998), 20, 21, 31.

10. Wright, "Company F," 597.

11. *New York Monuments Commission for the Battlefields of Gettysburg and Chattanooga: Final Report of the Battlefield of Gettysburg*, vol. 2 (Albany: J. B. Lyon Co., 1900), 800.

12. O.R., 474, 475.

13. Letter of Hancock to Bachelder, Nov. 7, 1885, *Bachelder Papers*, 1134; see also O.R., 371.

14. O.R., 371.

15. Frank Aretas Haskell provided an interesting variation to this story (the account in the text is largely drawn from Hancock's own battle report and reminis-

cence). Haskell wrote: "Gen. Hancock and his Aides rode up to Gibbon's Division, under the smoke. Gen. Gibbon, with myself, was near, and there was a flag dimly visible, coming towards us from the direction of the enemy. 'Here, what are these men falling back for?' said Hancock. The flag was no more than fifty yards away, but it was the head of a Rebel column, which at once opened fire with a volley. Lieut. Miller, Gen. Hancock's Aide, fell, twice struck, but the General was unharmed, and he told the 1st Minn., which was near, to drive these people away."

Haskell seemed to have been everywhere at Gettysburg where something significant was happening. This is, in fact, not far from the truth, and his account was written within weeks of the battle. Any embellishments aside, the events were certainly fresh in his mind. Prior to writing, he would have had time to interview various participants (which he no doubt did), but there is no particular reason that he might not have been with Gibbon on that part of the field at that time.

He was Gibbon's aide, and Gibbon was, at that time, in immediate command of the entire Second Corps. What is incorrect is Haskell's assertion that the Confederates were only fifty yards off. They were more than 300 yards away at that time. Hancock rode toward them with his aide, Captain (not Lieutenant) Miller, and was probably fifty yards or less from the rebels when they fired their ragged volley at the mounted officers, hitting Miller twice.

16. Letter of Hancock to Bachelder, Nov. 7, 1885, *Bachelder Papers*, 1134.

17. Letter of Colvill to Bachelder, June 9, 1866, *Bachelder Papers*, 256; see also Lochren, "Narrative of the First Minnesota," 1:35.

NOTES TO CHAPTER 6

1. Colvill statement to Folwell, Dec. 22, 1904, p. 6; see also letter from Colvill to Bachelder, Aug. 30, 1866, *Bachelder Papers*, 256.

2. Determining the actual order of the companies from extant accounts of the charge helped to place events along the regimental battle line. The army manuals of the day provided a definitive order based on the commission dates of the company captains. This appears simple enough, but it is complicated by a number of factors. First, Company C had been detached as part of the divisional provost guard since January 1863. Did this negate their place in the line? Or was the commission date of its captain observed and their place in line maintained with the regiment simply closing up on the empty space?

There are also some instances—at least two on record—of first lieutenants commanding companies at the time of the charge. Thomas Sinclair of Company B had a captain's commission date of July 4, 1863. The previous captain, Mark Downie, had become the regiment's major (commission date May 6, 1863). Since Sinclair was serving as commander with a first lieutenant's commission, what did that do to his company's place in the line? Logic would say its position immediately went to last place because that was where the company would be as soon as he received his commission.

Christopher Heffelfinger's recollections, published in 1915, indicated that he commanded Company D during the charge, which is supported by one of Colonel Colvill's orders, dated June 13, 1863 (see Chapter 2). The records show that Captain DeWitt C. Smith commanded the company and First Lieutenant Heffelfinger was not commissioned the company's captain until after the battle. Smith was transferred to Company G in August 1863 because its captain, Nathan Messick, had been killed. However, Smith was severely wounded at Antietam and had been recovering in Minnesota ever since and was referred to by some as "recruiting" back in Minnesota. Even after Smith was placed in command of Company G, there is no indication that

he was ever able to rejoin the regiment. He finally resigned from the regiment on October 7, 1863, and became an army paymaster. He was subsequently killed by Confederate guerillas.

Heffelfinger also said that Lieutenant Martin Maginnis commanded Company H during the charge. However, he talked about Captain John N. Chase, of Company H, and an incident just prior to Pickett's Charge on the third day of the battle. Daniel Bond also mentioned Chase as being present. In addition, Chase was indicated as being present on both the June 28 Consolidated Morning Report muster roll as well as on the June 30 payroll muster. His service record in the National Archives also indicates he was present with the regiment during the Battle of Gettysburg. If Chase was in the battle, then he did command Company H. Heffelfinger indicated that his own Company D was on the left flank of the regiment. This is accurate and supported by what the order of companies should have been by captains' commission dates and also the account of John Plummer of Company D, written shortly after the battle.

In my calculations I have treated the detached Company C as if it were not, at that time, part of the regiment. This was normal in other instances, including muster rolls, which simply indicated "on detached service." Therefore, I have considered only the remaining nine companies when shuffling them in line according to captains' commission dates.

In addition to Heffelfinger's account, there are several other articles, papers, books, and so on, in which veterans of the regiment indicate certain companies that were near their own, or mention a company on the end of the line. Many (most) of these cannot be reconciled with the order in which the companies should have been placed. The order changed numerous times throughout the war, and most of these accounts were written from twenty-five to fifty or more years after the war. One, written by Jasper Searles in 1890, noted that Company I was on the right flank during the charge and that it was commanded by a lieutenant. Searles was not in the charge, nor even with the regiment during Gettysburg. He had been assigned to command the division's ambulance corps several months prior to the battle. He helped evacuate the wounded off the field during the night of July 2, 1863. A further bit of evidence is a photograph in the papers of Louis W. Hill, in the James J. Hill Reference Library in St. Paul, Minnesota (see p. 138), which shows several members of Company A, First Minnesota, during the 1897 dedication of the regiment's monument on the battlefield. The men are sitting and reclining on boulders in the Plum Run swale, and the caption states it is where these men fought during the stand on Plum Run. Among those pictured is Henry Coates, captain of Company A during the battle. Colonel Colvill mentioned speaking to Coates during the fight along Plum Run, thus affirming Company A's spot in the center of the line, since that is where Colvill was positioned.

When a regiment was at a halt and in line of battle, a company's captain always was posted on the far right of the front rank. Consequently the only captain who should have been close enough to talk with Colvill would have been the captain of the company directly to the left of the color guard (center) of the regiment. Confirming that this was Captain Coates of Company A helps to ascertain the physical placement of other companies in the line.

In addition, the boulders in the photograph can still be seen on the battlefield today and are in a straight line from the regiment's monument on Cemetery Ridge down to Plum Run. It was common for regiments to establish monuments in the direct center of their regimental line positions. Members of the monument committee could have used these boulders as a landmark to establish the central position of the monument. However, we must remember that the men in the photograph spent mere minutes down among the boulders during the battle, and they had a lot more on their minds at that time than making mental notes of boulder configurations. Some very likely saw the area again while burying the regiment's dead on July 4 and could have made a lasting mental note of a specific configuration of a jumble of boulders. But there are many individual boulders and clusters of boulders along Plum Run, and most of the men did not see the area again for thirty-four years.

Timothy Smith, a Gettysburg Licensed Battlefield Guide, speculates that on the day of the monument dedication, it is just as likely that the men walked straight down from the monument and found the cluster of boulders. They may have posed among them and probably were in the general area of where they fought. However, there is no guarantee that they were on the exact spot, the photograph's handwritten caption notwithstanding. Smith also speculates that because the First Minnesota was in its position a mere two hours or so, there is no guarantee the regiment's monument marks the exact center of the July 2, 1863, position, although it is undoubtedly close to the spot where they were posted and certainly could be the exact one.

The regiment was in the middle of acres of farm fields, with few natural landmarks. They could have gotten some visual bearings from farmhouses and the position of the Round Tops to the south, but a lot of the topography had changed by the time the monument committee did its work. Fences were gone, or fence lines had changed; Hancock Avenue had been added to the crest of Cemetery Ridge, and the tracks and right-of-way for an electric trolley ran across the field where the charge had taken place; trees were taller or growing in many places where they had not during the battle, while some areas still wooded during the battle had been cut down.

A second photograph (of the four photograph series in the Hill collection) has the same group of men standing in front of the lone, fanned-out tree that looks to be about twenty or thirty feet behind the boulders (to the right of center in the "boulder" photograph). This photograph has the same handwritten caption as the "boulder" photograph, indicating that the men are "Standing on the ground and on the very spot where they were wounded in that Immortal Charge at Gettysburg, July 2nd/63."

The photographic evidence aside, the captains of all the companies and their commission dates are a matter of record. The only captains who have no direct, firsthand accounts indicating they led their companies during the charge are John N. Chase (H), Wilbur F. Duffy (I), and DeWitt C. Smith (D). Smith and Chase were discussed above. Duffy was mentioned in Daniel Bond's reminiscence as having been in the battle. Bond said Duffy was part of General John Gibbon's staff and did not return to the regiment until after the battle. If this is the case, and one of his lieutenants led the company in the charge, Duffy would still be considered captain of his company—on detached service—and it seems likely his commission date would still be considered in determining his company's place in the battle line.

Records of Gibbon's staff members do not include the name of Captain Wilbur F. Duffy, nor does any other general's staff roster for the Battle of Gettysburg. However, the June 28 muster roll does specify that the captain of Company I was on "detached service." Duffy was also missing from the name list for Company I on the June 30 payroll muster. Perhaps Jasper Searles was correct in his contention that Company I was lead by a lieutenant during the charge, even if he was mistaken in his memory of its placement. In any case, it appears Duffy was at the battle but on detached service in some capacity.

A final conundrum is John Ball's exact rank at the time of Gettysburg. Regimental records show John Ball was appointed captain on May 6, 1863, but that he was not officially mustered in as captain until July 6, 1863—three days after the Battle of Gettysburg. Normal assignment by seniority would have made him captain of Company B, which was commanded by First Lieutenant Thomas Sinclair since Mark Downie's rise to the rank of major in May 1863. Ball requested, and was allowed, to stay with Company F and serve as its captain. July 6, 1863, would normally be his "commission date," but that seems to have been made officially retroactive to May 6, 1863.

Daniel Bond of Company F pointed out in his memoir that Ball was a lieutenant at Gettysburg and did not become a captain (receive his commission) until after the battle. However, Bond was a private, and former Orderly Sergeant James Wright of Company F stated in his reminiscence that Ball was a captain as of May 6, 1863. In his capacity as sergeant, Wright would have worked closely with the company commander. Not only would a private not have done so, but Bond made it clear that he had some issues with and some hard feelings toward Ball. It appears then that Ball was considered and functioned as a captain as of May 6, 1863.

One more thing muddles the matter, though. The Consolidated Morning Report for June 28, 1863, listed a Company F officer as "absent-sick" and that Company F did not have a captain present. In addition, the report noted that the regiment had one captain who was "unassigned" (that is, not attached to a company). The captain of Company F prior to Ball, Captain John J. McCallum, had been wounded at Fredericksburg and transferred to the Invalid Corps.

Since both lieutenants for Company F were listed as "present," the only person who was a commissioned officer who could have been "absent-sick" at that time was Captain John McCallum. Perhaps, even though transferred to the Invalid Corps, he had not yet been mustered out from the First Minnesota and was therefore carried on the rolls. It would seem to indicate that the "unassigned" captain was John Ball, who must have been in something of an "on paper" limbo since he wanted to stay with Company F and did not want to take the captaincy of Company B.

As unlikely as it seems, if McCallum were still carried on the rolls of the First Minnesota at the time of Gettysburg and his commission date was still considered when placing the companies in line, it would have altered the order of the companies in the charge. McCallum's commission date for captain was September 17, 1861—the same date as Captain Joseph Perium's of Company K. The order of placement would depend on which of the two had first been mustered in as captain on that day. If McCallum, the order for the companies during the charge would be: D, H, A, I, B, K, E, G; if Perium, the order would be: D, H, A, I, K, B, E, G. This, again, assumes that no reshuffling was done after Company F was sent out as skirmishers and the regiment simply closed up.

The author feels McCallum's status did not figure in, but rather that John Ball was considered a captain as of May 6, 1863, and therefore the order of companies during the charge conforms to the order delineated in the text. This contention is supported by fitting the historical accounts of the charge into place on the line, according to the company of the author of the particular account, as well as the hard evidence of the photograph with Henry Coates, mentioned above, and the accounts relating to him.

3. According to Lochren's 1890 regimental history and Colvill's 1904 narrative, General Hancock asked Colvill, "What regiment is this?" and Colvill answered, "First Minnesota." No mention was made of this in Colvill's 1866 telling of the story, nor in his letter published in the *Minneapolis Daily Tribune* in July 1884. It does

not make sense that Hancock would ask this, receive an answer, and then circulate a letter throughout the army several days after the battle asking what regiment made the charge—which he did.

Ultimately, in the heat of the moment, it probably did not matter much to Hancock who they were, just as long as they were armed and wearing blue uniforms. Likewise, Hancock could have blurted out the question and not really listened to the answer or possibly not heard it in all of the noise and confusion. That could have prompted him to circulate the letter after the battle. Hancock was then said to have pointed to the Confederate battle flags of Wilcox's brigade and ordered Colvill to advance and take the colors.

In Colvill's 1884 account he had Hancock on the left of the First Minnesota. He stated that when Hancock stopped trying to rally Third Corps troops, he "rushed to the right rear, near the battery" to look north for expected federal reinforcements. He did not see any coming. According to Colvill, it was at this point that Hancock said, "My God, are these all the troops we have here?" Colvill did not hear Hancock say this but was told about it later.

Hancock then hastened to the right front of the First Minnesota, and as Colvill remembered it, "His order was 'Minnesota Forward!' delivered with all his force and action." Colvill continued, "The men of the regiment all heard it, and saw him as he delivered it, and turned their heads toward me, expecting and ready for my order, which was immediately given."

Colvill's 1904 interview given to Folwell provided yet another variation. Colvill said that rather than "rushing" (which seemed to indicate on foot), Hancock remounted after trying to rally the fleeing men of the Third Corps. He "rode" to Lieutenant Evan Thomas's artillery battery to the right and slightly behind the First Minnesota and momentarily surveyed the situation facing his line. He apparently sent the wounded Captain Miller to an aid station, as Colvill mentioned that Hancock "had sent his orderly on some errand." Hancock then "galloped off northward," only to return "five minutes later" and pause briefly at the artillery battery again. He finally rode to Colvill to ask what regiment his was and to order it to charge.

A very interesting alternative account written in 1921 by eighty-nine-year-old Charles Muller, formerly of Company A, stated that about the time Sickles's Third Corps was falling back, "A full brigade of new troops came along from the direction of Gettysburg and filed on our left and about 20 yards in our front. We judged them to be new troops from the fact that they were full ranks and all had new uniforms." Undoubtedly this was Willard's brigade. Muller remembered that Hancock asked what troops these were but that he was addressing the new brigade. More probably, he was addressing the regiment closest to the left of the First Minnesota, which was the 111th New York. According to Muller, Hancock ordered that body of troops to attack, and "when the order was given, our Colonel Colvill dit stab to the front of our regiment and said, 'Boys, will we go along wit them?' and we answered 'yes,' and then the order was given 'forward, march.'"

Muller's Company A was at the center of the regimental line, so it seems unlikely—with three companies to his left and at least twenty yards or more before the line of 111th New York even started—that he actually heard Hancock addressing that regiment and asking who they were. This is especially true because of the artillery fire going on around them. He would, however, be close to Colvill as the colonel stepped through the regiment to the front to ask or order anything. Hancock did order the 111th New York to charge prior to ordering in the First Minnesota but probably ten to twenty minutes earlier. It is likely that in Muller's fifty-eight-year-old memories, events were somewhat merged.

In an 1886 newspaper letter, Henry O'Brien stated, "It was at this time that General Hancock ordered the 1st Minn. and 111th N.Y. to charge." O'Brien, like Muller, seemed to be tying the two charges together, even mentioning his own regiment first, although the 111th New York charged before the First Minnesota, and he undoubtedly saw Hancock ordering the 111th New York to charge and then saw them advance. O'Brien's Company E was the next company to the left of Muller's Company A. Muller and O'Brien probably found out sometime after the battle that it was the 111th New York directly south of them.

But, like Muller, O'Brien was writing a good number of years after the event (twenty-three years in O'Brien's case). One charge followed close on the heels of the other, but given Hancock's movements at that time, it had to be at least ten to fifteen, perhaps twenty, minutes after the advance of the 111th New York that the First Minnesota was ordered to charge. See Henry D. O'Brien, "Gettysburg," *National Tribune*, July 29, 1886, p. 3.

4. Lochren, "Narrative of the First Regiment," 35.

5. Lochren, "Narrative of the First Regiment," 36.

6. O.R., 236, report of General Henry J. Hunt; see also Bachelder map.

7. Pfanz, *Gettysburg*, 374.

8. Shoulder arms was the standard placement of weapons when standing at attention. The rifle-musket is held in the right hand with the arm extended down, but very slightly bent, and close to the body. The weapon's barrel rests on, and extends above, the shoulder. The soldier holds the weapon with the trigger guard facing forward, his index finger and thumb wrapped around the trigger guard and the other fingers holding the neck of the stock where it begins to flare out into the butt of the stock. The back of the hammer rests on the little finger. Dressing ranks on the colors is an action in which each man moves slightly to the right if he

is on the left of the regimental colors or to the left if he is on the right of the colors. It closes up any gaps and gives a tight, shoulder-to-shoulder line formation.

9. Right shoulder shift was the standard placement of weapons for marching or charging. The rifle-musket is placed flat on its side against the front of the shoulder, the lock (the hammer, lock-plate, and nipple of the weapon) facing upward. The soldier holds the flat side of the butt stock with an opened hand, with the little finger and ring finger curled under to hold the end of the butt. The butt of the stock is held about midchest height and the elbow is tucked in close to the body. This position kept the very long rifle-musket up and out of the way, especially out of the faces of those men behind. Needless to say, this was particularly important when the bayonet was attached.

10. Colvill letter in *Minneapolis Daily Tribune*, July 28, 1884, p. 2.

11. Colvill statement to Folwell, Dec. 22, 1904, p. 7. See also Plummer letter, *Minneapolis Atlas*, Aug. 26, 1863. Interviews with landowners in 1868 indicated that corn was growing in the first field that the First Minnesota crossed (the one within which they were actually posted) during the battle. However, these interviews were not always reliable. Some land had changed hands since 1863, and in other cases farmers simply did not remember what they had in a specific field at the time of the battle (information provided by Gettysburg National Military Park Ranger Thomas Holbrook, letter to author, June 12, 1997). While this survey showed the first field had corn, which would have been about knee-high at the time of the battle, and the second field had wheat, extant records from the participants in the charge seem to be clear that the first field was a "pasture" and the second field of wheat had already been harvested.

12. One soldier mentioned moving out of one field and into another, but not a single extant recounting of the charge

mentioned having to contend with fences. This would have been a major obstacle, and having to cross one—let alone two—would probably have caused the charge to fizzle and the regiment to never make it to the Confederate line.

In addition to the already mentioned Official Reports, and a letter from Hancock to John Bachelder, Dec. 17, 1885, further proof of the condition of the fences can be seen in the background of the Rufus Zogbaum painting of the *Charge of the 1st Minnesota at Gettysburg*, hanging in the governor's reception room of the Capitol in St. Paul, Minnesota. You can see the remnants of a post-and-rail fence that has been torn down. Zogbaum did a lot of research for his painting—on the field and by interviewing members of the regiment who had made the charge. He pursued historical accuracy and likely was told by one or more of the veterans of the First Minnesota that the fences on the charge field had been pulled down.

13. Timing is based on the author's own double-quick charge over the original ground.

14. Stubble is the term generally used for harvested wheat as opposed to stalk field used for harvested corn; information provided to author by Iowa farmer Donovan Marsh. Farmers in this area of Pennsylvania could get two crops of wheat in a year—winter wheat and summer wheat; information provided to author by Gettysburg Military Park Ranger Thomas Holbrook. Farmer Edward H. Bassett of Company G mentioned in his diary, while approaching Gettysburg, "The crops look splendid. There is lots of wheat here and it is ready to cut."

15. Folwell's notes from interview with William Lochren where he discussed specifics of Colvill's statement of Dec. 22, 1904. Other renditions of the story support Lochren over Colvill, including those quoted in text below—"unknown sergeant" said "Marching as file-closer, it seemed as if every step was over some fallen comrade" and Colvill himself, later

in the Folwell statement, as he was looking back up the slope, "I saw numbers of our men lying upon it [the slope] as they had fallen," which seems, in the context of what else he said, to indicate a number greater than twelve or fifteen.

16. Lucia L. Heffelfinger Peavey, *Memoirs of Christopher B. Heffelfinger* (Santa Barbara, Calif., 1915; Minneapolis, 1922), 34. A study of the casualty lists reveals that there were certainly as many, if not more, leg wounds in the First Minnesota as head and upper body wounds. It could be these lower extremity wounds occurred as the regiment started down the slope, and the upper body wounds increased as the men reached the bottom of the slope into the ravine. This would make sense taking into account the trajectory of the Confederate rifle fire, with the Confederates moving more slowly and the First Minnesota coming down the slope at the double-quick.

The rifle-musket had a prominently arching trajectory. If the sights were set for 300 yards, there would be lower-body wounds at the beginning of the charge, chest and head wounds for about 100 yards, followed by nearly 200 yards of fire going over the men's heads. The final 30 to 50 yards would see more head wounds. With wild and/or panic firing and the close combat in the Plum Run ravine, it is not surprising that the wounds of the First Minnesota soldiers ran from head to feet. See Jack Coogins, *Arms and Equipment of the Civil War* (1962; reprint, Wilmington, N.C.: Broadfoot Publishing Co., 1990), 38–39.

17. "Unknown Sergeant" letter, *St. Paul Pioneer*, Aug. 9, 1863, p. 2.

18. Marvin diary, July 2, 1863.

19. Marvin described his wound in a letter to his brother, George, July 25, 1863: "The ball entered about 1 1/2 inches back of the two little toes & about 2 inches from the outside of the foot & passed, I think, between the bones or cords & came out at the point of the heal underneath my ancle." Marvin Papers.

20. Lochren, "Narrative of the First Regiment," 35.

21. Letter of Daniel Sullivan, "Fort Schylear, N.Y., July 31, 1863," typed transcript from private collection. The military training manuals of the day gave two different speeds or cadences for the double-quick-step march, depending on the need for haste: 165 steps and 185 steps per minute. David J. Murphy, a Civil War reenactor who writes the column "On the Line" for the historical-reenacting newspaper *The Civil War News*, noted, "The double quick step of 165 per minute is a brisk walk, while that of 185 steps is a light jog. In reenacting when the order double quick time is given the result is usually a wild, disorganized charge. Double quick time is an organized advance during which the lines are kept dressed"; Murphy, "On the Line," July 1999, p. 25.

While members of a veteran Civil War regiment were much better and more consistently drilled as a unit than any of today's reenactors, it is probable that the First Minnesota did spread out as they moved down the slope of Cemetery Ridge. Lochren made it clear that it rapidly became a flat-out race to get to the bottom of the slope as fast as possible.

22. The general research notes in the John Bachelder Papers state that the First Minnesota's charge was made at the left oblique—the same maneuver that Company F made when deploying as a skirmish line. Depending on the configuration of Wilcox's line, this could have caused the right of the First Minnesota to make contact before the left. A logical analysis indicates that it should have caused the left of the line to hit Wilcox's line first. However that does not allow for the likelihood that Wilcox's right was then being engaged by Willard's 111th New York. Given the fact that Wilcox's line was still moving in its divergent advance from Barksdale's brigade, it would have been approaching Plum Run on a north-northeast axis. The First Minnesota might very well have had to charge in a slight left

oblique, or west-southwest direction, to hit Wilcox's brigade head on. The reference to left oblique in the Bachelder notes could also simply be a misunderstanding of some source (possibly Wright) that Company F advanced at the left oblique. It is significant that the First Minnesota's monument on the field of the charge faces west-southwest. Perhaps the reference to the charge being made at the left oblique refers to the regiment's position in relation to the rest of the federal line extending north on Cemetery Ridge and not the regiment's own frontal axis.

23. Sullivan letter, "Fort Schylear, N.Y., July 31, 1863."

24. Lochren, "Narrative of the First Regiment," 35.

25. Colvill statement to Folwell, Dec. 22, 1904, p. 7. It is difficult to discern clearly from any account exactly how the volley took place. In 1904 Lochren contended that he did not remember a "volley fired into the faces of the rebels, nor the return volley of the confederates"; notes accompanying Colvill's statement, Folwell Papers. It could be that only those close enough to hear Colvill's order, Company A in the center, actually delivered a volley and that the rest of the regiment started a ragged fire-at-will after hearing the volley. Lochren was in Company K on the right of the regiment, with Company B between K and A.

The only hope of the charge succeeding was the shock value of the leveled bayonets. If the regiment stopped to fire a volley, it might make the volley more accurate but would slow the forward momentum and shock of the charge. In his statement to Folwell, Colvill mentioned that the regiment was ordered to fire "within a rod" of the dry stream bed of Plum Run. This would have been a mere five-and-a-half yards! The Confederates probably had not backed up much more than that distance on the other side of Plum Run.

In a letter from Colvill to John Bachelder, June 9, 1866, Colvill said that they delivered the volley "in their very faces" (which certainly describes six to twelve yards' distance), but then he added, "and then we charged." This would apparently indicate that they stopped to deliver the volley, and then he ordered "charge bayonets" with only a few yards between the First Minnesota and the rebels. Other accounts, such as Charles Muller's, indicate that they fired and "then we went at them with our bayonets." It seems likely that either Colvill ordered the men to fire on the run, and then the momentum continued for a few yards, or he brought them to the lip of the ravine with the recoiling rebels on the other side of Plum Run, ordered them to fire, and then each man loaded, sought cover, and bayoneted or clubbed a rebel as he saw the opportunity.

26. George Clark, "Wilcox's Alabama Brigade at Gettysburg," *Confederate Veteran* 17, no. 5 (May 1909): 229.

27. Muller, "History," 11.

28. Martin Maginnis, "The First Minnesota: The Most Gallant Charge of the War," newspaper article from paper identified only as "Gouverneur, N.Y. newspaper, 1881[?]," Taylor Papers.

29. William Colvill, "The Old First Minnesota at Gettysburg," *Minneapolis Daily Tribune*, July 28, 1884, p. 2.

30. O.R., Part 2, p. 616 (Cadmus Wilcox's report).

31. Sullivan letter, "Fort Schylear, N.Y., July 31, 1863."

32. Colvill to Bachelder, June 9, 1866, *Bachelder Papers*, 256.

33. Colvill, "The Old First at Gettysburg."

34. Colvill, "Old First at Gettysburg" (all quotes in this paragraph). Logic would indicate that the "gully" Colvill wrote of was the channel, or flow path, of Plum Run. Today the only portion of the run in this area that is that narrow is where a small rivulet enters the main run. Also, using the photograph mentioned in note 1, above, the boulders where the center of the First Minnesota made its stand are several yards from Plum Run. It is therefore likely that Colvill rolled into a gully or depression in the area of the boulders or

perhaps between two boulders. Presumably Colvill would have said, "into the dry stream bed" if that was what he meant.

Ultimately we cannot know how closely the channel of Plum Run today matches the channel in the summer of 1863, although it is probably similar. Soil erosion from Cemetery Ridge is a definite factor, given the degree to which the boulders in the 1897 photo have been buried by sediment since that time. Recent soil sampling studies in this area indicate that sediment buildup has reached as much as sixteen inches in places; Herbert G. Frost, untitled article, *Friends of the National Parks at Gettysburg* [newsletter], Spring 2000, p. 8. Little of some of the boulders is still visible above the soil. Even in the 1897 photo, Plum Run does not appear to run directly beside the nest of boulders.

A rough map by Folwell accompanies the text of Colvill's statement, Dec. 22, 1904. Colvill provided the information, and Folwell had it checked by Lochren. Folwell used a tight line of dashes to indicate the First Minnesota's position before the charge, to the left of Thomas's artillery battery on Cemetery Ridge. An arrow points forward, and there is another, more spread-out line of dashes, along the tongue of high ground that forms the lip of the Plum Run ravine. Logic says the regiment would have halted here, as Folwell's map indicates. It gave the tactical advantage of the high ground in relation to the advancing rebels, and it provided the cover of a scattering of boulders and rocks. Perhaps, after firing the volley, the regiment moved farther down into the swale, the center of the regiment taking up the position among the boulders shown in the 1897 photograph.

An intriguing sidelight was provided by the "unknown sergeant" who wrote to the *Saint Paul Pioneer*. His account was published, Aug. 9, 1863: "I know we reached the brink of the little run and gave them one volley which swept them from the face of the earth; but a new line rises from the bed of the run at our feet."

Clearly this indicates that at least the portion of the line occupied by this sergeant actually reached and stood on the lip of Plum Run's "ditch."

There was a Corporal William G. Sargent in Company K, which was third from the right in the regiment's line, providing his name is spelled correctly in the regimental roster. The signatory of the story in the newspaper is simply "Sergeant," spelled like the rank. The writer also referred to being a "file closer," a position always filled by a company sergeant. Of course, a corporal could fill the position in an understaffed regiment or company. The June 28, 1863, Consolidated Morning Report for the regiment lists only two sergeants for Company K (the standard was five) and six corporals (the standard was eight).

The writer also mentioned that a "brigade advances down the hollow to our right." This was something a member of the regiment could learn from others after the battle, even if he did not see it himself, but it has the sound of an eyewitness: the fact that he specifically says "a brigade," which would have been Lang's brigade and/or the Ninth Alabama of Wilcox's brigade. He also provided graphic information about the effect of the flank fire: "our men fall, many pierced by balls, both from the right side and front, which crossed each other in their courses through the body."

Plum Run is fed by a rivulet that creates a fork in the general area of the First Minnesota's charge. The rivulet runs southwest from the top of Cemetery Ridge and starts curving until it runs more or less due west ten or fifteen yards before joining Plum Run. This is on the right of the First Minnesota's position in the ravine. It could be that the "Sergeant" who wrote the letter to the newspaper—whether it was Corporal Sargent or not—was on the right of the First Minnesota's line and stood on the lip of this rivulet.

35. "Unknown Sergeant" letter, *St. Paul Pioneer,* Aug. 9, 1863, p. 2.

36. Peavey, *Memoirs of Christopher B. Heffelfinger,* 39.

37. Arabella M. Willson, *Disaster, Struggle, Triumph: The Adventures of 1000 "Boys in Blue," From August, 1862 to June, 1865* (Albany: Argus Co., 1870), 169.

38. O.R., 472, 476.

39. Pfanz, *Gettysburg,* 406.

40. Letter of Major Charles A. Richardson to Bachelder, May 8, 1868, *Bachelder Papers,* 340.

41. Richardson to Bachelder, May 8, 1868, *Bachelder Papers,* 340.

42. General notes, *Bachelder Papers,* 1976; see also Terrence J. Winschel, "Their Supreme Moment: Barksdale's Brigade at Gettysburg," *Gettysburg Magazine,* July 1989, p. 76.

43. Richardson to Bachelder, May 8, 1868, *Bachelder Papers,* 340; see also *New York Monuments Commission for the Battlefields of Gettysburg and Chattanooga: Final Report of the Battlefield of Gettysburg,* vol. 2 (Albany: J. B. Lyon Co., 1900), 886. Jasper Searles made the claim that a man from Company F shot Barksdale, although no one from the company itself seemed to say so; Jasper Newton Searles, "The First Minnesota Volunteer Infantry," in *Glimpses of the Nation's Struggle,* vol. 2 (St. Paul: St. Paul Book and Stationary Co., 1890), 104; Colvill asserted that "one of my men" shot Barksdale both to John Bachelder in 1866 (*Bachelder Papers,* 257) and in his 1884 newspaper account, Colvill, "Old First at Gettysburg." In a letter to Lochren, Dec. 31, 1889, a man named L. Z. Rogers from Waterville, Minnesota, claimed William W. Brown of Company G shot and killed Barksdale. Rogers related a story that Brown had told him in 1865 in which he said he shot an officer on a bay horse during the regiment's fight in the ravine. Brown apparently never said that the officer was Barksdale, but Rogers did. Lochren chose to include that tidbit of information in "History of the First Regiment," simply stating that "by some it has been claimed" that Brown shot Barksdale.

A much stronger claimant, considering where the regiment fought and where Barksdale was wounded on the field, was named by Charles W. Dey, formerly of Company C, 126th New York. Dey stated that Barksdale was shot by Corporal Menah C. Van Liew of Company C, 126th New York. Charles W. Dey, "Willard's Brigade," *National Tribune,* Sept. 24, 1880, p. 7.

44. Winschel, "Their Supreme Moment," 77.

45. Busey and Martin, *Regimental Strengths and Losses,* 188.

46. O.R., 631.

47. Letter of Colonel Francis Heath to John Bachelder, Oct. 12, 1889, *Bachelder Papers,* 1651–52. The relating of this episode has an interesting historical progression. Heath's original official report was rejected because it was too harsh in its criticism of other federal units. Whether it went through more than one revision after that is not known, but what was finally accepted was a bare-bones report of a dozen or so lines. The episode mentioning Humphreys is not in the short official report.

In the letter to Bachelder in 1889, Heath said definitively that it *was* Humphreys who rode up and ordered him to have his regiment stop the retreating Third Corps troops at bayonet point. Other earlier versions of the story indicated that Heath thought it was Humphreys. John Day Smith, a former corporal in Company F, author of the 1909 regimental history, stated that he gave the story "no credence whatever." He went on to say that, "A West Point officer as strict and punctilious as General Humphreys would not be likely to do what is charged in this distorted account." Even Smith did not question the veracity of his former colonel, however—he simply stated that it must have been some other officer who ordered Heath to stop the fugitives at bayonet point, not Humphreys.

Given the circumstances at that moment and the fact it was a period in military history where men were shot for cowardice and desertion, as well as one in which severe physical punishments, such as having to carry a log on the shoulders for hours or being locked up in a "sweat box," were administered, it does not seem beyond belief that a divisional commander would order friendly troops to menace, or even fire upon, his retreating, panicked troops.

In defense of Humphreys, the reader is reminded that Hancock met Humphreys on Cemetery Ridge before coming across the First Minnesota, which was posted to the south of the Nineteenth Maine. This would seem to imply that Humphreys moved more or less directly east in his personal retreat from the Emmitsburg Road and not northeast, which he would have had to do to run across the Nineteenth Maine. Then again, since the exact timing of events, some of which undoubtedly were simultaneous, is difficult to establish and since Humphreys was mounted and therefore mobile, it could have been possible for Hancock to come upon him south of the First Minnesota before or after the encounter with Heath of the Nineteenth Maine.

48. Adams, "The Nineteenth Maine at Gettysburg," 253–54.

49. Letter of Colonel Francis Heath to John Bachelder, Oct. 12, 1889, *Bachelder Papers*, 1651–52.

50. Busey and Martin, *Regimental Strengths and Losses*, 39.

51. Heath to Bachelder, Oct. 12, 1889, *Bachelder Papers*, 1652.

52. Paul Stevenson, *Wargaming in History: The American Civil War* (New York: Sterling Publishing Co., 1990), 29.

53. Heath to Bachelder, Oct. 12, 1889, *Bachelder Papers*, 1652.

54. Silas Adams, a former member of the left company, Company F, of the Nineteenth Maine, said that Heath's account was not quite right. Adams stated that the company did not refuse itself, but rather it was about-faced and marched "three or four rods to the rear." This would have been about twenty-two yards. Adams said

that artillery batteries had "joined us upon our left." The only battery that should have been there was Evan Thomas's Battery C of the Fourth U.S. Artillery, which had been there for some time before the Nineteenth Maine advanced to the position.

A little farther to the east was Rorty's battery, but Adams most likely was talking about Thomas's battery. Adams said he was about thirty to thirty-five feet from the right gun of the battery and that the battery had to pull back to conform to his company's movement because it was unsupported once they had moved back. There is no other record of the right guns of Thomas's battery pulling back, but it could have happened in response to the left of the Nineteenth Maine moving back, especially since the unknown Confederate troops were so close.

Another divergence from Heath's version is that Adams said the left of the Nineteenth stayed in contact with the artillery battery until Heath ordered the charge. Heath indicated that the left of his regiment refusing itself and his order to fall back farther up Cemetery Ridge, after the threat on his right flank was reported, were two different events. Adams's version suggested they were the same event.

Probably what happened was that Company F on the left flank fell back the twenty or so yards that Adams mentioned, then the battery pulled back to conform to their line. While that was happening, Heath ordered the rest of the regiment back so that it wheeled into line with Company F.

And finally, Adams believed that it was not the musketry of Company F that caused the mystery Confederate regiment to disappear into the smoke (Adams referred to it as a "brigade") but rather the fact that the First Minnesota charged on the left and drove Wilcox back, thus uncovering the right flank of the Confederate unit and compelling them to fall back. The First Minnesota, in fact, stopped Wilcox, and the mystery unit and Lang's command both continued forward and, essentially, uncovered their own right flanks. As indicated in the text, Lang then started withdrawing, and Heath ordered the Nineteenth to charge.

The difficulty in attempting to reconcile the different threads of this episode is a testament to the chaos of combat and the perceptions and recollections of participants at different points on the battlefield.

55. Colvill, statement to Folwell, Dec. 22, 1904, p. 7.

56. O.R., 618.

57. Pfanz, *Gettysburg*, 386, 387.

58. Heath to Bachelder, Oct. 12, 1889, *Bachelder Papers*, 1652.

59. Pfanz, *Gettysburg*, 422, 423.

60. O.R., Part 2, p. 631.

61. O.R., Part 2, p. 631–32.

62. O.R., Part 2, p. 631–32.

63. Gary W. Gallagher, ed., *Fighting for the Confederacy: The Personal Recollections of General Edward Porter Alexander* (Chapel Hill: University of North Carolina Press, 1989), 240.

64. Richardson to Bachelder, May 8, 1868, *Bachelder Papers*, 340.

65. Ezra De Freest Simons, *A Regimental History: The One Hundred and Twenty-Fifth New York State Volunteers* (New York: E. D. Simons, 1888), 122. A dissenting voice to this chronology comes from George M. Sweet, formerly a sergeant of Company I, 125th New York Regiment, writing in 1915. Sweet claimed the brigade was not falling back but rather that Willard had just ordered the bugler to sound the charge when he was killed. Sweet wrote that the death held up the charge by a minute, but then "the charge was sounded, and as the 2,000 muskets came down to the charge a wild hoorah sounded along the line as we sprang ahead and over the low stone wall, behind which Gen. Barksdale's men were partially covered."

Sweet wrote that his brigade pursued Barksdale's brigade (which immediately fell back) for about "30 rods," or about 165 yards, taking 500 prisoners. He then claimed that his 125th New York halted, "turned by the right flank and closed up a gap between the 125th N.Y. and the 111th N.Y., and held that position until 9 P.M., when we were relieved by another brigade. I do not know whose, as it was very dark." George M. Sweet, "Willard's Brigade at Gettysburg," *National Tribune*, Aug. 12, 1915, p. 7.

Sweet's account of when Willard was killed and the 125th New York closing up with the 111th New York and maintaining its advanced position on the field until 9:00 P.M. varies greatly from the regimental history, the reports of *The Official Records*, and the histories for each of the regiments of Willard's brigade contained in the 1900 book series *New York at Gettysburg*.

66. There is a monument at the place where Willard fell, and it is on a site that still perplexes the author. The monument is nearly in the direct center of the First Minnesota's line of battle along Plum Run. It stands to reason that if the remainder of Willard's brigade had come back directly through the First Minnesota's line that someone would have mentioned it. The brigade would also have had to contend with the fact that they would be coming back through Wilcox's Confederate brigade and that certainly should have rated a mention in someone's battle report or memoirs. The only way that the site can be correct is if Wilcox had retreated completely and the First Minnesota already had withdrawn by the time Willard's men moved across the ground, which would have been in near or total darkness. That is a remote possibility.

The author feels that Willard made his return while at least part, if not all, of Wilcox's brigade was still in place and possibly while the First Minnesota was still fighting. The actual site of Willard's death is probably at least several hundred feet south of the monument site. It was dusk when the brigade was moving back, and they were disorganized, lost in clouds of smoke, and subjected to intense artillery and rifle fire.

In addition, Willard's body quickly was taken back to the federal lines to prevent demoralization of the troops due to its ghastly, mangled condition. There was probably not time, nor did the circumstances permit anyone, to take exact note of where they were. It seems likely that the monument committee did the best it could, but the monument on Willard's supposed death site was placed nearly a decade before the First Minnesota's monument, so there were no points of reference from that. The site of the First Minnesota's monument undoubtedly is accurate, given the amount of time the regiment was posted there while the men could still see around themselves and the unique jumble of boulders directly west in Plum Run's ravine where Company A (the left center of the regiment) made its stand after the charge.

The one perplexing thing is a reference in the 125th New York's regimental history, published in 1888. Ezra D. Simons, the regiment's chaplain, said in the introduction to his book that the monument-to-be "will stand near the famous old stone wall, where Willard fell." Maps of the wartime battlefield, made soon after the war, indicate that the only stone fence or wall along this stretch of Plum Run was twenty to twenty-five yards northwest of the site of Willard's monument. Any area much farther away could not be construed by anyone as being "near" and certainly not a site a hundred yards or more south of the current monument.

However, a 1915 newspaper account by George M. Sweet, former sergeant of Company I, 125th New York, indicated that it was a "low stone wall." There were many rail and snake-rail fences around the battlefield, and many of these had a low, stacked-stone base over which the crossed posts and rails were laid. Maps show a snake-rail fence enclosing one of Abraham Trostle's farm fields directly to the west of Plum Run in the area of the battlefield where Willard's brigade en-

gaged Barksdale's brigade. It could be that the map indicates a simple, wooden snake-rail fence but that it actually had a low stone base. Many wooden fences had been knocked down in this part of the battlefield by this point in the battle, and it is likely that all Willard's men saw of this fence was its "low stone wall." George M. Sweet, "Willard's Brigade at Gettysburg," 7.

67. Plummer letter, *Minneapolis Atlas*, Aug. 26, 1863.

68. Sullivan letter, "Fort Schylear, N.Y., July 31, 1863."

69. Muller, "History," 13.

70. Patrick Henry Taylor, letter to parents, dated "Two Taverns, five miles from Gettysburg, July 6, '63"; also obituary of Patrick Henry Taylor, *Cass County* (Missouri) *Democrat*, Dec. 26, 1907.

71. Thomas L. Elmore, "A Meteorological and Astronomical Chronology of the Gettysburg Campaign," *Gettysburg Magazine*, July 1995, p. 19; see also John Day Smith, *The History of the Nineteenth Regiment of Maine Volunteer Infantry, 1862–1865* (Minneapolis: Great Western Printing Co., 1909), 73.

72. Gregory Coco, *A Strange and Blighted Land: Gettysburg—The Aftermath of a Battle* (Gettysburg: Thomas Publications, 1995), 82–83; see also William A. Frassanito, *Early Photography at Gettysburg* (Gettysburg: Thomas Publications, 1995), 340–41.

73. Plummer letter, *Minneapolis Atlas*, Aug. 26, 1863.

74. Colvill, "Old First Minnesota."

75. "Unknown Sergeant," *St. Paul Pioneer*, Aug. 9, 1863, p. 2.

NOTES TO CHAPTER 7

1. The time spent along Plum Run seemed to be very short for some men in the First Minnesota. Charles Muller of Company A indicated that he fired only two rounds, the second at point-blank range into a color sergeant just on the other side of a bush from him. He looked around for his comrades, but, "I begin to

see for my friends but they must of then have gone or wer shot down, then I started to run out of it to [too]"(Muller, "History," 12a). John Plummer of Company D wrote, "We had not fired but a few shots before we were ordered to fall back." William W. Brown of Company G fired five rounds, the last dropping a mounted officer (letter of L. Z. Rogers to William Lochren, dated "Dec. 31, 1889," William Lochren Papers, MHS).

2. Wright, "Company F," 599.

3. Francis Baasen letter with partial list of casualties, *St. Paul Pioneer*, July 16, 1863, p. 1.

4. Alfred P. Carpenter letter, dated "Warrenton Junction, Va., July 30th, 1863," typed transcription, MHS.

5. Bassett, *From Bull Run to Bristow Station*, 28.

6. Heffelfinger, *Memoirs of Christopher B. Heffelfinger*, 36.

7. Marvin diary, entry dated Thursday, July 2, 1863.

8. Muller, "History," 13.

9. Letter of C. P. Adams to William Lochren, dated "Hastings, Minnesota, September 8th, 1863," Lochren Papers.

10. *Central Republican* (Faribault, Minn.), Aug. 5, 1863; see also Adams to Lochren, "Hastings, Minnesota, September 8th, 1863," Lochren Papers.

11. Patrick Henry Taylor diary, entry for July 2, 1863, typescript of diary entries for June 30, 1863–July 5, 1863, MHS.

12. Patrick Henry Taylor letter to sister, July 19, 1863, Taylor Letters, typed transcriptions, Morrison County (Minnesota) Historical Society.

13. Plummer letter, *Minneapolis Atlas*, Aug. 26, 1863.

14. Plummer letter, *Minneapolis Atlas*, Aug. 26, 1863.

NOTES TO CHAPTER 8

1. Wright, "Company F," 601.

2. Wright, "Company F," 603.

3. Taylor Diary, entry for July 3, 1863, typescript of diary entries for June 30, 1863–July 5, 1863.

4. Taylor, letter to parents, dated "Two Taverns, five miles from Gettysburg, July 6, '63," Taylor Letters.

5. This was actually Private Lafayette W. Snow of Company B.

6. Taylor, letter to sister, dated "Camp near Snicker's Gap, Va. July 19, 1863," Taylor Letters.

7. John Michael Priest, *Into the Fight: Pickett's Charge at Gettysburg* (Shippensburg, Pa.: White Mane Books, 1998), 43, 196.

8. Wright, "Company F," 603.

9. Wright, "Company F," 604.

10. Wright, "Company F," 607.

11. John Gibbon, *Personal Recollections of the Civil War* (New York: G. P. Putnam's Sons, 1928), 146.

12. Frank Aretas Haskell, *The Battle of Gettysburg* (1878 [?]; reprint with introduction by Bruce Catton, Boston: Houghton Mifflin Co., 1969), 80. An interesting variation of this story was told by former Lieutenant William Harmon, Company C, quoted in the *Minneapolis Journal*, June 30, 1897. Harmon claimed that he was at Gibbon's headquarters (undoubtedly true) and overheard all the talk between Meade, Gibbon, and the other generals having lunch. After Meade made his comment to have all provost guards return to the line, Harmon declared that Gibbon turned to him and said, "Do you hear that, Harmon?" Harmon replied in the affirmative, and Gibbon told him, "Well see that your company is there."

A small point, but Haskell's account probably is accurate because he was also there, and it was written within two weeks of the battle. Haskell had no particular investment in relating the story, other than his obvious admiration for Farrell, and it makes more sense that Gibbon would have given the order to the commander of the provost guard.

13. As with most other incidents, exact timing is elusive. Most Union sources claimed it was around 1:00 P.M., most Confederates about 1:30 P.M. The Reverend Dr. Michael Jacobs, a professor at

Gettysburg College who noted the event, stated he heard the first signal gun at 1:07 P.M. Newspaper correspondent Charles Carlton Coffin of the *Boston Journal* said that his watch (set to Washington, D.C., time) showed 1:05 P.M. The author chooses to rely on the man who commanded Longstreet's artillery: Colonel E. Porter Alexander. He stated that his watch showed 1:00 P.M. when the cannonade commenced.

14. Bond, "Reminiscences," 92.

15. George R. Stewart, *Pickett's Charge: A Microhistory of the Final Attack at Gettysburg, July 3, 1863* (Boston: Houghton Mifflin Co., 1959), 114.

16. Stewart, *Pickett's Charge*, 150.

17. Harmon interview, *Minneapolis Journal*, June 30, 1897. Once again, it is Harmon's version in a newspaper thirty-four years after the battle balanced against Lieutenant Haskell's report in a manuscript written within two weeks of the battle. Haskell did not mention the decapitation. In fact, Haskell said he saw the shell explode in the air over the crest of Cemetery Ridge. In Harmon's defense, Gibbon's orderly was killed very early in the cannonade. When the other officers were mounting and riding to their commands, Gibbon was left to wonder where his orderly and horse were. He ran up to the crest of Cemetery Ridge from his headquarters. There were two shots fired as the signal for the beginning of the cannonade; perhaps Haskell saw one explode, and Harmon saw the other kill Gibbon's orderly.

18. Wright, "Company F," 608-9.

19. "Unknown Sergeant," "Battle of Gettysburg and the First Minnesota," *St. Paul Pioneer*, Aug. 9, 1863, p. 2.

20. Heffelfinger, *Memoirs of Christopher B. Heffelfinger*, 38.

21. *New York Times* reporter Samuel Wilkeson, quoted in Richard Wheeler, *Witness to Gettysburg* (New York: Harper and Row, 1987), 232; see also Glenn Tucker, *High Tide at Gettysburg* (1958; reprint, New York: Konecky & Konecky, 1993), 351.

22. Marvin diary, entry for "Friday, July 3rd, '63."

23. Marvin diary, entry dated "Friday, July 3rd, '63."

24. Bond, "Reminiscences," 93.

25. Plummer letter, *Minneapolis Atlas*, Aug. 26, 1863.

26. Tucker, *Hancock the Superb*, 150–51. The author wishes to note that, in our more "practical" times, Hancock's overt display of "machismo" might seem almost ludicrous, if not downright suicidal. It is not improved on by the fact that a mounted flag bearer (carrying the corps flag) rode behind him. The flag bearer's place was with the general, and he had to accompany the general on his ride. On the other hand no place on the battlefield was especially safe, and we must allow for the different values and mindset of the time. Hancock's ride, while a truly remarkable thing in itself, was not out of the realm of behavior expected of a nineteenth-century general in combat.

As cool and professional as Hancock was under fire, it could not have been a feat he relished. But it had its desired effect; he provided solid inspiration to his troops, and it helped them to bear up during the bombardment. A more important point is that Hancock, a seasoned combat veteran of the Mexican War as well as the previous two years of civil war, knew the serendipitous nature of artillery fire. Unlike aimed rifle fire, where being mounted was a real disadvantage, artillery would find you and kill you wherever you were, if fate decreed it. Proof enough are the many men crouching behind fences or hugging the ground who were blown to pieces. Hancock and his mounted flag bearer were not injured during their ride and were never struck by more than flying dirt.

27. Priest, *Into the Fight*, 189–98.

28. Gibbon, *Personal Recollections*, 148–49.

29. Lochren, "First Minnesota at Gettysburg," 52.

30. Wright, "Company F," 609.

31. Stewart, *Pickett's Charge*, 173; see also Priest, *Into the Fight*, 199. Tradition holds that Pickett's Charge had a total of 15,000 men assaulting the federal position. This seems to be based on a thumbnail estimate by James Longstreet earlier on July 3, 1863. He thought he would have three divisions to make the charge. He ended up with two and a half, all of which were understrength. Roughly 1,400 men were also in Wilcox's and Perry's brigades, which went in as support late in the charge but were quickly driven back. Even adding these two brigades to the total does not approach the 15,000 figure.

32. Wright, "Company F," 610.

33. Carpenter letter, "Warrenton Junction, Va., July 30th, 1863."

34. It must have seemed like that many to Bond at the time, but he certainly knew better when he wrote his memoir after the war. The number of rebels actually engaged in the fighting of Pickett's Charge was, as the text indicates, between 10,000 and 11,000.

35. See note 1, chapter 6, of Ball's rank at Gettysburg.

36. Bond, "Reminiscences," 94–95.

37. Carpenter letter, "Warrenton Junction, Va., July 30th, 1863."

38. Stewart, *Pickett's Charge*, 207.

39. Tucker, *Hancock the Superb*, 156; O.R., 366. A. M. Gambone speculated that Hancock could have been a victim of "friendly fire," likely by the Vermont troops. Gambone noted that a contemporary account by an officer on the scene stated that Hancock was riding south at the time, and given that he was facing that direction he could not have been hit in the front by Confederate fire. However, the officer also said that Hancock was addressing Brigadier General George Stannard when he was hit. Hancock could have turned his horse to come up beside Stannard, with both facing the rebel lines. Gambone also noted that according to the book *Reminiscences of*

Winfield Scott Hancock, written by Hancock's wife after his death, Hancock turned away from Stannard and toward the Copse of Trees when he was hit. This would certainly have faced him in the right direction to receive a Confederate bullet. A. M. Gambone, *Hancock at Gettysburg . . . and Beyond* (Baltimore: Butternut and Blue, 1997), 141. It seems unlikely to this author that, even given the flanking movement of the Vermonters, Hancock and Stannard would have been in front of the federal line of fire. One wonders why Stannard and/or his aides were not hit, since the Vermont troops were firing volleys.

There was also at least one Confederate who claimed to have shot Hancock out of the saddle, as unlikely as it seems. A secondhand account reported Sergeant W. R. Wood of Company H, Fifty-sixth Virginia firing his last round at "a mounted Federal officer" who was advancing "at the head of a column of apparently fresh troops" and stated that "the Federal officer immediately fell over and would have been dragged by his horse but for assistance rendered by Federal officers, who extricated him"; "Who Wounded Gen. Hancock?" *National Tribune,* Apr. 18, 1889, p. 5.

While the Vermont troops were fresh, Hancock ordered them into a flanking movement but did not lead it personally. The description of his wounding and being caught by officers as he tumbled from his horse is accurate, but the same scenario likely befell any number of mounted officers that day. The biggest problem with the account is that the Fifty-sixth Virginia Regiment was occupied on its own front, helping to punch through the Union line at The Angle. The accurate shot at Hancock would have been through more than 330 yards of Union and Confederate troops stretching to the south of Sergeant Wood.

40. Letter of John Gibbon to Francis A. Walker, March 14, 1884, *Bachelder Papers,* 1031.

41. Gibbon, *Personal Recollections*, 152–53.

42. Buell, *Warrior Generals*, 304.

43. Carpenter letter, "Warrenton Junction, Va., July 30th, 1863."

44. I use the term "Pickett's Charge" because of its general acceptance. Throughout the author's inquiries, even allowing for people who are not sure to what it refers, most seem to be at least familiar with the term "Pickett's Charge." Overall command of the assault was on the shoulders of Lieutenant General James Longstreet, commander of the Army of Northern Virginia's First Corps. As a result, it was often known as "Longstreet's Assault," especially in the nineteenth century. Longstreet had given direct field command of the charge to the commander of his only fresh division, Major General George E. Pickett. The charge was composed of Pickett's division plus two divisions from Lieutenant General Ambrose P. Hill's Third Corps, commanded in the charge by Brigadier General Isaac Trimble and Brigadier General J. Johnston Pettigrew.

45. Wright, "Company F," 615.

46. *Central Republican* (Faribault, Minnesota), July 29, 1863, p. 2. It seems unusual that the Confederates would still be shelling the federal line with their own troops right up to, and even breaching, that line. Confederate Colonel E. Porter Alexander indicated that he ordered his artillery to cease firing when it became evident by the smoke and sound of musketry that the two lines had met. But he did shell the Vermont troops who were flanking Pickett's men. Perhaps Messick was hit by a piece of shell that overshot the Vermonters.

More than one account stated Messick was hit by a shell fragment. If the fragment was small enough to enter the head, travel through and exit without blowing the side of the head off, it is possible the projectile was actually a .69 caliber bullet and not a shell fragment. Christopher Heffelfinger, who was a close friend of Messick, indicated that Messick was "shot through the neck." Perhaps when Heffelfinger saw the body he only noticed the exit wound behind the lower part of the right ear. It could also be that Heffelfinger never saw Messick's body (not likely) and the death wound merely was described to him.

A more unpleasant, but perfectly plausible, scenario is that Messick was killed by "friendly fire." This was not entirely unknown in the Civil War (or any other war) because of the smoke and confusion of warfare at that time, and Pickett's Charge did disintegrate into a frenzied, moblike melee by the end. The Sixty-ninth Pennsylvania was posted directly in front of the Copse of Trees, the Fifty-ninth New York to its left. Between the two regiments was a gap of perhaps twenty-five or thirty feet. This was covered by Cowan's artillery battery, posted about thirty yards behind the regiment's position at the stone wall.

One of the most unnerving things for soldiers on both sides was to have their artillery posted behind them and firing over their heads. Because of the unreliable quality of Confederate ammunition, there was great risk in doing this. The Union army did it more frequently, and Gettysburg was such an occasion. Artillery commander for the Union army General Henry J. Hunt had ordered the artillery to hold its fire for fifteen or twenty minutes during the opening of the cannonade before Pickett's Charge. It was Hunt's intention to save enough long-range ammunition to cut the assault to pieces with artillery cross fire before it ever reached the federal line.

Knowing the demoralizing effect on troops of being shelled and not having their own artillery return fire, General Hancock ordered his artillery to open fire immediately. Consequently, by the time the rebel assault columns started across the fields, the Second Corps artillery had little more than close-range canister ammunition left in their limber chests.

Canister rounds turned the cannons into huge shotguns, belching out a spray of iron or lead balls. It was not the kind of ammunition anyone, under normal conditions, would try to fire over a line of their own troops, particularly troops standing and fighting. However, it is clear that Cowan's guns did fire canister over the federal troops. In his official report he indicated that he started firing canister when the rebels were within 200 yards, and his last shot (a charge of double canister) was fired when a squad of rebels penetrated the federal line and was less than ten yards from the muzzles of his guns.

Cowan wrote that, just before this last round was fired, "The infantry in front of five of my pieces, and posted behind a slight defense of rails, some ten yards distant, turned and broke, but were rallied, and drawn off to the right of my battery by General Webb in a most gallant manner." It might have looked as though they turned and broke to Cowan, but he was describing the pell-mell rush of Hall's and Harrow's brigades, under orders, to the area of The Angle where the Confederates had breached the federal line. All of the rebels in front of Hall's and Harrow's position were funneling toward the opening in the line, hurried along by the Vermont troops outflanking them on their right.

Given the width of Cowan's six-gun battery (the standard was about eighty-two yards, although Cowan's battery was undoubtedly packed much more tightly), it would be difficult to believe that some federal troops were not hit or killed by the discharge of his guns. Captain Wilson Farrell of Company C was mortally wounded in the head while rushing his company into the fight in this area at about this time.

Men of the Sixty-ninth Pennsylvania claimed that they received fire from both Hall's brigade as it rushed into their sector and Cowan's battery with its canister fire. (See accounts by Privates Anthony McDermott and John Buckley of the Sixty-ninth Pennsylvania, *In Pickett's Charge! Eyewitness Accounts*, ed. by Richard Rollins [Rank and File Publications, 1994],

348–49). General Hunt was at Cowan's battery when the rebel squad was rushing the guns, firing his pistol into the oncoming Confederates and screeching, "See 'em?!—See 'em?!!" at Cowan. The major leading the oncoming rebels was yelling, "Take the guns! Take the guns!" and Cowan's gunners were dropping left and right from Confederate musket fire—a tense moment for an artillery officer determined to not have his battery captured.

After the double-canister charge was fired and the oncoming rebels had all been chopped down, Hunt was pulled out from under his freshly killed horse and given the mount of a nearby artillery sergeant. Tellingly, he said to Cowan as he rode off, "Look out or you will kill our men!"; see Stewart, *Pickett's Charge,* 222–23.

47. Lochren, "Narrative of the First Regiment," 37.

48. Letter from Henry O'Brien to John Bachelder, dated "East St. Louis, Mar. 23, 1883," *Bachelder Papers,* 936; see also letter from O'Brien to Lochren, dated "East St. Louis, Nov. 2, 1889." O'Brien was emphatic that the bullet through his hand cut the flagstaff in half, not the shot through Dehn's hand. He was less clear about the order of his wounds; in the 1883 letter he claimed he was hit in the hand, then the head; in the 1889 letter, the head and then the hand.

49. Wright, "Company F," 612.

50. Lochren, "Narrative of the First Regiment," 37.

51. O.R., 425; see also *Minnesota in the Civil and Indian Wars,* 1:373. Every indication is that Company C did not join in the repulse of Pickett's Charge until it was well under way. More than one source pointed to Farrell being hit while running into the fight with his company, which seems to have been during, or shortly after, the shift of Harrow's and Hall's brigades to the right into the melee around the Copse of Trees. The company was obviously pinned down during the cannonade, like everyone else, and was back at Gibbon's

headquarters on the east slope of Cemetery Ridge. But forty to fifty minutes elapsed between the ending of the cannonade and the time that the Confederates broke the Union line at the Copse of Trees and the Angle. See Stewart, *Pickett's Charge*, 185, 229 (maps).

Lieutenant William Harmon, in his *Minneapolis Journal* interview, said, "We all lay low while the artillery duel lasted. When it was over, Captain Farrell ordered me to form the company and adding that he would take command himself, something he rarely did. We had hardly begun to advance when he was killed. Just as we were going into the action, I caught sight of Heffelfinger, so it happened by chance that we fought near the rest of the First Minnesota, though we had not been with them during the battle."

The elapsed time cannot be reconciled, unless Farrell decided to hold his company to do its work as provost guard until the moment he felt it was needed, which could have been when he heard rifle fire over the ridge. If this is the case, no one (including Harmon) mentioned it.

52. R. M. Eastman, "Cemetery Hill, How the 1st Minn. Gathered in the Prisoners," *National Tribune*, Nov. 16, 1905, p. 3. Eastman supported Lieutenant Harmon's statement that Captain Farrell was mortally wounded early, when the company was advancing and before it was really engaged, writing that Farrell, "was mortally wounded before arriving at the front." However, O'Brien wrote that Farrell was, "killed within a few feet of the (stone) wall" that marked the federal battle line in front of the Copse of Trees. Henry D. O'Brien, "At Gettysburg, Troops at the Stone Wall, The High Water Mark of the Rebellion," *National Tribune*, Sept. 15, 1892, p. 4.

It must be remembered that O'Brien was in a different company and was himself seriously wounded at the end of the battle. Given that Eastman and Harmon were both in Farrell's company and Eastman was unwounded and Harmon only slightly wounded, they were obviously in a better position to know where Farrell was when he fell.

Eastman also mentioned that the provost guard of the Second Division, Second Corps, actually was composed of a detail of about thirty men from the Nineteenth Maine, as well as the roughly fifty officers and men of Company C, First Minnesota.

53. Bond, "Reminiscences," 96–97.

54. "Amid Flying Shot and Shell: Standards Borne by Minnesota Regiments," *Saint Paul Pioneer Press*, July 21, 1893.

55. Henry O'Brien figured prominently in the award of the Medal of Honor to a third man from the regiment. Young Private Alonzo Pickle, who turned twenty the day of the charge on July 2, 1863, saved O'Brien's life a year after Gettysburg. Both men were part of the First Battalion of Minnesota Volunteers. This two-company battalion was formed after the three-year enlistment of the First Minnesota had expired on April 29, 1864. Ninety-five of the original regiment (thirty-six original members who reenlisted and fifty-nine who were recruited later and still had time to serve on their enlistments) formed the First Battalion along with 140 new recruits.

During the Battle of Deep Bottom (part of the Siege of Petersburg, Virginia) on August 14, 1864, the First Battalion was among the units ordered to charge the Confederate breastworks. Lieutenant O'Brien went down with a bullet in his chest. After the assault failed and the federal troops started falling back, Corporal Pickle took the time to go to O'Brien. The seriously wounded lieutenant was close to the Confederate works, but Pickle lugged him off the field to safety under intense, but blessedly inaccurate, Confederate rifle fire.

Pickle was awarded his Medal of Honor on June 12, 1895. O'Brien received his, for Gettysburg, on April 9, 1890. Marshall Sherman's capture of the rebel flag at Gettysburg must have carried the most weight or caught the attention of the right people, as he received his Medal of Honor during the war, December 1, 1864. It probably was prompted, in part, by the sacrifice made by this brave veteran, who had reenlisted in the First Battalion to fight to the end of the war. During the Battle of Deep Bottom, Sherman was shot in the left leg, and he later lost the limb to amputation.

56. William Harmon, "Co. C at Gettysburg," *Minneapolis Journal,* June 30, 1897.

57. Wright, "Company F," 612.

58. Harmon, "Co. C At Gettysburg," *Minneapolis Journal,* June 30, 1897.

59. Wright, "Company F," 615.

60. A color guard, for a standard-size regiment, was composed of eight corporals and one sergeant. The sergeant was selected by the colonel and was known thereafter as the color sergeant or color bearer. A regiment carried two flags: the national flag with the regiment's name painted on the middle red stripe and a state flag, which often had the names of the battles the regiment fought in painted on it. The color sergeant carried the national flag, and the first corporal of the color guard carried the state flag.

Most regiments went through more than one set of colors during the war, due to the rough treatment of combat. Research done by Stephen Osman, site manager for Historic Fort Snelling near Minneapolis, suggests that the First Minnesota probably carried only a well-worn national flag at Gettysburg. All references to "the flag" at Gettysburg were in the singular, and the state colors for the regiment about this time are in too good condition to have been through the rough treatment of Gettysburg. The photo of the regiment's national colors after the battle is evidence of that. Also, O'Brien wrote that "two (flags) were seldom carried by one regiment at that period of the war." Henry D. O'Brien, "At Gettysburg, Troops at the Stone Wall, The High Water Mark of the Rebellion," *National Tribune,* Sept. 15, 1892, p. 4.

At Gettysburg the First Minnesota had a color guard composed of only the color

sergeant, Ellet Perkins, and three corporals. Perkins was shot in the thigh during the charge on July 2, Corporal John B. Stevens was shot in the chest, and a third (unknown) color corporal was also shot down after taking up the colors. The last member of the color guard, Corporal John Dehn, had the flag going into the repulse of Pickett's Charge. The entire color guard for the regiment was shot and disabled during the battle.

61. Holcombe, *History of the First Regiment,* 378; Wright, "Company F," 618.

62. Holcombe, *History of the First Regiment,* 378. The spliced flagstaff is still on display in the rotunda of the Minnesota State Capitol in St. Paul.

NOTES TO CHAPTER 9

1. Busey and Martin, *Regimental Strengths and Losses,* 239, 280; "Battle Facts," in *Illustrated Gettysburg Battlefield Map and Story* (Gettysburg: TEM, 1984).

2. Stewart, *Pickett's Charge,* 255.

3. O.R., 366.

4. David M. Jordan, *Winfield Scott Hancock: A Soldier's Life* (Bloomington: Indiana University Press, 1988), 101-2. Hancock's ordeal was a case study in medicine of the period. His wound was initially probed on the battlefield with the unwashed and probably filthy finger of Dr. Dougherty, the doctor inserting his index finger into the wound up to the first joint. By the end of July the general was staying at his parents' house in Norristown, Pennsylvania, weak, pale, emaciated, and feverish. The wound was not healing, was continually draining, and was undoubtedly infected. Hancock had endured the torture of any number of doctors probing the wound, trying to find the minié ball and remove it.

On August 21 he had the good fortune of being visited by Dr. Louis W. Read, a native of Norristown who was an army surgeon home on leave. Hancock believed he was dying and very likely was, so he felt he had nothing to lose in suggesting that Read give a try at extracting the bullet. Read noted that all other doctors had probed with Hancock in bed, his leg flexed at a right angle to his body. He suggested that if he probed with Hancock in the position he was in when hit—mounted—that he might have some success in finding the ball.

With Hancock stripped up to the waist, astride a chair on top of his parents' dining room table, Dr. Read took his bullet probe and sighted, like a rifleman, across the room from Hancock. Walking toward the general, he inserted the probe into the ugly wound. The instrument "dropped fully eight inches into the channel and struck the ball, which was imbedded in the sharp bone which you sit upon." The next day, Read extracted a large minié ball, likely a .69 caliber, and Hancock began to improve immediately. Within two weeks the general was out of bed and moving around on crutches.

5. Holcombe, *History of the First Regiment Minnesota,* 381.

6. Harmon, "Co. C at Gettysburg," *Minneapolis Journal,* June 30, 1897.

7. R. M. Eastman, "Cemetery Hill, How the 1st Minnesota Gathered in the Prisoners," *National Tribune,* Nov. 16, 1905, p. 3.

8. Tucker, *High Tide at Gettysburg,* 377; O.R. (report of Lieut. Gen. James Longstreet), 360.

9. Stewart, *Pickett's Charge,* 263–68.

10. Wright, "Company F," 613.

11. Coco, *Strange and Blighted Land,* 42.

12. This is pure speculation on the part of the author. Daniel Bond was much less charitable in his memoir, calling Coates and Chase "cowards." Bond obviously saw them return but probably knew nothing of their having secured permission to go to the field hospital to check on the men of the regiment. Bond tended still to be full of opinion and venom toward a number of his comrades, even after the many intervening years before he wrote his reminiscence of the war. Christopher Heffelfinger, in his memoir, indicated that

he disapproved strongly of Coates and Chase even asking for permission to leave the regiment to go to the hospital, as well as Messick allowing them to go.

13. Ermin D. Narewood, "Attack and Counter Attack" in Letters to the Editor column, *Gettysburg Magazine,* Jan. 1994, p. 121.

14. F. A. Conwell and J. J. McCallum, "Letters from Adj. McCallum and Chaplain Conwell to Mrs. Messick, on the Death of her Husband," *Central Republican,* Aug. 5, 1863, p. 1.

15. John W. Busey, *The Last Full Measure: Burials in the Soldiers' National Cemetery at Gettysburg* (Hightstown, N.J.: Longstreet House, 1988), 46–48; Heffelfinger, *Memoirs of Christopher B. Heffelfinger,* 40.

16. Jasper Newton Searles, "The First Minnesota Volunteer Infantry," in *Glimpses of the Nation's Struggle,* vol. 2 (St. Paul: St. Paul Book and Stationary Co., 1890), 111.

17. The casualty lists show that two officers and thirty-three enlisted men were killed outright during the charge on July 2. These would have to comprise the total of the bodies buried from the charge fields and along Plum Run on July 4. One of the officers, Second Lieutenant Waldo Farrar, is in a marked grave in the Gettysburg National Cemetery. The other, Captain Louis Muller, is in a marked grave in St. Michael's Catholic Cemetery in Bayport, Minnesota. Of the enlisted men, only four are in marked graves in the Gettysburg National Cemetery.

Lieutenant Colonel William G. LeDuc, chief quartermaster of the Eleventh Corps and a prominent citizen of Hastings, Minnesota, wrote a letter on Sept. 6, 1863, to Governor Henry A. Swift of Minnesota regarding the burials of the First Minnesota men at Gettysburg. LeDuc made an impassioned plea against the removal of the Minnesotans from the battlefield graves. He mentioned that he read of such a plan in "a St. Paul paper" that he happened to see. Although he did not seem aware of the impending establishment of the national cemetery, he wrote, "Where can these noble & brave men so well trust their mortal forms as in the earth wet with their patriotic blood. Rear whatever enduring monument you may think fitting (and you can make nothing so lofty as their heroism so splendid as their achievements or so worthy as their self sacrifice) but rear it upon the field illustrious by their glorious deeds and which shall be visited in after years with uncovered head and reverent foot steps."

In his next sentence he said, "Twenty-five nameless heroes of the 1st Minnesota lie buried under one tree and in one grave." This appears to support Jasper Searles's statement of burial in a "common grave." The fact that LeDuc noted in the letter that he had "just returned from Gettysburg" and that he used the term "nameless heroes" indicated that by September 1863 any temporary headboards for individuals in the mass grave were either gone or effaced enough by weather as to be illegible. A map of burial sites, surveyed and drawn in mid-July 1863, showed a small number of federal burials in the area of the First Minnesota's position before the charge and another site halfway down the slope of Cemetery Ridge toward Plum Run. See Coco, *Strange and Blighted Land*, 98. Either of these could be the site of the mass grave mentioned by Searles and LeDuc, and it can be assumed that the twenty-two bodies marked "Unknown" in the national cemetery plot are from this mass grave site.

18. O.R. (report of Brigadier General William Harrow), 422.

19. Holcombe, *History of the First Regiment*, 373.

20. Wright, "Company F," 616–17.

21. Heffelfinger, *Memoirs of Christopher B. Heffelfinger*, 40.

22. Henrietta Stratton Jaquette, ed., *South after Gettysburg: Letters of Cornelia Hancock, 1863–1868*, 2d ed. (New York: Thomas Y. Crowell Co., 1956), 14.

23. Jaquette, ed., *South after Gettysburg*, 20, 27; Franklyn Curtiss-Wedge, ed., *History of Goodhue County* (Chicago: H. C. Cooper, Jr., 1909), 507; Wright, "Company F," 851. Cornelia Hancock also met former Orderly Sergeant James Wright many years after the war. In 1910, while attending the National Encampment of the GAR in Atlantic City, Miss Hancock noticed Wright wearing a trefoil pin on his hat. She asked to speak with him, as a former Second Corps nurse, and was thrilled to find out he was from the First Minnesota. She related having cared for Colonel Colvill, and Wright knew upon hearing her name that "she was one of those to whom Col. Colvill felt particularly grateful for care and nursing."

24. Colvill's wound was so severe that it disabled him for the rest of his life. Nearly all photos of him taken after Gettysburg show him with a cane. The minié ball smashed into his right foot directly at the ankle joint, and the ball either exited at the instep of the foot or a good number of bone fragments were ejected from there. Colvill contended that the ball was extracted from his ankle joint two weeks after his wounding, and the one under his left shoulder blade was removed one week after the battle (Colvill letter, *Minneapolis Daily Tribune*, July 28, 1884).

In any case, a medical examination for an increase in his disability pension in 1892 indicated an exit wound of some kind in the instep of the right foot. The ankle and foot were "thickened" and the muscles, tendons, and ligaments of the foot and ankle were drawn up and paralyzed so that his right foot remained in a sort of claw or downward arching crescent. After Gettysburg he had to wear a special boot or shoe on his right foot that had an especially high heel so as to keep his foot almost "on point," like a ballet dancer. Colvill often had problems with the foot becoming inflamed and swollen and usually had to keep the entire leg resting horizontally when he sat for any period of time. The examining committee indicated, "it is equivalent to the loss of a leg."

Likewise, the severe wound that coursed down from his right shoulder, injuring his spine and extending under his left shoulder blade, caused him pain for the rest of his life. Colvill suffered from severe headaches, probably caused by nerve damage and his body attempting to readjust and compensate for damaged muscles in his back and shoulders.

25. All quoted material from Tillie Pierce Alleman, *At Gettysburg, or What a Girl Saw and Heard of the Battle: A True Narrative* (New York: W. Lake Borland, 1889; facsimile edition, Baltimore, Md.: Butternut and Blue Press, 1987 [new introduction], 1994), 101–5. The new introduction to the facsimile states that the book was first published in 1888, as does the new title page. However, the original title page within the facsimile has a copyright/publication year of 1889. This is significant because Alleman quoted figures for casualties, and how many men were in the charge, that first appeared in *Regimental Losses in the American Civil War* by William F. Fox, published in 1889. (See Appendix 4 for a discussion of Fox, his book, and the statistics of casualties and the number of men in the charge.) The fact that she included these figures from a book published in 1889 indicates that she sought out the specific information, or someone who knew her and her connection to Colvill and the First Minnesota made her aware of the figures. In any case, it adds more to the veracity of her story and to the fact that the book—as the original title page shows—must have been published in 1889.

26. Alleman, *At Gettysburg,* 101–2.

27. Holcombe, *History of the First Regiment,* 424.

28. Regardless of conflicting scenarios on how Colvill left Gettysburg after the battle, one more piece of evidence in support of Alleman is found in the *Minneapolis Tribune,* July 3, 1897, p. 1. The story relates the dedication of the regiment's main monument at Gettysburg and states, in part: "On the platform Col. William Colvill, who commanded in that great charge, was seated beside a gray-haired lady, and many were the inquiries among his old comrades as to who was the lady to whom the gallant colonel was so attentive. It finally became known that she was Mrs. Alleman, who lived on the Gettysburg field at the time of the battle. A young miss of 18 [*sic*], she was engaged in administering comfort to the wounded, and among others gave a cup of cold water to Col. Colvill, and had him removed to her father's residence and cared for him until he was taken to his friends in New York."

29. Marvin diary, entry dated Sunday, July 5, 1863.

30. Muller, "History," 18a, 19.

31. Muller, "History," 19.

32. Muller, "History," 19, 19a, 20.

33. In Heffelfinger's memoirs (p. 41) he maintained that Shippensburg was twenty-eight miles from Gettysburg and that it was northeast. A modern map shows the town as northwest of Gettysburg and about twenty miles away as the crow flies. It is possible that Heffelfinger meant twenty-eight miles over available roads, but it seems inconceivable that his father could have made a twenty-eight-mile hike and arrived in Gettysburg by about 4:00 P.M., no matter how early he started in the morning. Heffelfinger was the sixth of thirteen children and twenty-nine years old at the time of Gettysburg, so his father had to be at least in his late fifties and more likely in his sixties. However, the author concedes that he cannot know the physical conditioning of this mid-nineteenth-century farmer (and former cooper), nor the determination of a father concerned for a son whom he knows has just fought in a terrible battle.

34. In fact, Alexander Ramsey was Senator-elect, having been elected to the U.S. Senate by the state legislature in January 1863 to succeed Henry M. Rice, the

first Senator from the new state. Lieutenant Governor Henry Adoniram Swift was interim governor after Ramsey went to the Senate in the fall of 1863 and until the election in 1864 when Stephen Miller was elected governor. An official letter to Swift from the Minnesota secretary of state (July 1, 1863) said that Ramsey officially had resigned his office of governor and Swift was now "Governor de facto." So Ramsey was still in St. Paul during the Gettysburg Campaign, receiving official correspondence and functioning as governor until the first day of the battle. For that reason, the initial reports were addressed to him as governor; letter from D. Blakely, headed "State of Minnesota, Office of Secretary of State, Saint Paul, July 1, 1863," Henry A. Swift Papers, 1855–1868, MHS.

35. There were two soldiers named Burgess in the regiment, both of Company K. One was Private Samuel M. Burgess, wounded at Antietam in 1862 and discharged for disability on January 27, 1863. The other was Color Sergeant George N. Burgess, killed at Savage Station on June 29, 1862. There was never a captain in the regiment named Burgess.

36. Lochren Papers.

37. Hamlin Papers.

38. Goddard Letters.

39. Goddard Letters.

40. *Battles and Leaders of the Civil War,* vol. 3 (1883; reprint, Edison, N.J.: Castle Books, 1995), 423.

41. Roland R. Maust, "The Union Second Corps Hospital at Gettysburg, July 2 to August 8, 1863," *Gettysburg Magazine,* Jan. 1994, p. 66–68; Coco, *Strange and Blighted Land,* 195.

42. *Battles and Leaders,* 424.

43. "Amid Flying Shot and Shell: Standards Borne by Minnesota Regiments," *Saint Paul Pioneer Press,* July 21, 1893.

44. Gary W. Gallagher, ed., *The Third Day at Gettysburg & Beyond* (Chapel Hill: University of North Carolina Press, 1994), 167; O.R., 79.

45. O.R., 79.

46. Bond, "Reminiscences," 100.

47. Gallagher, ed., *Third Day at Gettysburg,* 170; O.R., 79, 84.

48. Lochren, "Narrative of the First Regiment," 38.

49. *Battles and Leaders,* 426, 427.

50. Tucker, *High Tide at Gettysburg,* 387.

51. *Battles and Leaders,* 428.

52. Andrew A. Humphreys, *From Gettysburg to the Rapidan: The Army of the Potomac, July 1863 to April 1864* (1883; reprint, Baltimore: Butternut and Blue), 4.

53. Gallagher, ed., *Third Day at Gettysburg,* 171.

54. Gallagher, ed., *Third Day at Gettysburg,* 172.

55. Gallagher, ed., *Third Day at Gettysburg,* 173.

56. Gallagher, ed., *Third Day at Gettysburg,* 178.

NOTES TO THE EPILOGUE

1. O.R., 105–6, 108.

2. C. E. Davis, letter to father, headed "Camp 1st Minnesota Inf. Aug. 12, 1863," microfilm, C. E. Davis Papers, MHS.

3. Holcombe, *History of the First Regiment,* 391.

4. Heffelfinger, *Memoirs of Christopher B. Heffelfinger,* 44.

5. Wright, "Company F," 701.

6. Wright, "Company F," 703. For most of the war, the soldiers carried and used shelter halves. Each man was paired off with another, each having a shelter half—a canvas sheet that could be laced to another one and with a cross stick and two uprights create a "dog tent," known today as a pup tent, capable of sheltering two men.

7. E. A. Walker to George W. Knight, Provost Marshal's Office, 3rd District, Brooklyn, N.Y., Aug. 31, 1863, First Minnesota Infantry Regiment Letters, 1861–1865, MHS.

8. Wright, "Company F," 703.

9. Wright, "Company F," 703.

10. Bond, "Reminiscences," 113.

11. Wright, "Company F," 715.

12. E. A. Walker to George W. Knight, Camp near Warrenton, Va., Nov. 5, 1863, First Minnesota Infantry Regiment Letters.

13. Wright, "Company F," 759.

14. Humphreys, *From Gettysburg to the Rapidan*, 26.

15. Wright, "Company F," 761.

16. Bassett, *Bull Run to Bristow Station*, 31–32.

17. Wright, "Company F," 768.

18. Wright, "Company F," 762.

19. O.R.(Report of Major Mark W. Downie), 281–82.

20. Lochren, "Narrative of the First Regiment," 40.

21. Wright, "Company F," 816.

22. Wright, "Company F," 818–19.

23. Heffelfinger, *Memoirs of Christopher B. Heffelfinger*, 47–48.

24. C. E. Davis, letter to sister Belle, "Camp 1st Minnesota Regt, Friday, Dec. 4th, 1863," Davis Papers.

25. Lochren, "Narrative of the First Regiment," 41.

26. O.R., 698.

27. Bassett, *Bull Run to Bristow Station*, 36.

28. Holcombe, *History of the First Minnesota*, 419.

29. Heffelfinger, *Memoirs of Christopher B. Heffelfinger*, 56–57.

30. Bond, "Reminiscences," 157.

31. Holcombe, *History of the First Minnesota*, 420.

32. Walker to Knight, Camp near Brandy Station, Virginia, Dec. 14, 1863, First Minnesota Infantry Regiment Letters. The sum of money Walker referred to was the combined bounty offered by the federal government and the state of Minnesota. Being a year with a 27 percent inflation rate, $700.00 in 1864 is around $7,625.00 in 2000 dollars.

33. Wright, "Company F," 843.

34. Wright, "Company F," 844.

35. Wright, "Company F," 850.

36. Wright, "Company F," 850.

37. Wright, "Company F," 866.

38. Bond, "Reminiscences," 166.

39. Heffelfinger, *Memoirs of Christopher B. Heffelfinger*, 62–63.

40. Walker to Knight, Fort Snelling, Minnesota, Mar. 27, 1864, First Minnesota Infantry Regiment Letters.

41. Holcombe, *History of the First Minnesota*, 18.

42. Walker to Knight, Fort Snelling, Minnesota, Mar. 27, 1864, First Minnesota Infantry Regiment Letters. Adams's plan seems not to have worked. Walker's muster-out date was May 5, 1864, at Fort Snelling.

43. The brevet rank was an honorary rank that, except in unique circumstances, carried no actual authority and for volunteer forces no extra pay. During the Civil War it served the place of medals given for valor and heroic acts in the modern U.S. Army. Unfortunately it eventually became a much abused reward, often given to officers stationed in Washington, D.C., or on office staffs, who had never heard a shot fired. On March 13, 1864, in an obvious inducement for reenlistments, hundreds of brevet promotions were handed out—253 in the headquarters of the Army of the Potomac alone. It soon became a standing joke in the army: "that bloody day, the 13th of March," as if another Gettysburg had been fought on that date; see Francis A. Lord, *They Fought for the Union* (Harrisburg, Pa.: Stackpole Co., 1960), 230–31. It is clear that Colvill and Adams earned their brevets in the manner intended.

44. Report to the State Adjutant General's Office by Josias Redgate King, William R. Johnson, and John W. Pride, Adjutant General's Office Papers—First Regiment, MHS.

45. Kenneth Maitland Davies, *To the Last Man: The Chronicle of the 135th Infantry Regiment of Minnesota* (St. Paul: Ramsey County Historical Society, 1982), 172. See also website: http://www.dma. state.mn.us/redbull/2BDE/2-135/history/lineage.html

46. Wright, "Company F," 818.

NOTES TO APPENDIX 1

1. Elmore, "A Meteorological and Astronomical Chronology of the Gettysburg Campaign," 7.

2. Michael O'Malley, *Keeping Watch: A History of American Time* (Washington: Smithsonian Institution Press, 1990), 67.

3. New Encyclopaedia Britannica, 15th ed., s.v. "time."

NOTES TO APPENDIX 2

1. The discussion of Civil War weapons and tactics was constructed from the following sources: Wayne Austerman, "Case Shot and Canister: Field Artillery in the Civil War," *Civil War Times Illustrated*, 26, no. 5 (Sept. 1987): 16–18, 20, 22, 24, 26–29, 43–46, 48; Bruce Catton, *Mr. Lincoln's Army*, 186–93, 269; Jack Coggins, *Arms and Equipment of the Civil War* (1962; reprint, Wilmington, N.C.: Broadfoot Publishing Co., 1990), 21–39, 61–85; Gwynne Dyer, *War* (New York: Crown Publishers, 1985), 77–81; John Gibbon, *The Artillerist's Manual, Compiled from Various Sources and Adapted to the Service of the United States*, 2d ed., rev. and enl. (New York: D. Van Nostrand, 1863); Paddy Griffith, *Battle Tactics of the Civil War* (New Haven: Yale University Press, 1989), 137–63; Garry James, "The Union's Most Ready Rifle," *Civil War Times Illustrated*, 28, no. 5 (Sept./Oct. 1989): 10, 12, 14; Francis A. Lord, *Civil War Collectors Encyclopedia* (New York: Castle Books, 1963), 14–17, 19–47, 237–55; Lord, *They Fought for the Union*, 140–43, 154–68.

For a full discussion of the effect of the weaponry and munitions on a soldier and medical treatment during the Civil War, see George Worthington Adams, *Doctors in Blue: The Medical History of the Union Army in the Civil War* (1952; Baton Rouge: Louisiana State University Press, 1996); Earl J. Hess, *The Union Soldier in Battle: Enduring the Ordeal of Combat* (Lawrence: University Press of Kansas, 1997).

NOTES TO APPENDIX 3

1. Bruce Lincoln, *Discourse and the Construction of Society: Comparative Studies of Myth, Ritual, and Classification* (New York: Oxford University Press, 1989), 24–25.

2. William Betcher and William Pollack, *In a Time of Fallen Heroes: The Re-Creation of Masculinity* (New York: Macmillan Publishing Co., 1993), 119.

3. James A. Aho, *Religious Mythology and the Art of War: Comparative Religious Symbolisms of Military Violence* (Westport, Conn.: Greenwood Press, 1981), 10.

4. Lochren, "Narrative of the First Regiment," 8–13.

5. Holcombe, *History of the First Regiment*, 273–74.

6. Lochren, "Narrative of the First Regiment," 40.

7. Frank Aretas Haskell, *The Battle of Gettysburg* (1878?); reprint with introduction by Bruce Catton. Boston: Houghton Mifflin Co., 1969), 109.

8. Letter of Lt. Col. William G. LeDuc, dated "Office of Chief Quartermaster, Eleventh Corps, Sept. 6th, 1863," Swift Papers.

9. Charles Anderson Page, "The 1st Minnesota—The Recent Battles—But 87 out of 220 Left—Sketch of the Organization," *New York Tribune*, July 10, 1863, p. 1.

10. Report from the Veteran Committee of the First Minnesota—J. R. King, Co. G 1st Minn., Wm. R. Johnson, Co. E 1st Minn., J. N. Pride, Co. E 1st Minn., Adjutant Generals Office Records, MHS.

11. "In Honor of the Fallen Soldiers of the Minnesota First," *Stillwater Messenger*, July 14, 1863, p. 2.

12. Samuel Wilkeson, "Details from Our Special Correspondent," *New York Times*, July 6, 1863, p. 1.

13. Page, "The 1st Minnesota," *New York Tribune*, July 10, 1863, p. 1.

14. "Our Army Correspondent, Letter from Lieut. Baasen of the First Regiment," *Saint Paul Pioneer*, July 16, 1863, p. 1.

15. "From the First Minnesota," *Saint Paul Daily Press*, Sept. 9, 1863, p. 1.

16. "The First Minnesota at Brooklyn, New York: The Boys Having a Grand Time," *New York Herald,* reprinted in *Saint Paul Pioneer,* Sept. 5, 1863, p. 1.

17. "The Military Force in the City," *Brooklyn Daily Eagle,* Aug. 29, 1863, p. 2.

18. "The Draft in Brooklyn: The Drawing Commenced," *Brooklyn Daily Eagle,* Aug. 31, 1863, p. 2.

19. "The First Regiment, The Return Home," *Saint Paul Pioneer,* Feb. 16, 1864, p. 1.

20. Program for the "Dedication of the One Hundred Thirty-Fifth Infantry Colvill Memorial," Star Tribune News Research Library archive.

21. "Battle of Gettysburg and the First Minnesota," *Saint Paul Pioneer,* Aug. 9, 1863, p. 2. Thermopylae was a 480 B.C. battle in which a small group of Greeks, commanded by the Spartan King Leonidas, fought to annihilation to hold back an invading Persian army. Fontenoy was a 1745 battle fought in what is today Belgium. A brigade of Irish troops, expatriates fighting with the French against the British and Dutch, charged the much larger British force. Enormous casualties were incurred on both sides, but the British and Dutch armies were forced to retreat and lost the battle. "The Old Guard" was Napoleon's Imperial Guard—his elite force. Upon seeing massive allied reinforcements coming onto the field at Waterloo, Napoleon ordered the Old Guard into a direct frontal assault on the center of the British line, hoping to win the battle before the reinforcements could deploy. The Old Guard was butchered by artillery and infantry fire and then outflanked by infantry and cavalry on the left and right. With the defeat of Napoleon and the Guard's devastating casualties, it ceased to exist as a fighting force. "Chevy Chase" is myth, ballad, and history. The heroic ballad, of unknown authorship and dating from fifteenth-century oral tradition, probably relates to the Battle of Otterburn in 1388. It could also be an amalgam of various fights in the long history of wars along the border of Scotland and England.

22. Lochren, "Narrative of the First Regiment,"35–36, 38. Lochren's narrative was quoted in the 510-page, 1916 regimental history. Fortunately, both for the historical record and giving George Willard and his men their due, a more complete discussion of the fighting was also made, which included Willard's brigade and their fight with Barksdale. However, this part of the narrative made it sound as though Willard's brigade was fended off and Barksdale continued toward the First Minnesota's position. It is interesting to note, whether by design or simple typographical error, Lochren's original text said, "No other troops were then near us," and the same passage reprinted in the 1916 regimental history said, "The other troops were then near us" but went on in the next paragraph with Lochren's original, "There was no organized force here to oppose them; nothing but our handful of two hundred and sixty-two men."

23. "No Feat of Arms Like It, Ride of the Six Hundred Out-done at Gettysburg," *Saint Paul Pioneer Press,* July 3, 1897, p. 2.

24. "No Feat of Arms Like It," *Saint Paul Pioneer Press,* July 3, 1897, p. 2.

25. "One of the Grandest Charges in History, Graphic Account of the Work of the First Minnesota at the Battle of Gettysburg," *Minneapolis Journal,* Apr. 13, 1901, p. 5.

26. "Story of the Regiment that Never Ran," *Minneapolis Journal,* June 26, 1897, p. 12.

27. "The History of a Regiment of Heroes," *Saint Paul Pioneer Press,* July 3, 1897, p. 2.

28. "Losses at Gettysburg Greatest in History," *Minneapolis Sunday Times,* Apr. 6, 1902, p. 13.

29. "War Hero Is Dead," *Saint Paul Pioneer Press,* May 1, 1908.

30. "Commander at Gettysburg—Some Prevalent Misconceptions Cleared Up by Official Records," *Minneapolis Journal,* Dec. 9, 1903, p. 9.

31. Interview with Mr. W. H. Adams, box 75, Folwell Papers.

32. "Says Colvill was in Command: Major C. B. Heffelfinger Writes to Correct Statement of W. H. Adams Concerning the Old First at Gettysburg," *Minneapolis Journal,* clipping from scrapbook, "December 1903" given as date indicator, MHS.

33. Jarich G. Oosten, *The War of the Gods: The Social Code in Indo-European Mythology* (London: Routledge & Kegan Paul, 1985), 4.

NOTES TO APPENDIX 4

1. Colvill, statement to Folwell, Dec. 22, 1904, p. 3, 10.

2. William Fox, *Regimental Losses in the American Civil War: 1861–1865* (Albany: Albany Publishing Co., 1889), 402.

3. Lochren Papers.

4. The full title is *New York Monuments Commission for the Battlefields of Gettysburg and Chattanooga. Final Report on the Battlefield of Gettysburg.*

5. William Fox, *New York Monuments Commission for the Battlefields of Gettysburg and Chattanooga: Final Report on the Battlefield of Gettysburg,* vol. 1 (Albany: J. B. Lyon Co., 1900), 101–7; see also Busey and Martin, *Regimental Strengths,* 7–9.

6. Fox, *Regimental Losses,* 402.

7. These included: Corporal Stephen Martin, Company K, diary, July 2, 1863 ("300" seemed to refer to the charge on July 2); Cornelia Hancock, nurse attending Colonel Colvill after the battle, in a letter to her sister dated "Gettysburg – July 8TH, 1863": "Three hundred and eighty-four men went into battle," indicated for the entire battle, not just the charge; Captain Charles Edward Davis, Company E,

letter to brother George dated Friday, July 17, 1863 ("We went in with 25 officers and 310 men" probably for the entire battle); letter to the *St. Paul Pioneer* signed "Sergeant," dated July 28, 1863 ("270 officers and men all told" specified for the charge on July 2); letter in the Faribault *Central Republican* dated Wed., July 29, 1863, from J. Jay Knox to Governor Ramsey ("352" engaged in the entire battle); Col. Colvill to John Bachelder, June 9, 1866 ("269," referred to the charge on July 2); Colvill letter, *Minneapolis Daily Tribune,* July 28, 1884 ("about 300" likely referred to the charge on July 2); Orville D. Thatcher—working in the War Department in the Adjutant General's Office—to Lochren, July 27, 1889 ("We carried into the fight some 320 odd, but that's a disputed point also," probably meaning the entire battle).

8. Taylor Diary, entry for Monday, June 15, 1863, p. 355.

9. Taylor Diary, entry for Monday, May 18, 1863, p. 349; see also Wright, "Company F," 527–28.

10. Bond, "Reminiscences," 90–91.

11. Busey and Martin, *Regimental Strengths,* 8–9.

12. John D. Billings, *Hardtack and Coffee: Or The Unwritten Story of Army Life* (1887; reprint intro. by William L. Shea, Lincoln: University of Nebraska Press, Bison Books, 1993), 355, 357.

13. Stephen Osman, e-mail to author, Sept. 14, 1998; see also Regimental Consolidated Morning Reports, State Adjutant General Records, MHS.

14. Wright, "Company F," 527–28.

15. Taylor to sister, July 19, 1863, Taylor Letters.

INDEX

Pale Horse at Plum Run was designed by Will Powers at the Minnesota Historical Society Press and set in Utopia by Judy Gilats at Peregrine Graphics Services, St. Paul, Minnesota. Printed by Maple-Vail Press. The maps are by Matt Kania, St. Paul.